WEB WORK

Information Science and Knowledge Management

Volume 1

WEB WORK

Information Seeking and Knowledge Work on the World Wide Web

by

CHUN WEI CHOO

BRIAN DETLOR

and

DON TURNBULL

Faculty of Information Studies,
University of Toronto, Canada

KLUWER ACADEMIC PUBLISHERS

DORDRECHT / BOSTON / LONDON

A C.I.P. Catalogue record for this book is available from the Library of Congress.

ISBN 978-90-481-5520-0

Published by Kluwer Academic Publishers,
P.O. Box 17, 3300 AA Dordrecht, The Netherlands.

Sold and distributed in North, Central and South America
by Kluwer Academic Publishers,
101 Philip Drive, Norwell, MA 02061, U.S.A.

In all other countries, sold and distributed
by Kluwer Academic Publishers,
P.O. Box 322, 3300 AH Dordrecht, The Netherlands.

Printed on acid-free paper

Printed in the Netherlands.

For:

Tuan Wei and Kerie (CWC)

Ben (BD)

Lisa, JoAnne, Scotty and Barbara (DT)

Table of Contents

Preface xi

SECTION I: INFORMATION SEEKING AND KNOWLEDGE WORK

Chapter 1: Information Seeking 3

1.1 Information Needs 3
1.1.1 Information Needs: Cognitive Dimensions 4
1.1.2 Information Needs: Affective Dimensions 5
1.1.3 Information Needs: Situational Dimensions 6
1.2 Information Seeking 8
1.2.1 Information Seeking: Cognitive Dimensions 9
1.2.2 Information Seeking: Affective Dimensions 10
1.2.3 Information Seeking: Situational Dimensions 12
1.3 Information Use 14
1.3.1 Information Use: Cognitive Dimensions 16
1.3.2 Information Use: Affective Dimensions 17
1.3.3 Information Use: Situational Dimensions 19
1.4 Human Information Seeking: An Integrated Model 21
1.4.1 Information Needs—A Summary 22
1.4.2 Information Seeking—A Summary 23
1.4.3 Information Use—A Summary 24
1.4.4 Some Implications for Practice 26

Chapter 2: The Structure and Dynamics of Organizational Knowledge 29

2.1 From Information to Knowledge 29
2.1.1 From Signals to Data 29
2.1.2 From Data to Information 29
2.1.3 From Information to Knowledge 31
2.1.4 From Information to Knowledge — in Organizations 32
2.2 The Structure of Organizational Knowledge 33
2.2.1 Tacit Knowledge 35
2.2.2 Explicit Knowledge 39
2.2.3 Cultural Knowledge 43
2.3 The Dynamics of Organizational Knowledge: Creating, Diffusing, and Using Knowledge 48
2.3.1 Knowledge Creation: Leveraging Tacit Knowledge 49
2.3.2 Knowledge Diffusion: Codifying, Abstracting, and Diffusing Knowledge 52
2.3.3 Knowledge Utilization: Communities of Practice 56
2.4 The Integration of Organizational Knowledge 60
2.5 Organizational Knowledge and Sensemaking, Decision Making 63
2.6 Summary 66

SECTION II: KNOWLEDGE WORK ON INTRANETS

Chapter 3: The Intranet as Infrastructure for Knowledge Work....71

3.1 What are Intranets? 71
3.1.1 Intranet Technology 73
3.1.2 Intranet Functionality 78
3.2 Benefits and Challenges of Intranets 79
3.3 The Intranet as IT Infrastructure 82
3.4 Intranets as Shared Information Work Spaces 86
3.4.1 Intranets as Content Spaces 87
3.4.2 Intranets as Communication Spaces 88
3.4.3 Intranets as Collaboration Spaces 90
3.4.4 Supporting Ba Through Intranets 91
3.5 Lessons Learned from CSCW 92
3.6 Intranet Case Studies 96
3.7 Conclusion 100

Chapter 4: Designing Intranets to Support Knowledge Work....101

4.1 Intranet System Development 101
4.2 Basing Design on the Analysis of the Information Environment 103
4.3 The Structure of the Organizational Information Environment 107
4.3.1 Taylor's (1991) Information Use Environment 107
4.3.2 Katzer & Fletcher's (1992) Information Environment of Managers 109
4.3.3 Rosenbaum's (1996) Structurationally Informed Value-Added Model 110
4.3.4 Davenport's (1997) Information Ecology Model 112
4.3.5 Common Elements 115
4.4 A Behavioral-Ecological Framework for Intranet Design 117
4.4.1 Information Ecology 117
4.4.2 Information Needs and Uses 119
4.4.3 Value-Added Processes 120
4.4.4 Summary 122
4.5 Empirical Testing of the Behavioral-Ecological Framework 123
4.6 Other Complementary Research 128
4.7 Conclusion 130

SECTION III: INFORMATION SEEKING ON THE WORLD WIDE WEB

Chapter 5: Models of Information Seeking on the World Wide Web 133

5.1 Information Foraging 133
5.2 Bibliometrics 137
5.2.1 Bibliometrics of Use 137
5.2.2 Bibliometric Coupling 138
5.2.3 Co-citation Analysis 138
5.2.4 Bibliometric Laws 139
5.2.5 Bibliometrics and Web Documents 142
5.2.6 Bibliometrics and the Web - Webometrics 144
5.2.7 Bibliometric Measures of Group Web Use 146
5.3 User Browsing 147
5.3.1 Marchionini's Electronic Browsing Model 147
5.3.2 Ellis' Model of Information Seeking 148
5.3.3 Aguilar's Model of Scanning 151
5.3.4 A Behavioral Model of Web Information Seeking 152
5.4 Web Use Studies 154
5.5 Conclusion 158

Chapter 6: Understanding Organizational Web Use 159

6.1 Study Introduction 159
6.2 Questionnaires 160
6.3 WebTracker 167
6.4 Interviews 175
6.5 The Behavioral Model of Information Seeking 177
6.6 Effect of Web Training on Organizational Web Use 181
6.7 Conclusion 184

Coda 189

References 191

Index 213

Preface

This book brings together three great motifs of the network society: the seeking and using of information by individuals and groups; the creation and application of knowledge in organizations; and the fundamental transformation of these activities as they are enacted on the Internet and the World Wide Web. Of the three, the study of how individuals and groups seek information probably has the longest history, beginning with the early "information needs and uses" studies soon after the Second World War. The study of organizations as knowledge-based social systems is much more recent, and really gained momentum only within the last decade or so. The study of the World Wide Web as information and communication media is younger still, but has generated tremendous excitement, partly because it has the potential to reconfigure the ways in which people seek information and use knowledge, and partly because it offers new methods of analyzing and measuring how in fact such information and knowledge work gets done. As research endeavors, these streams overlap and share conceptual constructs, perspectives, and methods of analysis. Although these overlaps and shared concerns are sometimes apparent in the published research, there have been few attempts to connect these ideas explicitly and identify cross-disciplinary themes. This book is an attempt to fill this void.

The three authors of this book possess contrasting backgrounds and thus adopt complementary vantage points to observe information seeking and knowledge work. One author (Choo) has taught and researched in organization science and information science for several years, with a particular emphasis on information management, knowledge management, and organizational learning. A second author (Detlor) has substantial experience in consulting, designing, and managing information systems and is completing his doctoral research studying a large-scale project by a major high-tech company to support knowledge work on the World Wide Web and an intranet. The third author (Turnbull) has worked in the areas of World Wide Web software architecture and application design, and Web content design. He is completing his doctoral research on data mining Web usage metrics in order to discover patterns of Web-based information seeking by employees of a large corporation.

Purpose and Approach

As a text, the book has three objectives. First, it provides a review and synthesis of the important theoretical models that have been developed to understand information seeking and knowledge work in organizations. Second, it examines the role of the intranet as an infrastructure for supporting knowledge work, and proposes a new framework for designing intranets as information spaces for collaboration, communication, and sharing knowledge. Third, the text investigates the nature of information seeking on the Web, highlighting research and measurement opportunities that are inherent in the structure and operation of the Web, and suggesting how quantitative methods may add depth and rigor to the research.

The three sections of the book reflect these objectives:

Section I: Information Seeking and Knowledge Work
Section II: Knowledge Work on Intranets
Section III: Information Seeking on the World Wide Web

Thus, Section I describes the theoretical foundation and the broader contexts in which information seeking and knowledge work is situated in organizations. Section II has a much sharper focus, concentrating on the intranet as a new kind of information infrastructure that is particularly well suited to supporting knowledge work. Section III most directly addresses the research and application implications of the World Wide Web as an information source and channel that will dramatically alter how organizations function and how individuals access and use online information.

Overview of the Contents

The book consists of six chapters, two in each of the three sections. Section I begins with Chapter One, *Information Seeking*. It sets the scene by surveying what we have learned from decades of research on how people and groups look for and process information. The unifying perspective is that information seeking is social behavior, and that this behavior is shaped by factors that operate at the cognitive, affective, and situational levels. Thus, information needs are as much felt as they are thought about (Dervin 1993, Kuhlthau 1993). Information seeking is guided by perceptions of information quality and accessibility as well as by the conditions and requirements of a particular situation (MacMullin and Taylor 1984). Information use is the least predictable of all, being influenced by a variety of factors such as cognitive styles, affective preferences, and the roles and routines that regulate information use (Bryce 1996). Beneath all this complexity, the chapter presents a framework that places the findings of past research in an overarching structure.

Chapter Two, *The Structure and Dynamics of Organizational Knowledge*, examines the nature of knowledge in organizations as well as the processes by which knowledge is engaged and acted upon. Knowledge in organizations is not monolithic nor homogenous. Recent research suggests that organizational knowledge may be categorized as tacit knowledge, explicit knowledge, and cultural knowledge (Nonaka and Takeuchi 1995, Boisot 1998, Choo 1998, and Spender 1998). Thus, individuals and groups possess tacit knowledge derived from experience, skillful practice, and reflection. Physical objects and procedural routines codify explicit knowledge learned or invented by the organization. Finally, cultural knowledge is embedded in the organization's beliefs about its identity and purpose, its capabilities, and its environment. Chapter Two also contains an extended discussion of the major theoretical models that have been developed to explain the dynamics of creating, diffusing, and utilizing organizational knowledge.

Having laid the conceptual groundwork, Section II begins with a focused discussion of an emerging platform for supporting information seeking and knowledge work in organizations—the intranet. Chapter Three, *The Intranet as Infrastructure for Knowledge Work*, introduces the architecture and components of typical intranet implementations, and weighs the potential benefits that intranets can bring against the problems that can limit their effectiveness, drawing lessons from the research on computer-supported collaborative work (Baecker 1993). For many organizations, the first use of intranets is as a publishing medium, providing rapid and universal access to documents without incurring the costs of paper-based production. Intranets become more effective as knowledge infrastructures when they are designed and utilized as shared information work environments that act simultaneously and seamlessly as spaces for content access, communication, and collaboration. Chapter Three concludes with a number of examples of innovative companies that have adopted intranets to support knowledge work.

Chapter Four, *Designing Intranets to Support Knowledge Work*, reviews theoretical models that analyze the structure of organizational information environments (Davenport 1997, Taylor 1991, Katzer and Fletcher 1992). Common elements are identified and woven into a new framework for designing intranets as knowledge work platforms. The proposed "behavioral-ecological framework" emphasizes equally the information practices of individuals and groups, and the information ecology of the organization. It allows intranets to be designed simultaneously from the bottom-up, honoring the culture and spirit of the Internet, and from the top-down, ensuring that the organization as a whole leverages the sharing of knowledge. Applications and services on the intranet are developed as value-adding processes that support the information practices of users, as well as enhance the information environment of the organization. Chapter Four is an amplification and application of the concepts presented in Section I, where we looked at information seeking and knowledge work without discussing any particular platform or infrastructure.

Section III examines information seeking in the specific context of the World Wide Web. Compared with Section I, this section analyzes at a much finer granularity the actions that people actually take when they use the Web as an information source or channel. The section begins with Chapter 5, *Models of Information Seeking on the World Wide Web*. The message here is that the structure of the Web and the functionality of the Web browser facilitate as well as constrain information seeking, resulting in new modes and patterns that may be revealed through the quantitative analysis of Web browser actions and Web server events. Chapter 5 reviews and compares models of Web information seeking in three emerging areas of research: information foraging; bibliometrics; and user browsing activity. Recent research that combines concepts and approaches in these areas suggests that universal "laws" of information seeking on the Web may indeed be discerned.

Finally, Chapter Six, *Understanding Organizational Web Use*, presents findings from the authors' own study of how knowledge workers use the Web to seek external information as part of their daily work. The main approach in studying Web use was the utilization of three diverse data collection and analysis methods. Fifty-two users from nine companies took part in the study, mainly IT specialists, managers, and consulting staff. Participants answered a detailed questionnaire and were interviewed individually in order to understand their information needs and information seeking preferences. A custom-developed WebTracker software application was installed on each of their workplace PCs, and participants' Web-use activities were then recorded continuously during two-week periods. The WebTracker recorded how participants used the browser to seek information on the Web: it logged menu choices, button bar selections, and keystroke actions, allowing browsing and searching sequences to be reconstructed. In a second round of personal interviews, participants recalled critical incidents of using information from the Web. The strength of this approach was the triangulation of methods to obtain a rich and detailed understanding of how knowledge workers use the Web to seek information.

Audience

The book's primary audience would be faculty and students in masters and doctoral programs, in information science, information systems, library science, and management schools. The book would be an appropriate text for graduate and doctoral level courses in areas such as: management information systems, information management, information retrieval, knowledge management, library and information science, records management, digital libraries. Consultants and organizations designing and implementing intranets would find the book useful in providing research-based insights into how information seeking and knowledge sharing may be enhanced.

Acknowledgments

Behind the names that appear on a book's cover are the numerous groups and individuals who have given generously of their time, advice, and support. Every book is a collective effort; and this one is certainly no exception. We wish to thank: Ross Barclay, recently graduated from the Faculty of Information Studies, who developed the WebTracker software and provided helpful ideas and advice on collecting and analyzing Web usage data; Leyuan Tian, from the Shandong Academy of Science (People's Republic of China), who did part of the quantitative analysis of the Web usage logs; Katherine Young, Clément Arsenault and Linda Yarema for indexing the final manuscript; Betty van Herk and Paul Roos from Kluwer Academic Publishers for their help in editing and promoting the book; and the anonymous reviewers for their insightful comments and suggestions which greatly aided in the formation of a more rigorous and detailed final product. We are also grateful for the many discussions and exchange of ideas with a variety of individuals who helped solidify and shape the ideas on which this book is based, namely Casian Moscovici from National Public Relations, Mike Milton and Dennis Venerus of Bell Canada, Jim Pitkow and Peter Pirolli from Xerox PARC. Most of all, we are deeply indebted to the people in companies and organizations who participated as subjects in our field work—their willingness to open their doors (and their computers) to detailed scrutiny and data collection has been vital to our research. The research presented in this book was supported by a three-year grant from the Social Sciences and Humanities Research Council of Canada.

Chun Wei Choo
Brian Detlor
Don Turnbull

Faculty of Information Studies
University of Toronto
March 2000

Section I: Information Seeking and Knowledge Work

Chapter 1: Information Seeking

We often see "information" described as a "resource." This tends to imply that information is "something" that resides in documents, information systems, or other artifacts. The information is assumed to be constant, unchanging. Its meaning is fixed by its representation in the artifact. A complementary view is to look at information not as an object but as the outcome of subjective construction. Information resides not in artifacts but in the minds of individuals. People actively construct the meaning of information through their thoughts, actions, and feelings. Since individuals typically use information to solve a problem, perform a task, or increase understanding, the social settings in which the information is encountered determines its value and salience. When we treat information as an object, we are concerned with how to acquire the information that we need, and how to represent the information that we have in order to enable access and processing. When we treat information subjectively, we are concerned with understanding the human and behavioral processes through which information is enacted and engaged. A fuller understanding of information seeking as social behavior helps us to design better information processes and information systems. This chapter provides a first step towards that understanding.

We structure our discussion by dividing information seeking activity into three processes: the experiencing of information needs, the seeking of information, and the using of information. We examine the cognitive, affective, and situational factors that influence each of these processes.

1.1 Information Needs

Information needs are frequently thought of in terms of a person's cognitive needs—gaps or anomalies in the state of knowledge or understanding that may be represented by questions or topics. These questions could be posed to an information system or source. Satisfying the cognitive need then involves retrieving information whose subject matter matches that of a query. While the performance of organizational tasks, including planning and decision making, are the main generators of cognitive needs,

> "the nature of the organization, coupled with the individual's personality structure, will create affective needs such as the need for achievement, for self-expression and self-actualization. ... In such a wider view the individual would be perceived not merely as driven to seek information for cognitive ends, but as living and working in social settings which create their own motivations to seek information to help satisfy largely affective needs." (Wilson 1981, p. 9, 10)

Thus, information has to satisfy not just cognitive needs, but also affective needs and situational requirements (Wilson 1994). In this section we analyze information needs by examining its cognitive, affective, and situational dimensions (see Figure 1.1).

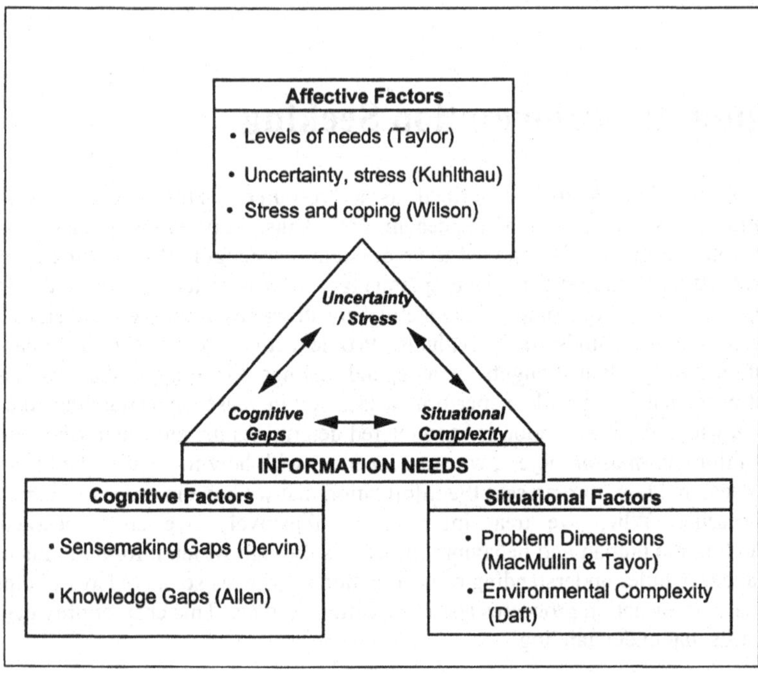

Figure 1.1 Information Needs

1.1.1 Information Needs: Cognitive Dimensions

Since the Second World War, a large number of information needs and uses studies have attempted to understand how different groups of people experience information needs and how these needs may be met. The information needs and uses of scientists, engineers, physicians and academics, as well as those of citizens, government officials, managers, and professionals have all been the subject of research inquiry. In recent years, Dervin (1983a,b, 1992) has been active in applying and promoting a sensemaking metaphor to describe how humans perceive information needs as cognitive gaps. In the sensemaking approach, people move through space and time, taking steps through experiences. As long as individuals can make sense of their experiences, movement ahead is possible. From time to time, movement is blocked by the perception of a cognitive gap—a situation in which people are unable to make sense of their experiences. To bridge this gap, individuals seek information to make new sense and use this information to help them continue on in their journey. Dervin and her associates have completed over 40 studies in the past two decades based on the sensemaking approach. Their research suggests that the ways in which people perceive their cognitive gaps and the ways that they want information to help are good predictors of their information seeking behaviors. Better yet, the ways in which people perceive and define their sensemaking gaps can be coded into universal categories that are applicable across different groups of information users. Table 1.1 below outlines eight situation gap categories identified by Dervin (1992).

Gaps	Description
Decision stop	where the person sees two or more roads ahead;
Barrier stop	where the person sees one road ahead but something or someone stands on the road blocking the way;
Spin-out stop	where the person sees self as having no road;
Wash-out stop	where the person sees self as on a road that suddenly disappears;
Problematic stop	where the person sees self as being dragged down a road not of his or her own choosing
Perceptual embeddedness	where the person judges how foggy is the road ahead
Situational embeddedness	where the person judges how many intersections are on the road, and
Social embeddedness	where the person judges how many people are also travelling.

Table 1.1 Sensemaking Gaps (Dervin 1992)

Allen (1996) suggests that information needs occur whenever an individual's knowledge fails. Allen analyzes information needs as knowledge gaps that are experienced when an individual's life situation interacts with his or her knowledge or cognitive structures, and reveals a deficiency in understanding. He identifies three categories of information needs based on knowledge gaps:

1. information needs that arise from failure of perception (that is, the individual is unable to perceive the situation);
2. information needs associated with exploring a topic area so as to identify alternative courses of action;
3. information needs that arise from choosing between alternative courses of action (that involves evaluating alternatives and their outcomes).

1.1.2 Information Needs: Affective Dimensions

Cognitive needs are draped in affective responses so that they are as much felt as they are thought about. When sense has run out, the lack of understanding creates a state of uncertainty. Kuhlthau (1993) describes how uncertainty causes a number of affective symptoms, including anxiety, apprehension, confusion, frustration, and lack of confidence. These affective states motivate and direct the individual's information seeking and information use experience. Affective responses influence, and are influenced by, the individual's ability to construct meaning, focus information needs, manage moods and expectations, and deepen personal interest in the search.

Taylor (1968) postulates that human beings experience four levels of information needs—visceral need, conscious need, formalized need, and compromised need. At the visceral level, the person experiences a vague sense of dissatisfaction, a gap in knowledge or understanding that is often inexpressible in linguistic terms. The visceral need may become more concrete and pressing as more information is encountered and its importance grows. When this occurs, the visceral need enters the conscious level, where the person develops a mental description of the area of indecision. Such a mental description is likely to be in the form of rambling statements or a narrative that reflect the ambiguity that the person still experiences at this level. To develop a focus, the person may consult with colleagues and friends, and when ambiguity is sufficiently reduced, the conscious need moves to the formalized level. At the formalized level, the inquirer is able to construct a qualified, rational statement of the information need, expressed for example in the form of a question or topic. Here the formal statement is made without the user necessarily having to consider what sources or information are available. When the user interacts with an information source or system, either directly or through an intermediary, the person may recast the question in anticipation of what the source or system knows or is able to deliver. The formalized question is thus modified or rephrased in a form that could be understood or processed by the information system. In this sense the question finally elicited represents the information need at the compromised level.

Wilson (1997) suggests that uncertainty and its affective symptoms constitute a state of stress with which the individual must cope. For example, research in health information seeking has contrasted "monitors" who prefer high levels of information input to cope with a stressful event and suffer less psychological arousal when they have the information, with "blunters" who prefer less information and suffer greater arousal when they receive a high information input (Miller and Mangan 1983). Wilson also examines the relationship between information needs and coping by applying Krohne's (1986, 1989) model of coping. When an individual's intolerance of uncertainty is high but the intolerance of arousal is low, the individual copes through "constant monitoring." On the other hand, when both uncertainty intolerance and arousal intolerance are high, the individual engages in "fluctuating coping."

1.1.3 Information Needs: Situational Dimensions

Information needs arise from the problems, uncertainties, and ambiguities encountered in specific situations and experiences. Such situations and experiences are the composite of a large number of elements that relate not just to subject matter, but also to situational factors such as goal clarity and consensus, magnitude of risk, amount of control, professional and social norms, time and resource constraints, and so on. As a result, the determination of information needs must not stop at asking "What do you want to know?" but must also answer questions like: "Why do you need to know it?" "What does your problem look like?" "What do you know already?" "What do you anticipate finding?" and "How will this help you?" MacMullin and Taylor (1984) suggest that problem situations be analyzed according to a number of problem dimensions that amplify information needs and form the criteria by which individuals assess the relevance and value of information. A list of these dimensions can be found in Table 1.2 below.

	Problem Dimensions: Problems lie on a continuum between...	Information Needs (Examples)
1	Design ...	Options, alternatives, ranges
	Discovery	Small, detailed sets of data
2	Well-structured ...	Hard, quantitative data
	Ill-structured	Probablistic data on how to proceed
3	Simple ...	Path to goal state
	Complex	Ways to reduce problem to simpler tasks
4	Specific goals ...	Goal operationalization and measurement
	Amorphous goals	Preferences and directions
5	Initial state understood ...	Clarify unclear aspects of initial state
	Initial state not understood	Soft, qualitative data to define initial state
6	Assumptions agreed upon ...	Information to help define problems
	Assumptions not agreed upon	Views of the world, definition of terms
7	Assumptions explicit ...	Range of options, frames to analyze problems
	Assumptions not explicit	Information to make assumptions explicit
8	Familiar pattern ...	Procedural and historical information
	New pattern	Substantive and future-oriented information
9	Magnitude of risk not great ...	Cost-effective search
	Magnitude of risk great	"Best" available information
10	Susceptible to empirical analysis ...	Objective, aggregated data
	Not susceptible	Experts' opinions, forecasts, scenarios
11	Internal imposition ...	Clarification of internal goals, objectives
	External imposition	Information about external environment

Table 1.2 Problem Dimensions (MacMullin and Taylor 1984)

Information needs would also vary according to the complexity of the situation in which the information is to be utilized. Situational complexity increases when many actors and entities are involved, and when these agents interconnect and interact in complicated and unpredictable ways. A specific instance of situational complexity is perceived environmental uncertainty, a variable that represents the external environment's perceived complexity and changeability. Perceived environmental uncertainty is conceptualized as lack of information about environmental factors; lack of knowledge about the outcome of an action; and inability to assess how environmental factors affect success or failure (Duncan 1972). The external environment may be divided into sectors, such as the customer, competition, technological, regulatory, economic, and sociocultural sectors (Choo and Auster 1993). Empirical studies suggest that information scanning tends to be focused on the market-related sectors, with information on customers, suppliers, and competitors appearing to be the most important (see for example, Ghoshal 1988, Lester and Waters 1989, Choo 1993, Olsen et al 1994).

1.2 Information Seeking

The experiencing of information needs does not always lead to information seeking. People may rely on their own memory or intuition to fill the information need. People may also suppress their information needs or avoid a problem situation so that no information seeking is necessary: "People can, and frequently do, engage in information avoidance. They interact with their environment by limiting their intake of information, ignoring information if it is associated with negative outcomes, and taking information shortcuts." (Allen 1996, p. 109) When information seeking does occur, it is purposive and goal-directed, and resembles a problem-solving or decision-making process. The individual identifies possible sources, differentiates and chooses a few sources, locates or makes contact with them, and interacts with the sources in order to obtain the desired information. In today's munificient information environment, an important question is how does the individual select between sources, and between information from different sources? In an economy where human attention is the scarce resource, how does an individual allocate time and energy when searching for information? Research suggests that when deciding between sources, an individual weighs the amount of effort required to use a source against the anticipated usefulness of the information from that source. At the same time, this evaluation of cost and benefit is modulated by the individual's personal interest and motivation, and by the complexity of the task or problem at hand. Figure 1.2 below illustrates the cognitive, affective, and situational dimensions of information seeking.

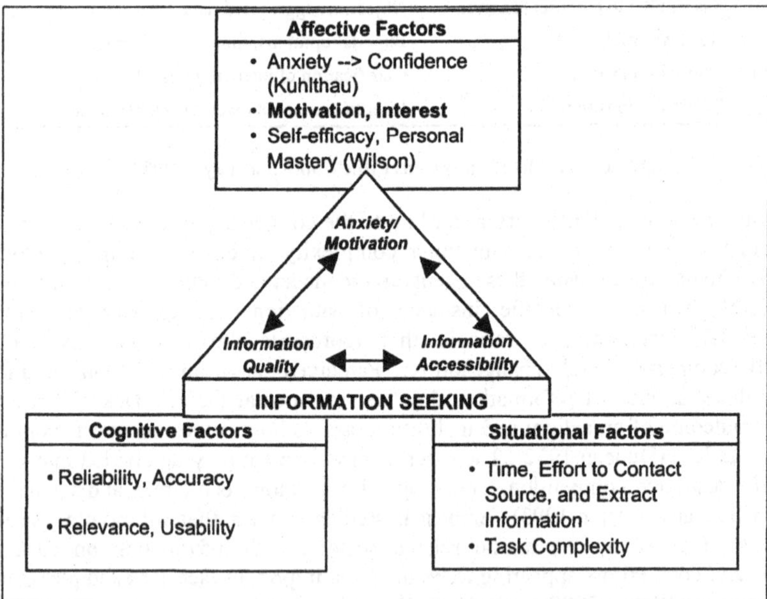

Figure 1. 2 Information Seeking

1.2.1 Information Seeking: Cognitive Dimensions

At the cognitive level, the individual would select a source that is perceived to have the greater probability of providing information that will be relevant and useful. Moreover, the individual would be concerned with the accuracy and reliability of the source. Research in information seeking often groups together some or all of the relevance and reliability related attributes under the rubric of perceived source quality, and examines to what extent this influences the selection of sources.

Zmud (1978) reviews the literature on the dimensions of information and identifies the following characteristics: quantity (measured by adjectives such as 'complete' or 'sufficient'), reliability ('true,' 'accurate'), timeliness ('current'), and format quality ('readable,' 'clear'). In his empirical study to validate these dimensions, four classes of information traits were derived: (1) an overall view of the quality of information consisting of a measure of relevancy; (2) the relevancy components comprising accuracy, factualness, quantity, and reliability/timeliness; (3) the quality of format; and (4) the quality of meaning in terms of its reasonableness ('logical,' 'sensible').The concept of information 'relevance' is fundamental in the development of information science. Saracevic (1970) includes in his summary list of definitions the notions that relevance is "a measure of usefulness of an answer" and "an indication of significance to an important purpose." Relevant information includes "ideas or facts so closely related to the problem at hand that disregarding them would alter the problem" (p. 120). He then defines relevance as a relationship in the form of an algorithm: "Relevance is the (A) gauge of relevance of an (B) aspect of relevance existing between an (C) object judged and a (D) frame of reference as judged by a (E) assessor" (p. 120-121). Eisenberg and Schamber (1988) interpret this definition as: "Relevance is a measure of utility existing between a document and a question as judged by a requester" (p. 166). In his study comparing the impact of source accessibility and quality on the use of information sources by decision makers, O'Reilly (1982) determined that relevance is a main dimension of perceived source quality (the other dimensions being accuracy, reliability, and timeliness).

Relevance is generally believed to be a good predictor of source and information selection and use, and the relationship between relevance and use has been explored in different ways. The objective view of information assumes that the content of a document or information item may be represented objectively and that this representation may then be matched with a query. Thus, a document is said to be relevant to a query when it is objectively judged to be so by a consensus of those practicing in a field (Harter 1986). An information retrieval system could then be designed to compute the amount of match between terms in a user's query and terms from a document in order to measure the degree that the document is "about" the topic of the query. The difficulty here is that any single representation of a document or query conveys different content and meaning to different people. In contrast, the subjective view sees relevance not as an objective, inherent property of the information item, but as a relationship between information and query that is constructed or determined by the user. Relevance is assumed to be:

- Subjective, depending on human judgment and thus not an inherent characteristic of information or document;
- Cognitive, depending ultimately on human knowledge and perceptions;
- Situational, relating to individual users' information problems;
- Multidimensional, influenced by many factors;
- Dynamic, constantly changing over time; and
- Measurable, observable at a single location in time.

(Schamber 1994, Harter 1992, Saracevic 1970, 1975)

To distinguish the subjective view, some authors have suggested the term pertinence to indicate the ability of an information item to go beyond "topic-relatedness" to satisfying some personal, visceral need of the individual (see our discussion of Taylor's levels of information needs earlier). Pertinence goes deeper than relevance by connecting with personal cognitve and affective needs, and by addressing particular demands of the situation in which the information need arises.

Taylor (1986) suggests that the reliability of a source represents the summation of many of the values of that source. He defines reliability as "the trust a user has in the consistency of quality performance of the system and its outputs over time." The system or source is "consistent in maintaining its accepted level of accuracy, of currency, of comprehensiveness (or selectivity as the case may be), and it can be relied upon to do so in the future" (p. 64). Nilan and his colleagues (1988) investigated the source evaluation criteria that information seekers apply. They interviewed subjects about the sequences of information seeking and use events that they have experienced. The transcripts were then content-analyzed to extract the criteria that the subjects used to evaluate their information sources. The initial research has identified a number of criteria for the acceptance or rejection of information, sources, and information seeking strategies (Nilan, Peek and Snyder 1988; Halpern and Nilan 1988). Among the fifteen source criteria that were reported most frequently, the top five were "Authority or expertise based on credentials," "Authority or expertise based on experience," "Only perceived source," and "Trust."

1.2.2 Information Seeking: Affective Dimensions

At the affective level, the individual's degree of personal motivation and interest in the problem or topic would determine the amount of energy that he or she invests in information seeking. Kuhlthau (1993) suggests that as the information search progresses, initial feelings of uncertainty and anxiety fall as confidence rises. If a clear theme is developed to focus the search, the individual may become more highly motivated, and if the search proceeds well, there is a growing feeling of satisfaction and accomplishment.

Kuhlthau postulates that information search is composed of six stages—initiation, selection, exploration, formulation, collection, and presentation—each of which is characterized by emotional responses. During initiation, the user first recognizes a need for more information, and feelings of uncertainty and apprehension are common. During selection, the user identifies the general area or topic to be investigated. Feelings of uncertainty are replaced by optimism and a readiness to search. Thoughts are on choosing a search strategy best able to satisfy the criteria of personal interest, information available, and time allocated. During exploration, the user expands personal understanding of the general area. Feelings of confusion and doubt may increase. The fourth stage of formulation is the turning point of the process in which the user establishes a focus or theme on the problem that can guide searching. Feelings of uncertainty diminish as confidence increases. During collection, the user interacts with information systems and services to gather information. Confidence increases and interest in the project deepens. With a clear sense of direction, the user is able to specify and look for particular, relevant information. In the final stage of presentation, the user completes the search and resolves the problem. There is a sense of relief, accompanied by satisfaction if the search is thought to have gone well, or disappointment otherwise.

Kuhlthau's model of the information search process is based on the principle that uncertainty—experienced both as a cognitive state and an affective response—rises and fall as the search process progresses:

> "Uncertainty due to a lack of understanding, a gap in meaning, a limited construct initiates the process of information seeking. Uncertainty is a cognitive state that commonly causes affective symptoms of anxiety and lack of confidence. Uncertainty and anxiety can be expected in the early stages of the Information Search Process. The affective symptoms of uncertainty, confusion, and frustration are associated with vague, unclear thoughts about a topic or question. As knowledge states shift to more clearly focused thoughts, a parallel shift is noted in feelings of increased confidence." (Kuhlthau 1993, p. xxiii)

Kuhlthau (1993) draws six sets of implications. First, information search is a process of constructing understanding and meaning. In doing so, the user moves from uncertainty and vagueness to confidence and clarity as the search progresses. Second, the formulation of a focus, guiding idea, or point of view is the pivotal point in the search process. Unfortunately, many users bypass the formulation activity altogether, beginning to gather information without first forming a sufficiently clear focus. Third, information encountered may be redundant or unique. Redundant information fits into what the user already knows or believes in, and is readily recognized to be relevant or not. Unique information is new and extends knowledge, but it may not match the user's constructs, requiring reconstruction. Too much redundant information leads to boredom, while too much unique information causes anxiety. Fourth, the range of possibilities pursued in a search is influenced by the user's mood or attitude towards the search task. A user in an invitational mood would tend to take more expansive, exploratory actions, while a user in an indicative mood prefers conclusive actions that lead to closure (Kelly 1963). A user's mood changes during the search process, from perhaps an invitational, exploratory mood in early stages to a more indicative mood as the search progresses. Fifth, the search process is a series of unique, personal choices based on the user's predictions or expectations about what sources, information, and strategies would be effective or expedient. Finally, the user's interest and motivation levels grow as the search progresses. Interest is higher in later stages when the user has defined a search focus and has enough understanding of the topic to become intellectually engaged. Interest may also be enhanced by introducing the notion of fun and play, but most information systems ignore this need.

Drawing from social learning theory, Wilson (1997) suggests that the construct of self-efficacy or sense of personal mastery (Bandura 1977) may influence information seeking. Thus, Bandura postulates that an individual's belief or feeling about his or her own effectiveness would affect whether the individual even tries to cope with situation. Wilson reasons that since a strong feeling of self-efficacy or personal mastery about using a source would lead to a more extended and intensive use of that source, doubt about one's capacity to use a source properly would lead to that source not being used, even if the source might be perceived to contain relevant information.

1.2.3 Information Seeking: Situational Dimensions

At the situational level, the selection and use of sources is influenced by the amount of time and effort that is required to locate or contact the source, and to interact with the source to extract information. These source attributes may be bundled together in a variable called perceived source accessibility.

In a landmark study by Gerstberger and Allen (1968) of how engineers select information sources for problem solving, the engineers kept 15-week records of the progress of their R&D projects, and ranked 9 information sources on the basis of their perceived accessibility, perceived ease of use, perceived technical quality, and amount of previous use. The study concluded that accessibility is the single most important determinant of source use; both accessibility and technical quality influence the choice of first source; and perception of accessibility is influenced by experience with the source. However, when the engineers consider whether to accept or reject ideas from sources as tentative solutions to their problems, the dominant factor now becomes the technical quality of the sources rather than accessibility. In other words, engineers use sources in proportion to accessibility, but they accept ideas from these sources in proportion to technical quality (Gerstberger and Allen 1968, p. 279; Paisley 1968). In Gerstberger and Allen's study, accessibility was defined as "The degree to which one can attain meaningful contact with the channel—in other words just how easy it is to approach, obtain, or contact the channel (without giving consideration to the reliability of quality of the information expected)" (Allen 1977, p. 182).

After reviewing the concept of perceived accessibility in organizational communication, library science, and management information systems, Culnan (1985) summarized that in organizational communication, source accessibility has generally been defined as both the social and economic costs associated with acquiring information, whereas in library and information science literature, accessibility is generally defined in terms of the 'physical' costs of use, especially the physical distance of the library from the user. Culnan (1985) proposes perceived source accessibility as the unifying concept for the design and evaluation of a wide variety of information systems and services. She defines perceived accessibility as the "expected level of effort required to use a particular information source" (Culnan 1985, p. 302). She proposes three dimensions of accessibility: gaining physical access to the information source (physical dimension); translating an information need or request into a language that is understood by the source (interface dimension); and being able to physically retrieve the potentially relevant information (informational dimension). A fourth dimension may be psychological: for example, the unpleasantness of having to deal with a disagreeable source, or the embarrassment of revealing one's ignorance or need for assistance.

Many user studies found that the perceived accessibility of a source was a major, and sometimes the most important, determinant of source use. For example, scientists, technologists, and managers are often sensitive to perceived source accessibility, so much so that a library or information center on the next floor or even a few offices away may be infrequently visited, even though the users recognize that the library may contain more complete and current information than their close-at-hand sources. This preference for accessible sources seems to conform to Zipf's Law or Principle of Least Effort, which states that human behavior is governed by an attempt to minimize the probable average rate of work required to achieve desired goals (Zipf 1949), a phenomenon that has been observed in a variety of human activities.

Quite apart from source characteristics, the complexity of the task or the uncertainty of the task environment would also influence information seeking. A complex task characterized by numerous interdependent task elements that can behave and interact unpredictably may require broader information gathering and processing. Analogously, a task environment marked by volatility and turbulence may induce greater information scanning. Task complexity depends on the knowledge, tools and techniques that are used to transform inputs into organizational outputs. Perrow (1967) describes how this task technology is defined by two underlying task characteristics: task variety and task analyzability. Task variety is the frequency of unexpected and novel events that occur in the conversion process. Task analyzability is the extent to which the conversion process is analyzable and can be controlled by set procedures or standard practices. Thus, in organizations which apply technology with high task variety and where the task is not analyzable, large amounts of information are used to handle exceptions and rich information media are used to resolve unanalyzable issues.

Figure 1.3 summarizes our discussion of information seeking in this section. The selection and use of information sources is influenced by two sets of source-related attributes: perceived source accessibility and perceived source quality. At the same time, the relative importance of perceived source attributes is modulated by the complexity of the task to be accomplished, and by the personal interest and motivation of the individual in the search.

A research project which applied this framework was a national study of how CEOs in the Canadian telecommunications industry scanned their business environments for information about trends and developments (Choo 1993). For these CEOs, the perceived quality of a source (in terms of its reliability and relevance) was a more important predictor of source use than perceived source accessibility. The CEOs invested time and effort in contacting and interacting with less accessible sources such as customers, competitors, and business associates. These personal sources were rated highly by the CEOs for their ability to provide accurate and usable information. The study suggested that the switch of emphasis from source accessibility to source quality was because the CEOs were trying to make sense of a complex and ambiguous business environment, and because they were personally motivated and interested in learning about external trends and developments.

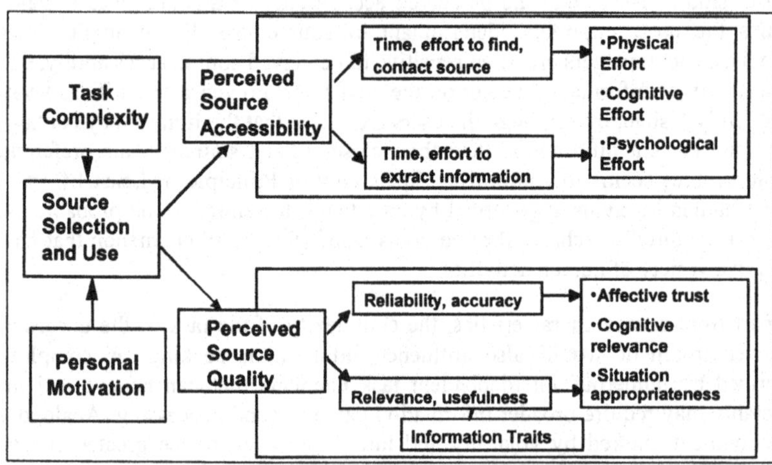

Figure 1. 3 Information Seeking: Perceived Source Accessibility and Quality

1.3 Information Use

Perhaps because it is so much an automatic part of every day experience, information use as a concept has been difficult to define satisfactorily. In a way, information need and information use are two sides of a coin, since the truest indication that information is needed is when it is used. Purposive information seeking focuses on the perceptions and behaviors that lead to information being found, including the identification, selection and use of information sources. Information use occurs when the recipient processes information by engaging mental schemas and emotional responses within a larger social and cultural context. The outcome of information use is a change in the individual's state of knowledge (increase awareness, understand a situation), or capacity to act (solve a problem, make a decision, negotiate a position). Figure 1.4 below illustrates the cognitive, affective, and situational dimensions of information use.

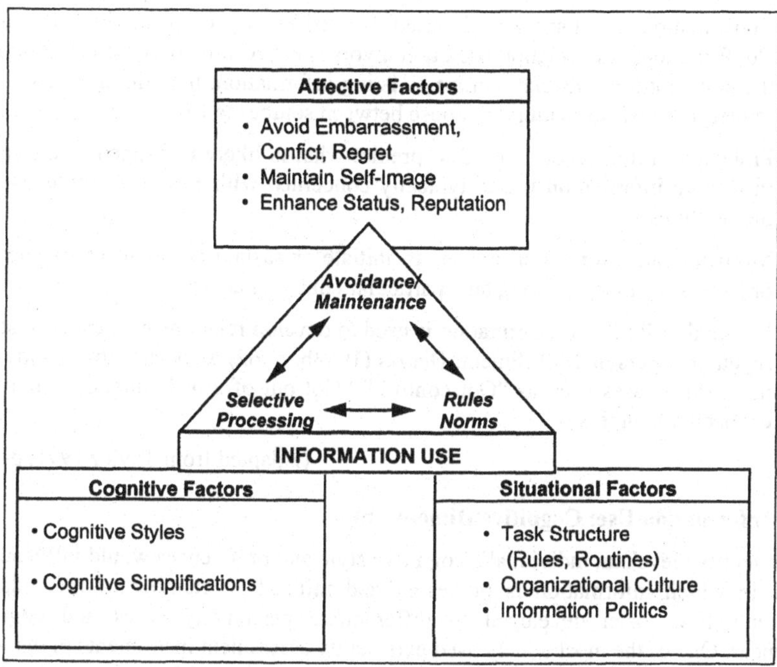

Figure 1. 4 Information Use

Taylor (1991) observes that the ways in which people use information may be described by just eight categories. The categories are not mutually exclusive, so that information used in one category may also address the needs of other categories.

1. Enlightenment. Information is used to develop a context or to make sense of a situation. Information is used to answer questions such as: "Are there similar situations? What are they? What is the history and experience of Corporation X in making product Y, and how is this relevant to our intent to manufacture Y?"
2. Problem Understanding. Information is used in a more specific way than enlightenment—it is used to develop a better comprehension of a particular problem.
3. Instrumental. Information is used so that the individual knows what to do and how to do something. Instructions are a common form of instrumental information. Under some conditions, instrumental information use requires information use in other classes.
4. Factual. Information is used to determine the facts of a phenomenon or event, to describe reality. Factual information use is likely to depend on the actual and perceived quality (accuracy, reliability) of the information that is available.

5. Confirmational. Information is used to verify another piece of information. Confirmational information use often involves the seeking of a second opinion. If the new opinion does not confirm existing information, then the user may try to reinterpret the information or choose between sources to trust.
6. Projective. Information is used to predict what is likely to happen in the future. Projective information use is typically concerned with forecasts, estimates, and probabilities.
7. Motivational. Information is used to initiate or sustain personal involvement, in order to keep moving along on a particular course of action.
8. Personal or Political. Information is used to develop relationships; enhance status, reputation, personal fulfillment. Dervin (1983b, p. 62) associates this information use with phrases such as "Got control," "Got out of a bad situation," and "Got connected to others."

(Adapted from Taylor 1991, p. 230)

1.3.1 Information Use: Cognitive Dimensions

At the cognitive level, an individual's cognitive style and preferences would influence the manner in which information is processed and utilized. A number of methods and instruments have been developed to differentiate personality types and cognitive preferences. One of the most widely used personality assessment instruments in the world is the Myers-Briggs Type Indicator (MBTI) classification, which is derived from the work of Carl Jung (Bayne 1995). MBTI analyzes personality types based on four pairs of traits:

- Introversion versus Extraversion: Introverts draw mental energy from themselves whereas extroverts draw energy from others.
- Sensing versus "Intuiting": Sensing types rely on information perceived through their five senses. Intuitive types rely more on patterns, relationships, and hunches.
- Thinking versus Feeling: Thinking types use information to make logical decisions based on objective criteria. Feeling types depend on personal values to decide between right and wrong.
- Judging versus Perceiving: Judging types move quickly to closure by making use of the available information. Perceiving types keep their options open by taking their time to gather sufficient information.

These four pairs of attributes are combined to create a matrix of 16 personality types. Each personality type is expected to display distinctive styles and preferences when processing and using information, as outlined above.

Other cognitive style variables that have been examined include field dependence, and adaption-innovation styles. Field dependent individuals tend to respond uncritically to environmental cues, whereas field independent individuals orient themselves correctly in spite of environmental cues (Witkin & Goodenough 1981). In Kirton's Adaption-Innovation theory (Kirton 1989), adaptors support existing frames of reference and attempt to improve an existing system, while innovators are more prepared to challenge existing paradigms and try to reconstruct the system. When innovators select and use information, they are more likely than adaptors to explore new elements and generate new mental models.

In processing information, people rely on a limited number of shortcuts to reduce the complex task into simpler judgmental operations. These heuristics are two-edged, for while they reduce mental effort in decision making, their use can also lead to systemic biases or errors in judgment. Tversky and Kahneman (1974) describe three sets of heuristics that are commonly used: representativeness, availability, and anchoring and adjustment.

People use heuristics of representativeness when they are assessing the likelihood that an event or object belongs to a certain category. They do so by judging the similarity of the event or object to stereotypes that they believe to be representative of category members. Managers for example may quickly categorize a price lowering action by a competitor as an attempt to gain market share; supervisors may select someone based on perception of certain traits that they believe to typify a desirable worker. Representativeness heuristics may capture learning from experience, but can lead to systemic errors when they do not take into account the size of the sample, prior or base probabilities of the various categories in the population, the distinction between events that are independent or related, the tendency for extreme events to regress to a mean, and so on.

People use heuristics of availability when they are assessing the likelihood or plausibility of a particular development. They do so by recalling familiar, recent, and vivid instances. Consumers for example base their buying decisions on past satisfactory use rather than results of objective evaluations; air travelers worry for their own safety after learning about recently publicized accidents. Availability heuristics can save time and effort in searching for relevant precedents, but can lead to biases when they are unduly limited to instances that are easy to recall or information that is easy to retrieve.

People use heuristics of anchoring and adjustment when they are trying to estimate the value of a quantity. They do so by starting from an initially presented value (the anchor) and adjusting it to arrive at a final estimate. Managers for example may estimate sales and budgets for the next period by simple extrapolations of values obtained in the previous period. Decision makers may accurately recognize important changes in the environment but fail to revise their strategies or performance targets sufficiently as justified by the new information. Anchoring heuristics lead to errors when the adjustment is insufficient. Anchoring may also be qualitative, as when first impressions persist and remain difficult to modify.

1.3.2 Information Use: Affective Dimensions

At the affective level, we may expect that when people process information, they avoid using information that will arouse strong, negative emotions in others or in themselves.

People use information selectively to avoid embarrassment, conflict or regret; to maintain self-image; and to enhance personal status or reputation.

Argyris (1994) explains how in the name of maintaining "morale" and "considerateness," people in organizations often censor and control their use of information. When facing problems presenting potential threat or embarrassment, they often reason and behave defensively. Argyris reasons that this form of defensive reasoning serves no purpose except self-protection, although the people who use it rarely acknowledge that they are protecting themselves. Instead they believe they are protecting the group, the department, the organization, all for the sake of being positive.

Argyris (1994) describes a company that applied Total Quality Management (TQM) techniques to help its 40 supervisors identify nine areas for improvement. Much to the satisfaction of management, the resulting initiative met its goals one month early and saved more money than was anticipated. In conversations with the supervisors, Argyris was told several times how easy it had been to identify the nine areas since the supervisors had known where the worst inefficiencies were for the past three to five years. Although they had the information for many years, the supervisors never acted on it. When asked why, they cited the blindness of management, rivalry between departments, and a corporate culture that avoided getting others into trouble for the sake of correcting problems. The responsibility for fixing the problem areas and the blame for not doing so always lay elsewhere. Argyris observes that although the supervisors believed they were using the rigorous methods of TQM, their actual information practices were driven more by affective, defensive routines. Thus, they gathered data selectively, postulated only non-threatening causes, and tested explanations in self-serving ways. Argyris suggests that people learn this procedure over time, supported by affective norms such as being "caring" and "thoughtful."

The underlying reason for such behavior is psychological, and has to do with the mental and affective strategies that people learn early in life for dealing with emotional or threatening issues. In stressful situations, people depart from their espoused theory of action based on rational principles and commitments, and instead behave according to a theory-in-use that is quite different. While espoused theories vary widely, most theories-in-use have the same four governing values,

> "All of us design our behavior in order to remain in unilateral control, to maximize winning and minimize losing, to suppress negative feelings, and to be as rational as possible, by which we mean laying out clear-cut goals and then evaluating our own behavior on the basis of whether or not we've achieved them. The purpose of this strategy is to avoid vulnerability, risk, embarrassment, and the appearance of incompetence." (Argyris 1994, p. 87)

A specific example of affective responses influencing information use is when decision makers become increasingly locked into losing courses of action. Why do decision makers positively evaluate and continue a course of action when the objective information indicate withdrawal is necessary to reduce further losses? Staw and Ross (1987) identify a number of psychological determinants that induce escalation of commitment: prior reinforcement, self-justification, self inference, and a desire to save face. Prior reinforcement occurs when individuals have received reinforcement from benefits achieved early in a course of action, and the deterioration is slow and irregular. They stay on a failing course because they expect success in the end or because the behavior has been ingrained. In self-justification, decision makers "justify an ineffective course of action by increasing their commitment to it, ... in the hope of turning the situation around or saving their original decisions from being a failure." (Staw and Ross 1987, p. 51) In self-inference, individuals tend to become committed to a course when their earlier actions supporting the course have been explicit, volitional, visible, irrevocable, repeated, and significant (Staw and Ross 1987, Salancik 1977, Kiesler 1971). In face-saving, decision makers persist because they do not want to admit to themselves that they have made an error, much less expose their mistakes to others. In organizations where error-free decision making is valued, managers may attempt to hide their mistakes or postpone their discovery.

Another well-known information behavior is the not-invented-here (NIH) syndrome: the tendency of a longstanding group to reject new information from outside. Such behavior may be a natural consequence of individuals who over time, increase order and stability in their work environments so as to reduce the amount of stress and uncertainty that they need to face. As a result, the longer the individuals' tenure in a group, the stronger their emotional attachment to beliefs and decisions that they helped create, and the more resistant they become towards outside new ideas and information. In a study of 345 R&D professionals working on 50 projects in a large corporate research facility, Katz and Allen (1982) found that project performance increases up to 1.5 years tenure, stays steady for a time but by 5 years has declined noticeably, partly as a result of the NIH syndrome.

1.3.3 Information Use: Situational Dimensions

At the situational level, the degree to which a task has been structured by rules and routines will impact the use of information. Cyert and March (1992/1963) describe how organizations rely on standard operating procedures to guide information processing. They distinguish four major types of procedures: task performance rules, continuing records and reports, information-handling rules, and plans and planning rules. Task performance procedures specify methods for accomplishing tasks and may apply at many levels of the organization, from regulating the information behavior of managers to controlling the information use of operators and counter staff. Task performance rules are important because they encode past organizational learning, and ensure that the activity of each subunit is consistent and coordinated with the work of other subunits. Records and reports are maintained by the organization for the purposes of control and prediction. They have a control effect because members assume that the records are being kept for a purpose and that someone will check the records. As a database of past events, they also help to predict the future, assuming that past cause-effect relations will hold for the future. Records reflect the organization's model of the world, so that what records are maintained influence what aspects of the environment are noticed, and what alternatives are considered. Information-handling rules define how the organization's information is to be routed and filtered. Information routing rules specify who will communicate to whom about what, and often define 'proper' channels of information flow that reflect hierarchy or specialization. Information filtering rules specify what information is to be generated and transmitted, which are based again on the specializations and points-of-view of senders and recipients, and can influence the formation of organizational expectations. Plans and planning rules are used to derive an intended allocation of resources among the alternative activities of the organization, typically presented in the form of budgets. Cyert and March reason that by being simultaneously a goal, schedule, theory and precedent, a plan, like other standard operating procedures, helps to reduce the information processing load of dealing with a complex world. In summary, we note that task performance rules define what information is required and how it is to be used; records and reports policies define what information is captured and stored; information-handling rules define which information is to be passed on, to whom, and how it should be filtered; and planning rules define how information is used to allocate resources.

Schein (1997) defines organizational culture as a pattern of shared assumptions developed by the organization as it learns to cope with its problems of external adaptation and internal integration. Because the assumptions have worked well enough, they are considered valid and are therefore taught to new members as the correct way to perceive, think and feel in relation to those problems. While Schein's definition of culture emphasizes consensus, Martin (1992) suggests that organizational culture is simultaneously integrated, differentiated, and fragmented. In the integrated perspective, the organization agrees about basic values and assumptions which are consistent in content and in the ways they guide action. Integrated cultures provide cognitive clarification, helping individuals to make sense of their activities, and to be aware of role expectations and the organization's history (Martin 1992). In the differentiation perspective, subcultures form "islands of localized lucidity," with each subculture creating its own "coherent meaning system," and "providing clear solutions to problems shared by a group." (Martin 1992, p. 93) To preserve subcultural clarity and cohesiveness, ambiguous or contradictory information is channeled outside the boundaries of the group. In the fragmented perspective, a multiplicity of interpretations coexist and do not coalesce into a stable consensus (Martin 1992). Organizational cultures are temporary webs of individuals loosely connected by the issues they are interested in. Information use is highly selective and focused on specific issues. Individuals' participation and positions in these interest networks are constantly changing, and rather than pushing ambiguity away, they confront and deal with it directly. Whether organizational culture is integrated, differentiated or fragmented, it provides a shared framework that people use to notice and label actions and events, assign value and significance to developments, and collectively make sense of information.

Janis (1982) has observed how highly cohesive groups are susceptible to groupthink, when group members seek concurrence to such an extent that they compromise the processing and use of information, choosing to ignore or undervalue information that threatens group beliefs and solidarity. The symptoms of groupthink are divided into three types. First, group members share a feeling of invulnerability which leads to optimism and a willingness to take risks. Second, group members are close-minded, collectively rationalizing or discounting aberrant information and maintaining stereotyped views of opposing parties as weak and ineffectual. Third, group members press toward uniformity, sustaining a shared impression of unanimity through self-censorship as well as direct pressure against dissenting views. As a result of these affective illusions of invulnerability and solidarity, the group's seeking and use of information is compromised, and decision making becomes defective. Specifically, members fail to survey alternatives and objectives adequately; do not examine risks of preferred choice or reappraise alternatives that were initially rejected; search for information poorly; process information in a biased, selective way; and do not make contingency plans (Janis 1982). Groupthink is more likely when decision makers are members of a cohesive group, when organization structure insulates the group or lacks norms to require methodical procedures, and when the decision situation is highly stressful due to external threats. External threats draw the group even closer, with members increasing their reliance on the group for social and emotional support, thereby heightening the desire to seek concurrence and consensus.

An important part of organizational culture is organizational politics. In a contest for power, information may be used as a resource to protect or expand spheres of influence. Davenport, Eccles and Prusak (1992) found that the major reason for the inability to create information-based organizations was the failure to manage the politics of information use. Among the 25 organizations they studied, five models of information politics were observed: technological utopianism, anarchy, feudalism, monarchy, and federalism. The most common political model was a form of information feudalism, in which individual managers and their departments control information acquisition, storage, distribution, and analysis. Managers act as powerful feudal lords who not only rule over the creation and circulation of information, but also determine the meanings and interpretations that should be attached to information. Instead of feudalism Davenport et al recommend a form of information federalism as being the most appropriate model in today's environment. Federalism recognizes that politics is a necessary and legitimate activity for people with divergent interests to work out a collective purpose and the means for realizing it. Under federalism, managers negotiate among themselves the use and definition of information. Managers bargain with each other to cede some of their information assets in return for producing a larger pool of knowledge that they can tap into and exploit to advantage.

1.4 Human Information Seeking: An Integrated Model

The model of information seeking presented in this chapter is based on a number of guiding ideas. Information needs arise when people perceive gaps in their state of knowledge and ability to make sense of experience. Information seeking is the process in which they then purposefully search for information by identifying, selecting, and interacting with sources. Information use occurs when people process information which changes their state of knowledge or capacity to make sense. Information seeking and use is part of a larger human and social activity through which information becomes useful to an individual or group. Information seeking and use is situated action, so that the way the process develops depends on changing conditions in the context of information use, and this in turn depends on the changes in the context induced by human action.

The three processes of information needs, information seeking, and information use may be integrated into a general model of how humans seek information (see Fig. 1.5). Although information seeking and use is a dynamic, non-linear process that often appears disorderly, the model suggests that there is underlying structure in the ways people look for and use information. The model provides a framework for analysis by conceptually partitioning information seeking into three processes: experiencing information needs, information seeking, and information use. Within each process, the model examines the interactions of cognitive needs, affective responses, and situational demands.

1.4.1 Information Needs—A Summary

As shown in the top triangle of Figure 1.5, people experience information needs when they perceive gaps in their state of knowledge or their ability to make sense. Information needs are shaped by cognitive, affective, and situational factors. To analyze information needs cognitively, Dervin (1992) uses the metaphor of a person making journey through life being stopped in gap situations when the ability to make sense has run out. The way that a person perceives the gap is a good predictor of information seeking and use behaviors. From a large number of field studies, Dervin is able to identify a number of generic information gaps that people experience. These gaps include decision stops (e.g. when a person faces two or more roads ahead), barrier stops (when there is one road ahead but the way is blocked), and spin-out stops (e.g. when there is no road ahead). People who perceive themselves as being in these situation gaps will seek information to bridge the gap.

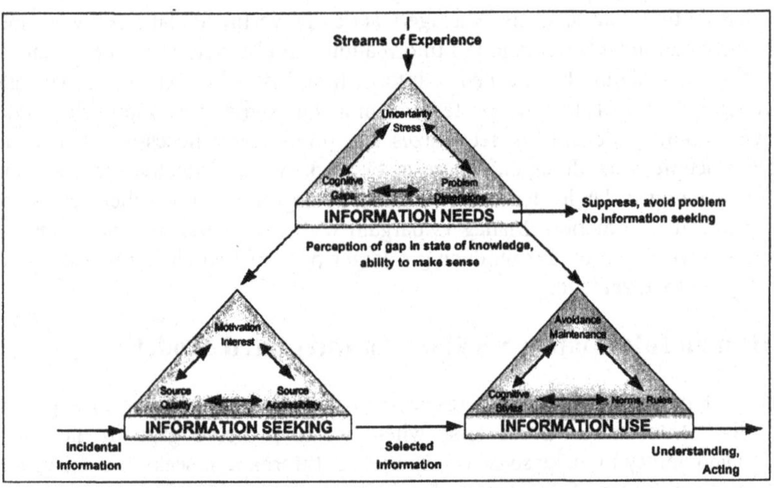

Figure 1.5 Human Information Seeking: An Integrated Model

When sense has run out, the lack of understanding creates a state of uncertainty. Kuhlthau (1993) found that uncertainty causes a number of affective symptoms, including anxiety, apprehension, confusion, frustration, and lack of confidence. Affective responses influence, and are influenced by, the individual's ability to construct meaning, focus information needs, manage moods and expectations, and deepen personal interest in the search. Wilson (1997) suggests that uncertainty and its affective symptoms can constitute a state of stress. Individuals cope with the stress in a variety of ways. For example, some prefer large amounts of information and suffer less stress when they have the information, while others prefer less information and suffer greater arousal when they receive much information.

Individuals experience information needs as they are immersed in specific problem situations. Such situations are composed of a large number of elements that relate not just to subject matter, but also to situational factors. For example, the problem situation lies on a continuum between well- or ill-structured, simple or complex, familiar or new; its assumptions may or may not be agreed upon; its goals may be specific or amorphous (MacMullin and Taylor 1984). Well-structured problems would require formal, quantitative data, while ill-structured problems need information on how to interpret or proceed. Problems with specific goals would require information that operationalizes or measures the goals, while problems with amorphous goals would first need information to clarify preferences and directions. Problem dimensions therefore elaborate information needs and form the criteria by which individuals assess the relevance and value of information.

1.4.2 Information Seeking—A Summary

The experiencing of information needs does not inevitably lead to information seeking. An individual may respond to information needs in one of three ways. First, the individual may choose to suppress this information need by for example, avoiding the problem situation, so that no information seeking ensues. Second, the individual may search his or her own memory for information that can address the need. Again, no external information seeking occurs. Third, the individual may decide to bridge the gap of knowledge or understanding through purposive information seeking. Purposive information seeking is directed towards the goal of solving a problem, making a decision, or increasing understanding. The individual identifies possible sources, differentiates and chooses sources, makes contact with them, and interacts with the sources to obtain the desired information. Purposive information seeking is depicted by the left-hand triangle in Figure 1.5.

At the cognitive level, the individual selects sources that are perceived to have the greater probability of providing information that will be relevant, usable, and helpful. Relevance and usability may depend on information attributes such as currency, comprehensiveness, and appropriateness to the specific problem situation. In addition, the individual selects sources that are perceived to meet accuracy and reliability requirements. Taylor (1986) defines source reliability as the trust a user has in the quality of the source and its information. Field studies suggest that individuals consciously or subconsciously employ relevance- and reliability-related attributes to evaluate perceived source quality as part of information seeking activity.

At the affective level, the individual's degree of personal motivation and interest in the problem or topic would determine the amount of energy spent in information seeking. Kuhlthau (1993) describes how initial feelings of anxiety and confusion could be replaced by feelings of increased confidence as the search progresses. If a theme is found to focus the search, the individual becomes more highly motivated. The individual's mood towards the search may also influence the breadth and depth of information seeking—a person in an invitational mood would explore more sources while a person in an indicative mood would seek information that leads to closure or action. If the information found enables the individual to see the problem more clearly and to develop a sense of direction, feelings of optimism and confidence increase as the search progresses. Wilson (1997) postulates that since a strong feeling of self-efficacy or personal mastery about using a source leads to greater source use, doubt about one's capacity to use a source properly would conversely lead to that source not being used, even if the source might be perceived to contain relevant information.

At the situational level, the use of sourçes is influenced by the perceived accessibility of the source. At least three different kinds of "effort" or costs may be pertinent: physical effort; intellectual effort; and psychological effort. The selection of sources then deepens on their perceived quality and perceived accessibility. Additionally, the complexity of the task or the uncertainty of the task environment would also influence information seeking. A complex task characterized by numerous interdependent task elements which interact unpredictably may require broader information gathering. Similarly, a complex, volatile external environment may induce greater information scanning.

Even as purposive information seeking is going on, information is also being acquired "incidentally" through the individual's habitual information gathering routines. Wilson (1977) suggests that everyone maintains a set of habits or routines for keeping his or her internal mental model up to date. Such routines could include for example, scanning the mass media, conversations with friends and colleagues, and personal observation. Although these activities are not directed at addressing specific information needs, useful information is often encountered in this incidental manner.

1.4.3 Information Use—A Summary

As shown in the right-hand triangle of Figure 1.5, information use is the final stage of the model when the individual acts on the information found to for example, answer a question, resolve a problem, take a decision, negotiate a position, or make sense of a situation. The outcome of information use is therefore a change in the individual's state of knowledge and capacity to act or make sense. Taylor (1991) proposes that the ways people use information may be described by one or more of just eight categories: develop a context; understand a particular situation; know what and how to do something; get the facts about something; confirm another item of information; project future events; motivate or sustain personal involvement; and develop relationships, enhance status, reputation or personal fulfillment.

At the cognitive level, the individual's cognitive style and preferences would influence the manner that information is processed and utilized. A number of classifications have been developed to differentiate personality types and cognitive preferences. The Myers-Briggs Type Indicator is a widely used instrument for classifying personality types into

16 categories. Each personality types is expected to process and use information in a distinctive manner. Another cognitive style variable is field dependence. Field dependent individuals tend to respond uncritically to environmental cues, whereas field independent individuals orient themselves correctly in spite of environmental cues. Kahneman and Tversky (1974) have observed that when people use information to make judgments they rely on heuristics to simplify information processing. In certain situations, these simplifications can produce errors or biases. For example, to judge whether an event belongs to a category, people rely on mental stereotypes, but they often ignore other relevant information such as the distribution of the categories in the general population. To judge the frequency or likelihood of an event, people over-rely on recent, vivid, easy-to-recall information. To estimate a quantity they make adjustments from an initial anchor or suggestion. Unfortunately the adjustments are often inadequate.

At the affective level, people avoid using information that arouses strong, negative emotions in others or in themselves. They use information selectively to avoid embarrassment, conflict or regret; maintain self-image; and enhance personal status or reputation. Argyris (1994) observes how people censor their use of information in emotionally-charged situations. They do this ostensibly to show "care" and "consideration," but they are in fact acting defensively to "avoid vulnerability, risk, embarrassment, and the appearance of incompetence." Two other examples of affective responses shaping information use are the escalation of commitment and the not-invented-here syndrome. In commitment escalation, people continue to evaluate positively and maintain a course of action even when the available information indicates that the action is no longer viable, and that withdrawal is necessary to reduce further losses. People persist because they want to save face: they do not want to admit to themselves, much less to others, that they have made an error. In the not-invented-here syndrome, members of a longstanding group reject new information from outside the group. This is because group members have developed strong emotional attachment to their beliefs and past decisions, thereby creating a stable environment that reduces the amount of stress and uncertainty that they need to face. The longer the individuals' membership in a group, the more resistant they become towards outside new ideas and information.

At the situational level, information use is determined by the extent to which rules and routines structure the task in which the information is utilized. Cyert and March (1992/1963) describe how task performance rules define what information is required and how it is to be used in task execution; records and reports policies define what information is documented and archived; information-handling rules define how information is to be routed and filtered; and planning rules define how information is used to decide about resource allocation. Schein (1997) and Martin (1992) describe the role of organizational culture as establishing a shared framework of assumptions, beliefs and values for constructing meaning. People use the framework to notice and label actions and events, assign value and significance to developments, and collectively make sense of information. An important part of organizational culture is information politics, and a major obstacle to creating information-based organizations is managing the politics of information use. Thus, Davenport, Eccles and Prusak (1992) found that the most common political model in organizations to be based on information feudalism, where managers act as feudal lords who control information production and use, including what the information means.

The result of information seeking is a set of noticed, selected information that is a very small subset of the total information that is received. How this information is then processed and put to use depends on the cognitive style and preferences of the individual, the emotional responses that accompany information processing, and the social and cultural context surrounding information use. The final outcome of information use is a change in the individual's state of knowledge or awareness, allowing the individual to make sense or take action. The actions and interactions of multiple individuals and groups generate new experiences. New experiences create new ambiguities and uncertainties, so that the cycle of information needing, information seeking, and information use is always in motion.

1.4.4 Some Implications for Practice

The behavioral model of information seeking presented in this chapter has many implications for improving information system design and information management practices in organizations. We outline just a few below, mainly to indicate the breadth of the challenge that lies ahead.

1. Design information systems not just to answer queries, but to provide useful and useable information that would help individuals solve work-related problems and deal with the requirements of specific problem situations.

   System designers need to look beyond analyzing flows of data, beyond developing algorithms to retrieve data. The value of information lies in its closeness to action. We therefore need to understand how the meaning of information is constructed, how the context of organizational work is negotiated, and how the value and usefulness of information is determined. For example, users should be able to query systems not just with account numbers or keywords, but also with life situations ("I am buying a house, what statutory information sources do I consult?"); task descriptions ("I am writing a project plan on P—get me the information I need"); or sensemaking questions ("What are the assumptions underlying our interpretation?").

2. Increase awareness about the nature of human information seeking and processing, including an understanding of cognitive styles and limitations, and the ways that habitual routines and emotional defenses can block learning.

   Cognitive diversity invigorates an organization, so the intention here is not to use a taxonomy of cognitive preferences and routines to pigeonhole people according to their presumed strengths and weaknesses. Instead, the goal is to ensure a balanced mix of styles, skills and sensibilities so as to increase the vigilance of information processing.

3. Educate everyone to manage information quality and information quantity.

   System designers need to understand how people assign value and salience to information. Users need to know how to evaluate the quality of sources and information, and how to balance between source quality and source accessibility. In restricting information quantity to prevent overload, users should also guard against premature closure: divergent information gathering (that consults many sources) is necessary to prepare the ground for convergent action-taking.

4. Develop an organizational culture that values and encourages information sharing.

   Some of the best information sources are one's colleagues in the same organization. Ironically, as organizations become more information-intensive, the more problematic it has become to encourage members to share their information freely. Organizations now have to work at creating and sustaining affective systems and cultural climates which promote the sharing of information and knowledge.

Chapter 2: The Structure and Dynamics of Organizational Knowledge

This chapter has three objectives. First, we examine the transformation of data to knowledge as the outcome of human enactment that imposes increasing levels of structure on signals and data. Second, we present a typology of organizational knowledge that differentiates between tacit knowledge, explicit knowledge, and cultural knowledge. Third, we introduce major theoretical models that attempt to explain the dynamics of creating, diffusing, and using organizational knowledge.

2.1 From Information to Knowledge

Information and knowledge are the outcomes of human action that engage signs, signals, and artifacts in social and physical settings. Knowledge builds on an accumulation of experience. Information depends on an aggregation of data. Transformation of information into knowledge is the result of two complementary dynamics: the "structuring" of data and information that imposes or reveals order and pattern; and the human "acting" on data and information that attributes sense and salience. Figure 2.1 uses these two dimensions to show the assumed progression of data into information into knowledge.

2.1.1 From Signals to Data

In the lower left of Fig. 2.1, we encounter signals—sights, sounds, and other sensory phenomena to which the human actor is exposed. From the vast amount of signals reaching a person, the actor selects and takes notice of only a small number. This noticing typically involves grouping or delimiting signals into packets of data. Thus, marks on a paper are recognized as words; illuminated pixels on a screen are registered as images. The structuring of signals is physical because it depends on conditions in the material environment (such as lighting, noise) and on technical requirements of the task being performed (such as speed, accuracy). At the same time, which signals are noticed and punctuated into data is influenced by the observer's past learning about parsing of signals, as well as by beliefs about what signals to expect. Data then are facts and messages observed by an individual or group. Data are often elements of larger physical systems (such as books, instrument panels) which give clues about what data to notice and how they should be "read."

Since the prior information and knowledge of the observer influences what signals are noticed and parsed, the data-information-knowledge sequence is more like a circle than a hierarchy.

2.1.2 From Data to Information

In the middle of Fig. 2.1, we show how the observer makes sense of noticed data through a process of "cognitive structuring" which assigns meaning and significance to the perceived facts and messages. What meanings are constructed depends on the schemas and mental models that the actor brings forth to frame, categorize, and contextualize the data. Schemas mediate between sensory experience and intellectual thought: "schema refers to an active organization of past reactions, or past experiences, which must always be supposed to be operating in any well-adapted organic response. That is, whenever there is any order or regularity of behavior, a particular response is possible only because it is related to other similar responses which have been serially organized, yet which operate, not simply as individual members coming one after another, but as a unitary mass." (Bartlett 1932, p. 201) Whereas schemas are concerned with content—they enable the actor to categorize objects and thoughts; mental models are concerned with form—they enable the actor to represent selected data and their relationships to other facts and messages, and thereby make inferences about what the data mean. Mental models (Johnson-Laird 1983) are constructed by individuals using words, images or both in order to represent data and their relationships in a convenient and accessible manner so that a viable interpretation may be composed and tested. Thus data become information when the former has been vested with meaning and relevance.

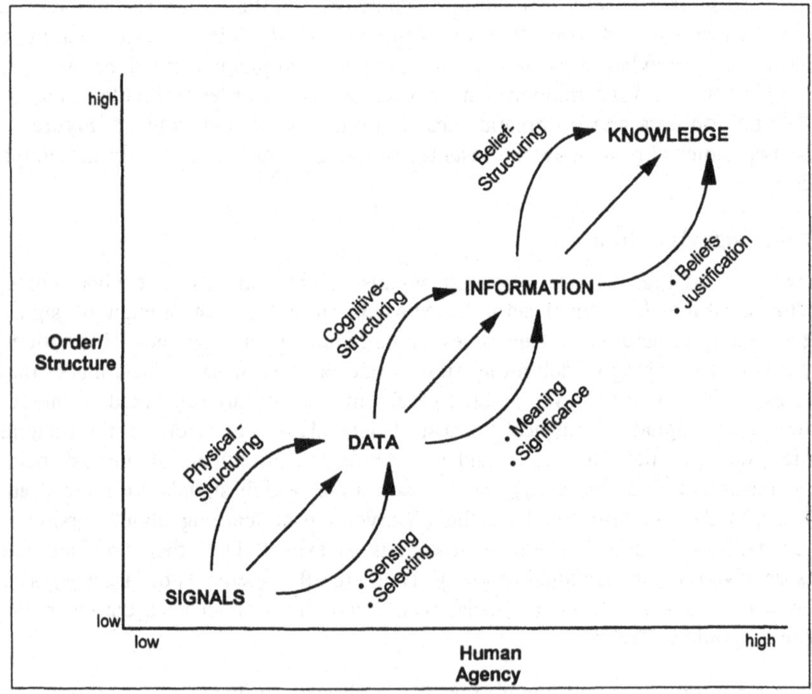

Figure 2.1 Data, Information, and Knowledge

2.1.3 From Information to Knowledge

As shown at the top of Fig. 1.1, information becomes knowledge when a human being forms justified, true beliefs about the world ("belief-structuring"). This view is derived from standard analysis in epistemology which defines propositional knowledge as justified true belief (Audi 1998, Moser et al 1998). This definition of knowledge specifies three conditions which are individually necessary and jointly sufficient. The belief condition requires that a person who knows that a proposition (which is an object of knowledge) is so believes that proposition. Beliefs are psychological states of the mind: while they may or may not be manifested in overt behavior, they do involve tendencies or dispositions to behave in certain ways under certain conditions. The truth condition requires that a person genuinely knows that a proposition is so only if that proposition is in fact the case. A proposition is true when for example there is a correspondence between the true statement and actual features of the world; or when the statement is "coherent" with some system of other statements (such as one's other beliefs). Since truth is relative, knowledge may vary dramatically from person to person (or from organization to organization), yet there will still be knowledge, in abundance. The justification condition requires that a person must have adequate indication or evidence that a proposition is true. Knowledge is not simply true belief — the justification condition disqualifies true beliefs that are supported only by lucky guesswork.

As an amplification, it may be helpful to note that epistemology distinguishes between propositional and non-propositional knowledge. Propositional knowledge is knowledge that something is so; non-propositional knowledge is knowledge of something. Propositional knowledge may be subdivided into empirical, a posteriori knowledge that is derived from sense-perception and introspection; and non-empirical, a priori knowledge that is derived from axiomatic bases and reasoning. Non-propositional knowledge of something may be derived from direct awareness of the objects, or knowledge by acquaintance (Russell 1912). Although propositional knowledge is traditionally defined as justified true belief, the justification condition is the focus of much epistemological debate. Many are suggesting that the definition of knowledge be made more rigorous by specifying the right kind of justification. Thus, there are contemporary attempts to analyze knowledge as: undefeatedly justified true belief; conclusively justified true belief (where belief is justified in such a way that what justifies it guarantees its truth); appropriately caused true belief (where the thing being believed plays a part in generating or sustaining that belief); and as reliably grounded true belief (where belief is the result of a reliable belief-producing process) (Audi 1998).

The treatment of knowledge in organizations is often based implicitly on empiricism—that concepts and propositions claiming to be knowledge are derived from experience and depend for their justification on experience. A related point of view approaches the human actor as a natural phenomenon whose epistemic activity is to be studied using empirical methods ("naturalistic epistemology" Quine 1969, Kornblith 1994). For example, Dretske (1981) applies information theory to characterize knowledge as information-produced belief: a person knows that a proposition is so only if some signal conveys this information to that person—information being an object that can be processed and transmitted from one place to another when events at these places are connected by some dependency. Goldman (1986) argues that a belief can be justified only if it is generated by belief-forming (cognitive) processes which have the reliable capability to arrive at true or correct answers to questions of interest. Examples of belief-forming processes include reasoning processes, memory processes, and perceptual processes. A pertinent question becomes just how reliable such a process must be in order that its resultant belief be justified. Since perfect reliability is not required, those processes that sometimes produce error can still confer justification.

2.1.4 From Information to Knowledge — in Organizations

How does information in organizations evolve into knowledge? Starting from interpreted information, organizational participants take actions based on construed meaning and import. As they observe and reflect on the outcomes of using different sets of information in a variety of work, social and personal situations, people discern patterns and form beliefs in order to understand them. Patterns, propositions, and hypotheses are the evolving material of personal and organizational knowledge. While a particular set of information refers to a specific experience, knowledge refers to an accumulation of experiences which has yielded concepts, beliefs, and evidence that sustain these beliefs. Through use, practice, and reflection, information becomes knowledge—in this sense, knowledge is the result of "belief structuring" which leads to a higher level of ordering and understanding than is the case for information (Fig. 2.1). Knowledge supplies beliefs and assumptions that are used to perceive situations or events, and to explain cause-effect relationships between actors and actions. Knowledge may be formal and informal, conscious and unconscious, cognitive and affective, prepackaged and situated.

Although an organization certainly possesses beliefs which it perceives to be true, these beliefs are often arrived at through weak belief-forming processes that may not meet the justification condition. Thus, organizations use belief-forming processes that rely on simplifications, individual opinions, or heuristics. Over time, beliefs can become entrenched or protected, so that an organization may continue to act on them unthinkingly, or fail to reexamine their validity when new information is available. These behaviors block the acquisition of new knowledge, and this is one reason why organizations are said to be hobbled by learning disabilities.

In organizations, the justification of knowledge as true belief becomes a public process. As individuals bring forth their personal beliefs in the act of sharing knowledge, they are called upon to justify those beliefs in the presence of others. According to von Krogh (1998) such public justification of personal knowledge is a fragile process because of four barriers: the need for a legitimate language to express the knowledge in understandable and acceptable terms; the existence of stories of failure that appear to challenge the personal beliefs; formal procedures that work against the justification process by controlling communications and steps; and the company's prevailing paradigm that seems to disagree with the personal beliefs. Justification may also be a political process, particularly when it involves individuals or groups who are perceived to possess higher power or status, and who can therefore lay stronger claims about the veracity or value of their beliefs.

An organization also possesses non-propositional knowledge, such as the knowledge of things, and the knowledge about how to do things. Clearly valuable to an organization is the knowledge that is contained in things such as products, patents, materials, and equipment. Less visible but just as strategic is the knowledge that an organization has developed about how to do things—knowledge that is embedded in the organization's routines and procedures.

Individuals in an organization develop a special kind of knowledge that is derived from practice and experience (and is therefore empirical and a posteriori), but which cannot be expressed as propositions or statements (and is therefore non-propositional). Although it is personal and elusive, organizations are very interested in this kind of knowledge because it is the source of creativity and innovation without which organizations cannot generate new knowledge.

Just as the philosophy of knowledge has divided knowledge into various types, the science of organizations has partitioned organizational knowledge into categories. We continue our exploration of organizational knowledge in the following sections by proposing a typology of organizational knowledge.

2.2 The Structure of Organizational Knowledge

Knowledge in organizations is not monolithic nor homogenous, but is developed from different origins and engaged in different ways. For example, there is knowledge comprising of what the organization believes about itself (identity, purpose), its capabilities, and its environment (communities, markets). There is knowledge embedded in the physical goods the organization produces and in the rules and routines that the organization adopts. Again, every person in the organization also possesses personal knowledge that is derived from experience, skillful practice, and personal insight. Recent work by researchers, including Boisot (1998), Choo (1998), and Spender (1998), suggest that organizational knowledge may be divided into:

1. tacit knowledge,
2. explicit knowledge, and
3. cultural knowledge.

The main features of each category of knowledge are outlined in Table 2.1, and these will be elaborated as we examine each category more closely in the ensuing sections. For now we make a few observations about the interactions across these three forms of knowledge.

Organizations may differ in their relative emphasis of these three categories of knowledge. A marketing services company may prize the tacit knowledge of its individuals in producing creative designs. A public sector organization may rely on explicit knowledge embedded in rules and routines to ensure consistency and accountability. A community-based organization may be held together by a strongly shared set of beliefs.

Type of Knowledge	Description
Tacit Knowledge	• The implicit knowledge used by organizational members to perform their work and to make sense of their worlds.
	• Tacit knowledge is hard to verbalize because it is expressed through action-based skills and cannot be reduced to rules and recipes.
Explicit Knowledge	• Knowledge that can be expressed formally using a system of symbols, and can therefore be easily communicated or diffused.
	• Explicit knowledge may be object-based or rule-based.
Cultural Knowledge	• The cognitive and affective structures that are habitually used to perceive, explain, evaluate, and construct reality.
	• The assumptions and beliefs that are used to describe and explain reality, as well as the conventions and expectations that are used to assign value and significance to new information.

Table 2.1. Categories of Organizational Knowledge

In many organizations, the effective utilization of knowledge typically involves all three forms of knowledge. Thus, highly skilled designers, when applying their creative intuition (tacit knowledge), would work with tools, plans, and specifications (explicit knowledge), at the same time following the adopted values and norms of the profession or organization (cultural knowledge). The direction of interaction can work in the other way too, as when the result of work or actions based on tacit knowledge leads to the organization redefining and reperceiving its roles and values. We describe an example of this in Section 2.3.1 (the Matsushita case). John Seely Brown of Xerox Corporation believes that the contribution of research is not just leveraging the tacit knowledge of its scientists, but also the invention of new cultural knowledge about the organization and its business:

> "The most important invention that will come out of the corporate research lab in the future is the corporation itself. As companies try to keep pace with increasingly unstable business environments, the research department has to do more than simply innovate new products. It must design the new technological and organizational 'architecture' that make possible a continuously innovating company. Put another away, corporate research must reinvent innovation ... [it] must prototype new mental models of the organization and its business." (Brown 1991, p. 105)

At the organizational level, much of the discussion on core competencies and core capabilities implies a close integration of all three types of knowledge. Leonard-Barton (1995) for example, dimensionalizes organizational core capabilities into: employee knowledge and skill; physical and technical systems; managerial systems; and values and norms—dimensions that we recognize as manifestations of tacit, explicit and cultural knowledge. Core capabilities set the organization apart from the rest, and give it a competitive edge. Indeed, we may reason that the more closely coupled the three categories of knowledge are in an organization, the more unique the advantage that the organization possesses, and the more difficult it is for others to copy that advantage. We examine each category of organizational knowledge in the following sections.

2.2.1 Tacit Knowledge

Michael Polanyi examines human tacit knowledge by "starting from the fact that *we can know more than we can tell*" (1966, p. 4, italics in original). Tacit knowledge permeates our personal and work lives, enabling us to drive the automobile, enjoy a poem, or deal with a problem situation. In all such cases of personal knowing, "*the aim of a skilful performance is achieved by the observance of a set of rules which are not known as such to the person following them*" (Polanyi 1962, p. 49, italics in original). Tacit knowledge is hard to transfer or verbalize partly because it cannot be broken down into particular rules or elements, and partly because it exists as an emergent quality of knowing something as a whole.

Tacit knowledge may be likened to knowing that is in our action, "implicit in our patterns of actions and in our feel for the stuff with which we are dealing" (Schön 1983, p. 54). Schön defines this 'knowing-in-action' with the following properties:

- "There are actions, recognitions, and judgments which we know how to carry out spontaneously; we do not have to think about them prior to or during their performance.
- We are often unaware of having learned to do these things; we simply find ourselves doing them.
- In some cases, we were once aware of the understandings which were subsequently internalized in our feeling for the stuff of action. In other cases, we may never have been aware of them. In both cases, however, we are usually unable to describe the knowing which our action reveals." (Schön 1983, p. 54)

From her analysis of the work practices of operators in pulp and paper mills, Zuboff observed how operators relied on action-centered skills that are based on tacit knowledge:

> "When operators in Piney Wood and Tiger Creek discuss their traditional skills, they speak of knowing things by habit and association. They talk about 'cause-and-effect' knowledge and being able to see the things to which they must respond. They refer to 'folk medicine' and knowledge that you don't even know you have until it is suddenly displayed in the ability to take a decisive action and make something work." (Zuboff 1988, p. 71, 187)

Tacit know-how is not limited to technical skills, but is just as important in undergirding the actions of professionals in architecture, engineering, management, psychotherapy, and so on (Schön 1983). Zuboff again provides an example of how bank account officers in the Global Bank Brazil made their credit decisions:

> "Our credit decisions have been more related to feeling than to technical skill. For big loans, the officer knows the client and the client's environment. He spends time with that person. They dine together, play golf together. That is why

> we specialize by industry and company size. This is why the officer comes to know things that are not written. Credit is given by the feeling in one's stomach." (Quoted in Zuboff 1988, p. 164)

In organizations, tacit knowledge is the personal knowledge used by members to perform their work and to make sense of their worlds. It is learned through extended periods of experiencing and doing a task, during which the individual develops a feel for and a capacity to make intuitive judgements about the successful execution of the activity. Because tacit knowledge is action-centered and distributed in the totality of the individual's action-experience, it cannot be isolated and packaged into elements or steps. Such interaction is situated in the social and physical setting where knowledge is engaged. Since tacit knowledge is experiential and contextualized, it cannot be easily codified, written down or reduced to rules and recipes.

Nelson and Winter (1982) suggest three reasons why knowledge used in an organization's operations and practices is likely to be tacit to a significant degree: "because it cannot be articulated fast enough, because it is impossible to articulate all that is necessary to a successful performance, and because language cannot simultaneously serve to describe relationships and characterize the things related" (p. 82). Speed of communication is a problem when the rate of information transfer is well below the rate needed to actually perform a task (such as serving a tennis ball). Articulation is a problem when the practical knowledge is limited in "causal depth": that is, enough is known to perform a task without requiring deep theoretical understanding underlying that skill. Relating parts to the whole is a problem when efforts to exhaustively explain details lead to incoherent messages and information overload. The relative significance of tacit knowledge is thus contingent on the situation surrounding its use:

> "The knowledge contained in the how-to-do-it book and its various supplements and analogues tends to be more adequate when the pace of the required performance is slow and pace variations are tolerable, where a standardized, controlled context for the performance is somehow assured, and where the performance as a whole is truly reducible to a set of simple parts that relate to one another only in very simple ways. To the extent that these conditions do not hold, the role of tacit knowledge in the performance may be expected to be large." (Nelson and Winter 1982, p. 82)

Although personal, tacit knowledge is invisible, its existence and importance are revealed through the skilled practice of individuals and in the ways that experienced employees innovate and deal with breakdowns or surprises in their work situations. Leonard and Sensiper (1998) suggest three ways that tacit knowledge is exercised in the service of innovation: problem solving, problem finding, and prediction and anticipation. In problem solving, experts overlay a problem with patterns derived from experience in order to quickly find a solution. In problem finding, tacit knowledge is used to frame a problem, often in a way that challenges assumptions or reveals hidden dimensions, so as to stimulate more radical innovation. In prediction and anticipation, tacit knowledge enables the prepared mind to follow hunches, listen to intuition, and take mental leaps to make discoveries or consider new ideas.

Despite it being difficult to articulate, tacit knowledge can be and is regularly transferred and shared. Tacit knowledge can be learned through observation and imitation. Thus, apprentices learn their craft by following and copying their masters; professionals acquire expertise and norms through periods of internship; and new employees are immersed in on-the-job training. Professionals reflect on what they know during the practice itself (for example, when they encounter an unusual case) as well as afterwards (for example, in a postmortem), and in doing so test and refine their own tacit knowledge (Schön 1983). Tacit knowledge can also be shared. Although not completely expressible in words or symbols, tacit knowledge may be alluded to or revealed through rich modes of discourse that include the use of analogies, metaphors or models, and through the communal sharing of stories. Storytelling are effective channels of tacit learning because narratives dramatize and contextualize knowledge-rich episodes, allowing the listener to replay and relive as much of the original experience as possible.

Tacit knowledge is vital to organizations because it is an important source of new knowledge: new knowledge in the form of discoveries and innovations is often the outcome of creative individuals applying their tacit insights and intuitions to confront novel or difficult problems. The most advanced computer-based information systems on their own cannot generate new knowledge, only human beings who have accumulated expertise and experience have the capacity to do so.

Organizations face a number of issues with respect to the management of its tacit knowledge. Tacit knowledge grows in the soil of experience, so that employees need to be given the time and opportunity to specialize and build up expertise in a certain area. As an alternative to cultivating its own tacit knowledge, an organization may consider contracting desired expertise on a "just-in-time" basis. This approach has limitations since tacit knowledge is not exercised in isolation, but needs to be contextualized and combined with the organization's explicit and cultural knowledge. Another basic concern is one of access: how does an organization find out and provide access to what its participants know, particularly when this personal knowledge defies codification and classification? As long as the personal knowledge remains tacit, it constitutes a unique competitive advantage for the organization, since the knowledge is hard for other organizations to copy. Unfortunately this uniqueness is not permanent nor protected, since the tacit knowledge is lost should the individual decide to leave the organization (and join a competitor!). The other side of the dilemma is that while tacit knowledge remains completely personal and internalized in individuals, the organization is limited in its ability to leverage and diffuse that knowledge for the development of a number of products or projects. In summary, the organization managing its tacit knowledge has to deal with three major challenges: how to deepen its own stocks of tacit knowledge; how to access and activate this knowledge; and how to maximize the value derived from its use.

Based on a field study of the biotechnology, engineering ceramics, and parallel computing industries, Senker (1998) identifies three main models for capturing tacit knowledge of a scientific and technological nature: science push; technology pull, and the introduction of automation. In science push, "the expansion of the public knowledge base provides the theoretical underpinning for procedures which had previously relied on tacit knowledge" (p. 236). She suggests that the rise of biotechnology is a prime example of science-push: over two decades of basic research in molecular biology and generic engineering produced a wealth of codified knowledge and laid the groundwork for the emergence of small, pioneering firms in the late 1970s, and the subsequent adoption by large firms. In technology pull, scientists and engineers explore the phenomena and problems arising in industrial products and processes, as well as the the practical methods developed in industry to solve problems. Senker sees many examples of technology pull in the semiconductor industry. For example, engineers investigating the cause of short circuits in electronic equipment in the late 1940s discovered whisker crystals. The subsequent research program into these crystals developed much of the fundamental science of crystal growth that proved invaluable to the electronics industry. In the introduction of automation, tacit knowledge is captured or "programmed" into an automated system. For example, a machine tool would record the actions of an experienced machinist on magnetic tape, which can then be played back by the machine to reproduce the same motions. More recently, numerical control machines use mathematical representations to specify the desired paths of cutting tools. In order to work well, NC machine tools often require skilled operators to adjust the tools, correct for tool wear and rough castings, and to correct programming errors and malfunctions. More ambitious attempts at "automating" tacit knowledge are computer-based expert systems which extract and codify heuristic rules-of-thumb from experts in order to replicate the performance of the human expert, at least in a narrowly-defined problem domain.

Spender (1996, 1998) maintains that tacit knowledge as conceptualized by Polanyi (that "we can know more than we can tell") is confusing because it bundles together two distinct properties of personal knowledge. Polanyi has suggested that tacit knowledge is both inaccessible to its possessor and incommunicable to another. For Spender (1998, p. 23),

> "it is this confusion between the inaccessibility of the relevant knowledge to its possessor and the ability of the possessor to convey that knowledge to another that renders this kind of explanation of tacit knowledge so unsatisfactory. We need to separate the internal communication or knowledge movement problem from the external interpersonal communication problem."

In order to exclude the external communication dimension Spender proposes a narrowing of the tacit knowledge category to "implicit knowledge." When people are solving problems, they often make use of implicit knowledge that they are not aware that they possess. This concept of implicit knowledge is supported by empirical evidence indicating that the human mind employs different methods and types of perceiving, remembering and learning, many of which lie outside the realm of mindful consciousness. Thus, Polanyi's original observation that tacit knowledge exists because "we know more than we can tell" may be rephrased as implicit knowledge exists because "we know more than we know we know." Spender further suggests that there are two kinds of implicit knowledge, one that is "individual and automatic," and the other that is "social and collective" (Spender 1996, p. 60-64). "Individual-automatic knowledge" is acquired through extended practice, and its performance is characterized by apparent effortlessness. Such knowledge is often inaccessible at the conscious level. Thus, expert typists can seldom arrange key caps correctly even though they use the keyboard all day; experienced drivers simultaneously monitor several fields of secondary attention; and skilled musicians are focused on interpreting the work they are playing and are unaware of the mechanics of performance. "Social-collective knowledge" is knowledge that is an inherent property of the social system in which the individual participates. In organizations, people assimilate the collective norms and values of their groups and communities, and use these norms as taken-for-granted until occasions when for example they are faced with morally difficult choices that require them to reflect on underlying values. Such collective knowledge is part of organizational culture, and is often communicated through narrative forms of discourse. (We call this collective knowledge cultural knowledge in this book.)

2.2.2 Explicit Knowledge

Explicit knowledge is knowledge that is expressed formally using a system of symbols, and can therefore be easily communicated or diffused (Nonaka and Takeuchi 1995). Explicit knowledge may be object-based or rule-based. Object-based knowledge may be found in artifacts such as products, patents, software code, computer databases, technical drawings, tools, prototypes, photographs, voice recordings, films, and so on. Knowledge is object-based when it is represented using strings of symbols (words, numbers, formulas), or is embodied in physical entities (equipment, models, substances). In the first case, the symbols directly represent or codify the explicit knowledge. In the second case, explicit knowledge may be unpacked from the physical object by for example, reverse-engineering a product, inspecting software code, or analyzing the composition of a substance. One important distinction between tacit and explicit knowledge lies in the transferability of the knowledge, as well as the mechanisms that accomplish this transfer. Grant (1996a, p. 111) suggests that "explicit knowledge is revealed by its communication. This ease of communication is its fundamental property". On the other hand, tacit knowledge is revealed through its application. If tacit knowledge cannot be codified and can only be acquired through observation and practice, then its transfer between individuals is necessarily slow, costly, and uncertain (Kogut and Zander 1992).

Explicit knowledge is rule-based when the knowledge is codified into rules, routines, or standard operating procedures. A substantial part of an organization's operational knowledge about how to do things is contained in its rules, routines and standard procedures. Although all organizations operate with standard procedures, each organization would have developed its own repertoire of routines, based on its experience and the specific environment it functions in. Cyert and March (1963/1992) distinguish between four major types of rule-based procedures: task performance rules, rules for maintaining organizational records, information-handling rules, and planning rules. Task performance rules specify methods for accomplishing organizational tasks. They form the bulk of the organization's rules and procedures and are important because they embody and facilitate the transfer of past learning. Performance rules also have a coordinating function, so that a solution implemented by one group is consistent with a large number of other solutions and tasks being performed elsewhere in the organization. Record keeping rules specify what records and how such records should be maintained by the organization. In the short term, records (such as financial statements or cost records) have a control effect. In the longer term, records are used to predict the environment by suggesting "simple hypotheses about the relation between the past and the future" (Cyert and March 1963/1992, p. 126). Information-handling rules specify the organization's communication system in terms of the characteristics of the information to be taken into the firm, the rules for distributing and summarizing internal and external information, and the characteristics of the information leaving the firm. Planning rules specify the periodic planning process as a standard procedure that produce intended allocation of resources among the activities of the organization (Cyert and March 1963/1992).

Nelson and Winter (1982) suggest that organizational routines or rule-based knowledge play the role of genes in an evolutionary theory of economic change which is based on three concepts:

> "The first is the idea of organizational routine. At any time, organizations have built into them a set of ways of doing things and ways of determining what to do. ... Second, we have used the term "search" to denote all those organizational activities which are associated with the evaluation of current routines and which may lead to their modification, to more drastic change, or to their replacement. ... Routines in general play the role of genes in our evolutionary theory. Search routines stochastically generate mutations. Third, the "selection environment" of an organization is the ensemble of considerations which affects its well-being and hence the extent to which it expands or contracts. The selection environment is determined partly by conditions outside the firms in the industry or sector being considered ... but also by the characteristics and behavior of the other firms in the sector." (Nelson and Winter 1982, p. 400-401)

In this evolutionary perspective, organizations remember by doing, so that the routinization of activity in an organization constitutes the most important form of storage of the organization's specific operational knowledge. Routines vary from well-specified technical routines for producing things; through procedures for hiring and firing, ordering inventory, or stepping up production; to policies on investment, R&D, or business strategies. As noted above, routines play the role that genes play in evolutionary biology. Routines as genes are persistent features of the organization that determine its range of possible behavior. They are inheritable in the sense that new "offspring" organizations (such as branch plants or regional offices) possess many of the features of their "parent" organization. They mutate as organizations make adjustments to their routines—sometimes by change, and sometimes as a response to external or internal change. They are selectable in the sense that organizations with certain routines may do better than others, depending on their fit with the environment.

An organization's explicit knowledge may take the form of intellectual assets, which Sullivan (1998, p. 23) defines as

> "the codified, tangible, or physical descriptions of specific knowledge to which the company can assert ownership rights. Any piece of knowledge that becomes

> defined, usually by being written down or entered into a computer, qualifies as an intellectual asset and can be protected. Intellectual assets are the source of innovations that the firm commercializes."

Examples of intellectual assets include plans, procedures, memos, sketches, drawings, blueprints, and computer programs. Intellectual assets may be categorized into commercializable assets and structural assets (Sullivan 1998) Commercializable assets are those that the organization can directly offer in the business or technology marketplace (through for example, technology licensing or joint ventures). Commercializable assets may in turn be divided into those that are legally protected and those that are not. Legally protected assets are called intellectual property, and this includes for example, patents, copyrights, trademarks, trade secrets, and semiconductor masks. Unprotected assets that are nevertheless commercializable refer usually to the organization's innovations which are still undergoing development. Structural assets are part of the organization's infrastructure and may include its administrative and technical methods, processes, procedures, as well as role, authority and reporting structures.

Explicit knowledge codified as intellectual assets are valuable to the organization because they add to the organization's observable and tradable stocks of knowledge. Moreover, because they have been committed to media, ideas may be communicated more easily, increasing the likelihood of discussion, experimentation, and enhancement, thereby inducing further cycles of knowledge creation and use.

Explicit knowledge serves a number of important purposes in an organization. First, they encode past learning. Good solutions and procedures learned from experience are formalized as routines to avoid reinventing the wheel. Rules and routines can also be more easily packaged into training programs and tools that help transfer knowledge to new employees. Second, explicit knowledge facilitates coordination between disparate activities and functions in the organization. An organization's tasks are highly interdependent: plans, specifications, contracts, rules, and routines, are used to define outputs, standards, and timelines so that the interdependency of an organization's work activities can be properly coordinated. Third, explicit knowledge in the form of routines and procedures reduce the information processing load associated with task performance by stipulating premises, criteria, options, and other information seeking and use requirements. Fourth, the equipment, plans, budgets, and rules and routines that constitute explicit knowledge signify technical skill and procedural rationality, and so help the organization to present a self-image of competence, legitimacy and accountability.

The movement of knowledge within and between organizations is often in the form of transferring explicit knowledge. Because explicit knowledge is articulated knowledge, it is often assumed to be readily understood by others and can therefore diffuse more easily beyond an organization's boundary. Sanchez (1997) suggests that this assumption may not always be warranted. Even though the knowledge has been made explicit, the receiving organization may experience problems of comprehension and valuation as they try to understand and appraise the significance of the articulated knowledge. There may be several reasons: firms develop their own languages and vocabularies that others might not understand; different firms possess different levels of technical capability; different firms are at different stages of growth and development; the usefulness of the knowledge depends on its linkages with other knowledge, resources and capabilities in the originating firm. Given these uncertainties, the assumption that explicit knowledge is fundamentally "less secure" than tacit knowledge may be simplistic.

In an increasingly knowledge-intensive network economy, organizations do not possess all the knowledge they need internally but instead rely on sharing or buying technologies or services through contractual and cooperative partnerships with other organizations. Knowledge therefore moves swiftly across organizational boundaries in a knowledge market. This poses a dilemma:

> "On the one hand, a firm would benefit by leveraging its knowledge quickly and widely both within and across its boundaries, while on the other hand the firm has an interest in maintaining control over strategically important knowledge whose diffusion to other firms would erode the distinctiveness of the firm's competencies based on its knowledge." (Sanchez 1997, p. 180)

To balance this tension, each firm should identify the kinds of knowledge that constitute its distinctive competencies, and maintain close control within the firm this explicit or articulated knowledge that is most critical, while leveraging as broadly as possible with other firms knowledge that is strategically less critical (Sanchez 1997).

Explicit knowledge plays a special role in the innovation-decision process. Innovation decision making is an information-seeking and information-processing activity (Rogers 1983, 1995) through which an individual moves from (1) initial knowledge about an innovation through subsequent phases of (2) forming an attitude toward the innovation; (3) deciding to adopt or reject the innovation; (4) implementing the new idea; and (5) confirming the decision. During the knowledge phase, an individual becomes aware of an innovation's existence and gains some understanding of how it functions. An innovation is thus first encountered as an objectification and embodiment of knowledge. Rogers (1983, 1995) calls this software information:

> "An innovation typically contains software information, which is embodied in the innovation and which serves to reduce uncertainty about the cause-effect relationships that are involved in achieving a desired outcome (such as meeting a need of the individual)." (Rogers 1995, p. 165)

Three types of innovation-embodied knowledge are involved here. First, there is awareness-knowledge, which is information that an innovation exists. Second, there is how-to knowledge, which consists of information necessary to use an innovation properly: answering questions such as what quantity of an innovation to secure, and how to use it correctly. Third, there is principles-knowledge, which is information explaining the principles underlying how an innovation works. Examples are concepts about biology of plant growth which underlie fertilizer adoption by farmers; principles of human reproduction which form a basis for family planning innovations; and basics of germ theory which support vaccination and health campaigns. To accelerate diffusion, all three types of innovation-based knowledge are likely to contain explicit elements, in order to promote awareness, visibility, and understandability; and to increase the chances of proper use and successful outcomes. Thus, an innovation may be introduced as a physical artifact (e.g. crop fertilizer, birth-control pill) that is accompanied by clearly laid out instructions on its deployment as well as background information on why the innovation works and what the benefits are.

2.2.3 Cultural Knowledge

While the classification of organizational knowledge as tacit and explicit is widely discussed, the category of cultural knowledge is less often encountered. Boisot (1998) attributes this to a "Western bias towards classifying as knowledge only that which can be given a codified and abstract formulation":

> "[This] has led knowledge assets—whether embodied in physical objects such as plant and machinery, or in organizational practices such as planning and budgeting systems—to be treated as if they were essentially technological in nature. They are not. *They are first and foremost cultural and only then technological.* The potential value of a knowledge asset is largely a function of how it is used and in what context. ... it does not make much sense to talk of knowledge assets independently of the cultures in which they are embedded. It takes culture as operating through institutional structures that must themselves be considered knowledge assets." (Boisot 1998, p. 119, italics in original)

At the beginning of the chapter, we presented a definition of knowledge as justified true belief. An organization's cultural knowledge thus consists of the beliefs it holds to be true and justifiably so (based on experience, observation, reflection) about itself and its environment. Importantly, an organization's cultural knowledge is used to answer questions such as "What kind of an organization are we?" "What knowledge would be valuable to the organization?" and "What knowledge would be worth pursuing?"

To elaborate, cultural knowledge in organizations consists of the cognitive and affective structures that are habitually used by organizational members to perceive, explain, evaluate, and construct reality. Cultural knowledge includes the assumptions and beliefs that are used to describe and explain reality, as well as the criteria and expectations that are used to assign value and significance to new information. These shared beliefs, norms and values form the framework in which organizational members construct reality, recognize the saliency of new information, and evaluate alternative interpretations and actions. Collins (1998) highlights two important roles of cultural knowledge: cultural knowledge is required to understand and use facts, rules, and heuristics; and to make inductions in the same way as others in order to enable concerted action. Cultural knowledge, by defining the limits and bases of legitimate discourse, also

> "constitutes the main conduit for the expression and existence of power, in the sense of defining what is legitimized as knowledge in the first place, and who are accorded sufficient reputation and status to have their views taken seriously in the second place." (Fleck 1998, p. 160)

Fleck's commentary echoes many others. For example, knowledge as power is a recurrent theme in much of Foucault's work (see for example Foucault 1980). Knowledge as paradigm received its most celebrated exposition in Kuhn (1970), who analyzed how normal science takes place within paradigms that define what kinds of problems are studied, what methods are acceptable, and what criteria are used to evaluation solutions.

According to Sackmann (1991, 1992) cultural knowledge in an organization consists of: dictionary knowledge, directory knowledge, recipe knowledge, and axiomatic knowledge. Dictionary knowledge comprises commonly held descriptions, including expressions and definitions used in the organization to describe the 'what' of situations, such as what is considered to be a problem, or what is considered to be success. Directory knowledge refers to commonly held practices and is knowledge about sequences of events and their cause-effect relationships that describe the 'how' of processes, such as how a problem is solved or how success is to be achieved. Recipe knowledge comprises prescriptions for repair and improvement strategies that recommend what action 'should' be taken for example, to solve a problem or to become successful. Axiomatic knowledge refers to reasons and explanations of the final causes or a priori premises that are perceived to account for 'why' events happen. Sackman's categories of cultural knowledge are closely related to the schemas, scripts, cause maps, and basic assumptions that are often associated with discussions of organizational culture.

Garud and Rappa (1994, p. 345) propose that the development of new knowledge based on technology is a socio-cognitive process which rests on three definitions of technology: "technology as beliefs, artifacts, and evaluation routines". Technology development is guided by beliefs about what is possible, what is worth attempting, and what levels of effort are required. Technology as physical artifact specifies the technology's form (such as shape or material of construction) and function (such as uses and applications). Technology as evaluation routines define testing routines and normative values that "filter data in a way that influences whether or not researchers perceive information as useful. Researchers with different beliefs attempt to sway each other with respect to the routines utilized to judge the technology" (Garud and Rappa 1994, p. 346). Evaluation routines also facilitate communication about the technology and allow the new technology to gain legitimacy in the eyes of researchers. Beliefs, artifacts, and evaluation routines interact with each other to shape the evolution of new technology. Garud and Rappa suggest that beliefs guide the creation of artifacts that in return raise commitment in the technology; beliefs are externalized as testing routines and standards; and routines legitimize and select the form that the technology takes. Overall, an organization's beliefs about what technology or new knowledge is feasible and worth attempting, a part of its cultural knowledge, would influence the direction and intensity of the knowledge development effort, as well as the routines and norms by which new information and knowledge would be evaluated.

In the context of knowledge creating, cultural knowledge plays the vital role of providing a pattern of shared assumptions (Schein 1991) so that the organization can assign significance to new information and knowledge. Cultural knowledge supplies values and norms that

> "determine what kinds of knowledge are sought and nurtured, what kinds of knowledge-building activities are tolerated and encouraged. There are systems of caste and status, rituals of behavior, and passionate beliefs associated with various kinds of technological knowledge that are as rigid and complex as those associated with religion. Therefore, values serve as knowledge-screening and -control mechanisms." (Leonard-Barton 1995, p. 19)

There are familiar accounts of organizations in which cultural knowledge is misaligned with its efforts to exploit tacit and explicit knowledge. For example, Xerox PARC in the 1970s had pioneered many innovations that Xerox itself was not able to exploit but other companies later commercialized into products that defined the personal computer industry. Thus, PARC had invented or developed: bit-mapped display technology required for rendering graphical user interfaces; software for on-screen windows and windows management; the mouse as a pointing device; the first personal computer Alto; and an early word-processing software Bravo for the Alto (Smith and Alexander 1988). Xerox did not fully apprehend the application potential of these inventions because its identity and business strategy was still focused on the photocopier market. Many of the researchers working on these projects subsequently left PARC, taking their knowledge with them.

Cultural knowledge also establishes a framework in which organizational discourse and sense-making can take place. Alvesson (1993) suggests that "cultural knowledge represents a prerequisite for the ability to master a particular symbolic and value environment, to decipher the cultural codes and manoeuvre freely in a social setting" (p. 1001). Cultural knowledge in organizations thus plays important roles such as

> (a) defining a shared language for creating community and social identity;
> (b) providing a resource for persuasion;
> (c) giving the organization a profile or intended image;
> (d) creating legitimacy and good faith about actions and outcomes; and
> (e) obscuring uncertainty and reducing ambiguity." (Alvesson 1993).

Organizations are in a sense, "systems of persuasion," and organizational knowledge work is symbolic action that must be symbolized in talk, action, titles, structures and cultural objects. Alvesson concludes that in both embracing and moving beyond knowledge work, organizations need

> "to develop rhetorical strategies and forms of symbolism in which the distinct claims are brought forward, made clear, credible and competitive, and to develop and control other vital abilities, orientations than those strictly knowledge-related. ... [This] is also a matter of influencing employees on a broader scale, including securing and developing work and organizational identities. Cultural-ideological forms of control which affect the ways people perceive their work, organizations and themselves and the values, norms and emotion which guide them become a crucial feature ..." (Alvesson 1993, p. 1011-1012)

It is misleading to approach cultural knowledge as a form of background knowledge where the information is regarded as self-evident, so that the logical steps by which other forms of knowledge have to be justified are not required (Douglas 1975). It is tempting to view cultural knowledge as a stable, relatively static background before which new information and knowledge is perceived and engaged. Douglas (1975) warns that this "stability is an illusion, for a large part of discourse is dedicated to creating, revising, and obliquely affirming this implicit background, without ever directing explicit attention upon it." (p. 4) Thus cultural knowledge is as dynamic as tacit and explicit knowledge in guiding and animating the use of organizational knowledge.

2.2.3.1 Cultural Knowledge in Knowledge Transfer

The movement of knowledge across organizational boundaries can involve tacit, explicit, and cultural knowledge to varying degrees. In a limited number of cases, the transfer is largely accomplished through a movement of explicit knowledge (e.g. an equation, a chemical formula). Transfers of such well-defined packages of codified knowledge typically requires a substantial amount of collateral knowledge in the receiving organization to decode the new information (in-house engineers and technologies are needed to understand and apply the new equation or formula). In a larger number of cases, the transfer of explicit knowledge is accompanied and facilitated by experienced human experts. Experts interpret the meaning of the new information, and deal with the detailed questions arising from trying to use the new information. Thus, tacit knowledge is necessary to assimilate and apply new explicit knowledge properly. There are important cases when the movement of explicit knowledge even when accompanied by tacit knowledge is not enough: cultural knowledge is also necessary. This is especially so when organizations are trying to learn new practices or systems of work that are woven into organizational networks of roles, relationships, and shared meanings. Consider Toyota's production system, an example of a tight integration of tacit, explicit, and cultural knowledge:

> "Toyota's knowledge of how to make cars lies embedded in highly specialized social and organizational relationships that have evolved through decades of common effort. It rests in routines, information flows, ways of making decisions, shared attitudes and expectations, and specialized knowledge that Toyota managers, workers, suppliers and purchasing agents, and others have about different aspects of their business, about each other, and about how they can all work together." (Badaracco 1991, p. 87)

When General Motors wanted to learn the Toyota production system, it established the NUMMI (New United Motor Manufacturing, Inc.) plant in 1984 as a joint venture with Toyota in order to facilitate the learning of 'intimate, embedded knowledge.' NUMMI took over a General Motors facility at Fremont California. Work at NUMMI was organized based on the Toyota's lean production system that seeks to utilize labor, materials, and facilities as efficiently as possible. The system is guided by the principles that quality should be assured in the production process itself with no defects overlooked or passed on, and that team members should be treated with consideration, respect, and as professionals ('full utilization of workers' abilities'). The NUMMI system combines employee involvement and continuous improvement processes. In order to ensure that each job is done in the most efficient way, the performance of the work is specified explicitly by sequences or procedures. NUMMI team members themselves are responsible for setting the work standards, and continuously improving the job standards for maximum efficiency.

O'Reilly and Tushman (1997) observed that at NUMMI, the organizational culture includes norms about continuous improvement and team responsibility. Instead of feeling unmotivated, workers felt a sense of autonomy and responsibility. Instead of feeling monitored, workers "controlled" their own behaviors. In lieu of industrial engineers (there are none at NUMMI; the old GM Fremont plant had 82 industrial engineers), NUMMI workers are trained in industrial engineering techniques and the team itself undertakes work redesign and improvements:

> "... these methods and standards are determined by work teams themselves: workers are taught how to time their own jobs with a stopwatch, compare alternative procedures to determine the most efficient one, document the standard procedure to ensure that everyone can understand and implement it, and identify and propose improvements in that procedure. At any given time, the task of standardized work analysis might be delegated to a team leader or a team member, but everyone understands the analysis process and can participate in it." (O'Reilly III & Tushman 1993, p. 90)

In a comparison of the Toyota-GM venture (NUMMI) and Volvo's Uddevalla plant, Adler and Cole (1993) noted that

> "...the Japanese production model explicitly focuses on strategies for organizational learning. Standardization of work methods is a precondition for achieving this end — you cannot identify the sources of problems in a process you have not standardized. Standardization captures best practices and facilitates the diffusion of improvement ideas throughout the organization—you cannot diffuse what you have not standardized. And standardization stimulates improvement—every worker is now something of an industrial engineer. At NUMMI, the skill development strategies for individual workers are managed as a component of this process, rather than as a way of maximizing personal opportunities. As a result, training focuses on developing deeper knowledge, not only of the relatively narrow jobs but also of the logic of the production system, statistical process control, and problem-solving processes." (p. 92)

Although much has been published about Toyota's production system, without the NUMMI experience, GM might have permanently missed the essence of Toyota's management process. Co-practice to learn the system was necessary because the capabilities were "tacit know-how in action, embedded organizationally, systemic in interaction and cultivated through learning by doing" (Doz and Hamel 1997, p. 570). Badaracco (1991) concluded that through NUMMI, GM had the chance to learn first hand Toyota's collaborative approach to worker and supplier relationsips, just-in-time inventory management, and efficient plant operations. For Toyota, the project helped it learn about managing US workers, suppliers and logistics, and about cooperating with the unions and the state and local governments.

"Scores of GM managers and thousands of workers have worked at NUMMI or at least visited the operation. It would have been much simpler for GM to buy from Toyota the manual *How To Create the Toyota Production System*, but the document does not exist and, in a fundamental sense, could not be written. Much of what Toyota 'knows' resides in routines, company culture, and long-established working relationships in the Toyota Group." (Badaracco 1991, p.100)

2.3 The Dynamics of Organizational Knowledge: Creating, Diffusing, and Using Knowledge

Analyzing knowledge as tacit, explicit, and cultural draws out the differences and dependencies between aspects of organizational knowledge that we otherwise cannot easily examine. Moreover, each category of knowledge brings forth its own issues for creating, representing, conveying, and sharing the knowledge that would need to be addressed by designers of organizational processes and information systems.

The three categories of organizational knowledge are intertwined. Tacit knowledge is embedded in the skills of an individual or the shared practices of a group. Rule-based knowledge is distributed across multiple participants and groups who work in a coordinated manner framed by rules and routines. Insofar as the performance of routines involve the exercise of personal skills and judgment to deal with situational specifics, tacit knowledge is required to apply rule-based knowledge. Cultural knowledge is shared by many members of the organization in order to give meaning and value to information, events and actions. Insofar as rules and routines are manifestations and codifications of organizational culture, rule-based knowledge is ensconced in cultural knowledge.

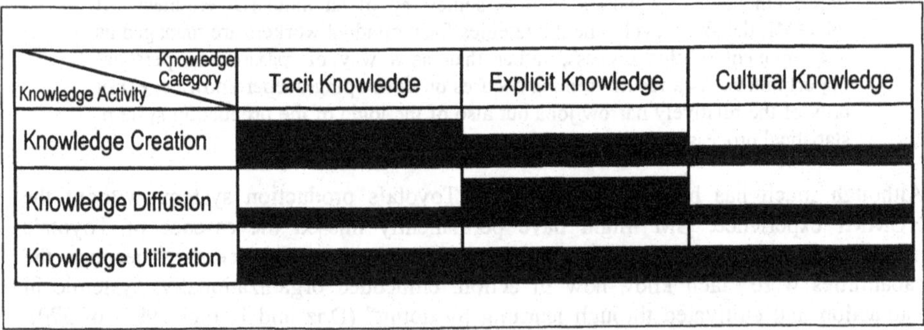

Figure 2.2 Creating, Diffusing, and Using Knowledge

An organization creates value by creating new knowledge, diffusing knowledge, and putting knowledge into practice. As shown in Figure 2.2, all three categories of organizational knowledge are fully involved in each of these activities. Recent research elucidates how the roles and interactions of tacit, explicit and cultural knowledge vary between these activities. On organizational knowledge creation, Nonaka and Takeuchi (1995) emphasize the importance of tacit knowledge as the source of new knowledge:

> "Tacit knowledge of individuals is the basis of organizational knowledge creation. The organization has to mobilize tacit knowledge created and accumulated at the individual level ... the key to knowledge creation lies in the mobilization and conversion of tacit knowledge." (p. 72, 56)

In knowledge diffusion, we expect explicit knowledge to play a vital role in facilitating the flow of knowledge across organizational boundaries. Explicit knowledge is defined by its property of ease of communication (Grant 1996a), and its use can speed up and reduce the cost of transferring knowledge (Kogut and Zander 1992). Boisot (1998) examines how the codification and abstraction of personal knowledge into public knowledge can greatly increase the diffusibility of knowledge.

In knowledge utilization, knowledge is assimilated into the technical and social practices of a work group. Part of it becomes internalized (as part of personal knowledge); part of it is codified as new tools, documents and artifacts; and part of it becomes shared ways of looking at things that happen in the course of using the knowledge. Thus, tacit, explicit and cultural knowledge are woven together in a community of practice (Brown and Duguid 1991, Brown 1993, Wenger 1998) that provides a context in which the use and meaning of objects, problems, and events gets constructed and negotiated.

2.3.1 Knowledge Creation: Leveraging Tacit Knowledge

Nonaka and Takeuchi (1995) suggest that the production of new knowledge involves "a process that 'organizationally' amplifies the knowledge created by individuals and crystallizes it as a part of the knowledge network of the organization" (Nonaka and Takeuchi 1995, p. 59). Two sets of activities drive the process of knowledge amplification: (1) converting tacit knowledge into explicit knowledge; and (2) moving knowledge from the individual level to the group, organizational, and inter-organizational levels. The process grows like a spiral as the dance between tacit and explicit knowledge takes place at higher and higher levels of the organization.

The basis of organizational knowledge creation is therefore the conversion of tacit knowledge into explicit knowledge and back again. Over time, human knowledge shifts between the tacit and the explicit through a process of social interaction between individuals that also produces new knowledge and expands its use. Nonaka and Takeuchi (1995) identify four modes in which new knowledge is created through conversion between tacit and explicit knowledge: socialization, externalization, combination, and internalization. We outline these processes, using examples from Nonaka and Takeuchi's discussion of how Matushita developed an automatic home bakery product.

Socialization is a process of acquiring tacit knowledge through sharing experiences. As apprentices learn the craft of their masters through observation, imitation, and practice, so do employees of a firm learn new skills through on-the-job training. When Matsushita started developing its automatic home bread-making machine in 1985, an early problem was how to mechanize the dough-kneading process, a process that takes a master baker years of practice to perfect. To learn this tacit knowledge, a member of the software development team, Ikuko Tanaka, decided to volunteer herself as an apprentice to the head baker of the Osaka International Hotel, who was reputed to produce the area's best bread. After a period of imitation and practice, one day she observed that the baker was not only stretching but also twisting the dough in a particular fashion ("twisting stretch"), which turned out to be the secret for making tasty bread.

Externalization is a process of converting tacit knowledge into explicit concepts through the use of abstractions, metaphors, analogies, or models. The externalization of tacit knowledge is the quintessential knowledge-creation activity and is most often seen during the concept creation phase of new product development. Externalization can also be triggered by dialogue or collective reflection. Returning to the Matsushita case, Tanaka could not specify in engineering terms the "twisting stretch" motion she had learned from the master baker. Nevertheless she was able to communicate this tacit knowledge to the engineers by creating the mental concept of "twisting stretch," and by indicating the power and speed of the kneading propeller in order to imitate this motion. For example, Tanaka would say, "make the propeller move stronger," or "move it faster," and the engineers would make the necessary adjustments through trial-and-error.

Combination is a process of creating explicit knowledge by bringing together explicit knowledge from a number of sources. Thus, individuals exchange and combine their explicit knowledge through telephone conversations, meetings, memos, and so on. Existing information in computerized databases may be categorized, collated, and sorted in a number of ways to produce new explicit knowledge. The Matsushita home bakery team drew together eleven members from completely different specializations and cultures: product planning, mechanical engineering, control systems, and software development. The "twisting stretch" motion was finally materialized in a prototype after a year of iterative experimentation by the engineers and team members working closely together, combining their explicit knowledge. For example, the engineers added ribs to the inside of the dough case in order to hold the dough better as it is being churned. Another team member suggested a method (later patented) to add yeast at a later stage in the process, thereby saving the cost of a cooler otherwise needed to prevent the yeast from overfermenting in high temperatures.

Finally, internalization is a process of embodying explicit knowledge into tacit knowledge, internalizing the experiences gained through the other modes of knowledge creation into individuals' tacit knowledge bases in the form of shared mental models or work practices. Internalization is facilitated if the knowledge is captured in documents or conveyed in the form of stories, so that individuals may re-experience indirectly the experience of others. Matsushita's home bakery product was a great success. It sold a record 536,000 units in its first year, topped the list of Mother's Day gifts, and was featured in a 1987 issue of Fortune magazine. The success story was disseminated throughout Matsushita by word of mouth and in-house publications, changing employees' perceptions about the potential of home appliances and inspiring them to develop other innovative products. The new tacit knowledge being internalized was that Matsushita could develop a product by interfacing directly with customers and by pursuing quality without compromise.

Although Nonaka and Takeuchi did not mention cultural knowledge, we can see how Matushita's cultural knowledge had been transformed by the success of the home bakery product. Hitherto, Matsushita's self-image was a company that manufactured price-competitive, standard products in mature markets. The home bakery episode showed that Matsushita was capable of genuine innovation by fully addressing customer needs and leveraging expertise from several groups. This inspired Matsushita to launch a new grand concept labeled "Human Electronics" that would develop consumer products which elevated the quality of human life using electronics. Other "quality of life" appliances that followed included an automatic coffee brewer that was integrated with a coffee bean grinder; an induction-heating rice cooker; and the popular "GAOO" large-screen television.

Nonaka and Takeuchi (1995) do include aspects of cultural knowledge in the way they segment tacit knowledge into technical and cognitive dimensions. The technical dimension encompasses practical know-how; while the cognitive dimension includes mental models, beliefs, and perspectives that are so ingrained that they are taken for granted, and therefore cannot be easily articulated. However, we maintain that a separate category of cultural knowledge is helpful for the following reason. Tacit knowledge is personal knowledge that is lost to the organization when the individual leaves. Cultural knowledge, although it is not codified, remains with the organization as its membership changes. As described earlier, cultural knowledge as beliefs and values endures in the form of a common vocabulary and language, shared practices, incentive and reward systems, evaluation routines and criteria, and so on.

As shown in Figure 2.3, the four modes of knowledge conversion follow each other in a continuous spiral of organizational knowledge creation. Knowledge creation typically begins with individuals who have developed some insight or intuition into how better to do their tasks. This tacit know-how may be shared with others through socialization. However, as long as the knowledge stays tacit, the organization is unable to exploit it further. Thus, the tacit know-how of the master baker's kneading technique had to be converted into explicit knowledge that is then used to design the kneading mechanism inside the bread-making machine. From the organization's perspective, externalization of tacit knowledge into explicit concepts is therefore pivotal. Drawing out tacit knowledge requires taking a mental leap, and often involves the creative use of a metaphor or analogy. An organization would have several sets of explicit knowledge generated by different groups or units at different points in time. These disparate bodies of expertise may be combined and reconfigured into new forms of explicit knowledge. As shown in the Matsushita case, such synthesis is often necessary to make the application of new knowledge operational, viable, and cost-effective. Finally, the new explicit knowledge generated through the innovation process is disseminated, re-experienced and re-internalized as new tacit (and cultural) knowledge.

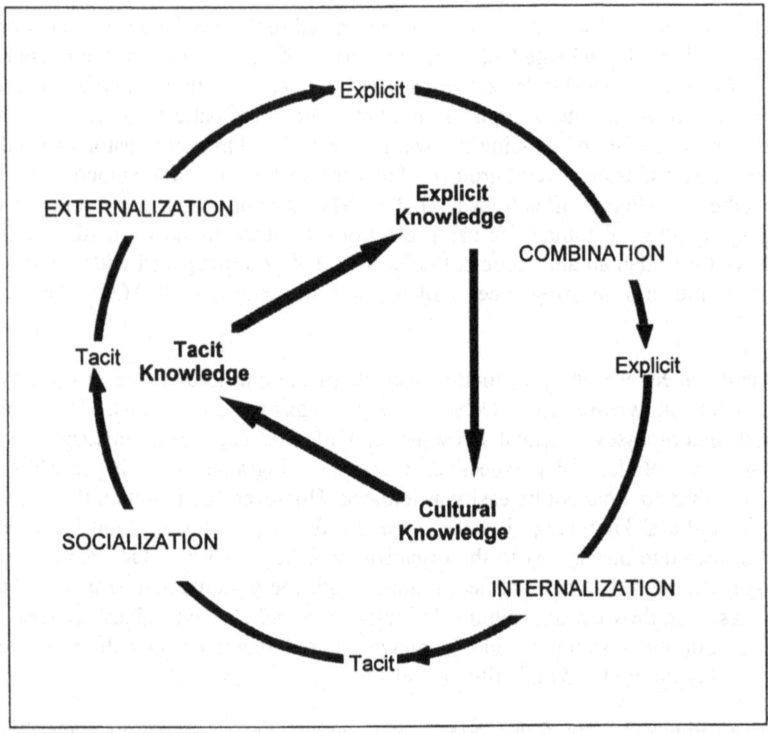

Figure 2.3 Knowledge Creation: Knowledge Conversion Cycle (Nonaka and Takeuchi 1995)

2.3.2 Knowledge Diffusion: Codifying, Abstracting, and Diffusing Knowledge

Boisot (1995, 1998) proposes an Information Space or I-Space model as a conceptual framework to describe the information flows that constitute the creation and diffusion of knowledge in organizations. The I-Space is bounded by the three dimensions of codification, abstraction, and diffusion. Within this I-Space, the locations and trajectories of an organization's knowledge assets might be positioned and mapped according to these three dimensions. The key hypothesis of the model is

> "that codification and abstraction are mutually reinforcing and that both acting together, greatly facilitate the diffusion of information. ... the more codified and abstract an item of information becomes, then, other things being equal, the larger the percentage of a given population it will be able to reach in a given period of time." (Boisot 1998, p. 55)

In the I-Space model, codification is the process which creates perceptual and conceptual categories that facilitate the classification of phenomena. Codification is equivalent to a selection from competing perceptual and conceptual alternatives. By assigning categories to phenomena, uncertainty is reduced, surplus data are shed, and the requirement for data processing is economized.Any task and the knowledge associated with it might be scaled according to the amount of data processing it entails. In the uncodified region of the scale are tasks that require the processing of an infinite number of bits of data (such as riding a bicycle). In the codified region of the scale are simple tasks that need only small amounts of data for their execution (such as turning an on-off switch) or structured tasks that follow sequences of instructions (such as using software). Economizing on data processing then involves moving from the uncodified end of the scale towards the codified, from the inarticulate towards the articulate, from the tacit towards the explicit. The effectiveness of codification depends not only on intellectual and observational skill but also on the complexity of the phenomena that is being partitioned into categories. When performed well, codification facilitates and accelerates information processing.

Whereas codification groups the data of experience into categories, abstraction is the process that minimizes the number of categories needed to draw on for a given task. Abstraction is accomplished by revealing the structure and cause-and-effect relationships that underlie phenomena. Both codification and abstraction reduce data processing, but abstraction does so by specifying which categories are likely to be relevant to a given data-processing task. Knowledge can be located on an abstraction scale according to the number of categories that need to be drawn on. In the unabstract or concrete region of the scale would be knowledge based on highly concrete experiences that is mainly perceptual and local in application. In the abstract region of the scale would be knowledge based on abstract thought that is mainly conceptual and broadly applicable. When performed properly, abstraction uncovers causal or descriptive structures and works together with codification to make knowledge even more articulated and hence more shareable.

The diffusion of information in I-Space refers to "the proportion of a given population of data-processing agents that can be reached with information operating at different degrees of codification and abstraction" (Boisot 1998, p. 52). Such a population is not limited to individuals inside an organization, but also includes firms, conglomerates, industries. Diffusibility here is the availability of information to those who want to use it: it is measured with respect to a potential audience for a set of messages being transmitted. Where a knowledge asset is located on the diffusion scale depends on many factors that influence the speed, extent, and trajectory of diffusion. These factors would include: the frequency and intensity of interaction within the population; the available means of communication; the sharing of social and cultural codes and contexts; and legal protection and restrictions. Generally, the lower-level technical factors would affect information diffusibility, whereas the higher-level social factors would affect uptake and adoption.

To help assess the degree of codification, abstraction, and diffusion of a knowledge asset, Boisot suggest using questions such as the following:

- Is the knowledge easily captured in figures and formulae? Does it lend itself to standardization and automation?

- Is the knowledge generally applicable to all agents whatever the sector they operate in? Is it heavily science-based?

- Is the knowledge readily available to all agents who wish to make use of it?

The more affirmative the answers to these questions, the greater the degree of codification, abstraction, and diffusion of the knowledge.

The creation and diffusion of new knowledge along the three dimensions of codification, abstraction, and diffusion trace a trajectory in the Information Space, as shown in Figure 2.4 (Boisot 1998, p. 59). New knowledge emerges from personal knowledge that is uncodified, based on concrete experience, and undiffused—it lies in the bottom left hand area of the I-Space cube. Successive efforts to articulate this knowledge increases its degree of codification and abstraction until it becomes proprietary knowledge. Initially the knowledge is available only locally (for example, within the organization), or it may be protected by legal restrictions—proprietary knowledge lies in the top left hand area of I-Space. However, because it has been made explicit and therefore diffusible, the proprietary knowledge gradually moves into the public domain, finding its way into reports, journals, instruction manuals, newspapers, and so on. Over time, it becomes public knowledge, located in the top right hand area of I-Space. Repeated use of this knowledge, often in a variety of settings, results in the assimilation of the knowledge as part of "common sense." Although common sense by definition is widely shared, each individual internalizes and makes use of this common sense differently to create personal intuitions and perceptions. Thus the cycle is complete as the new knowledge is returned into the tacit domain of personal knowledge.

Figure 2.4 also shows where tacit, explicit, and cultural knowledge may be positioned in the Information Space. Tacit knowledge is personal knowledge based on concrete experience that is uncodified and undiffused; so it is lies in the lower left hand corner of the I-Space cube. Through the processes of codification and abstraction, tacit knowledge is articulated as explicit knowledge. The I-Space model distinguishes between two forms of explicit knowledge: proprietary and public knowledge. Proprietary knowledge is explicit knowledge that is available internally in the organization, and is therefore undiffused — it lies in the top left hand corner of the cube. Public knowledge is explicit knowledge that has become generally available through a variety of communication channels and media — it lies in the top right hand corner of the cube. Finally, cultural knowledge is the set of widely shared beliefs and perceptions (the "common sense") that arises from the repeated utilization of public knowledge. Shared perceptions are developed by the industry or community as a whole, but also by particular organizations and by specific groups and individuals. These perceptions form the background knowledge from which new personal, tacit knowledge emerges. In this way the social learning cycle is simultaneously a cycle of the transformation between tacit, explicit, and cultural knowledge.

The I-Space cube is also used to develop organizational strategy based on controlling the codification and diffusion of knowledge assets. Boisot (1998) describes how BPX, the exploration arm of BP (British Petroleum), used the I-Space model to help develop its technology strategy in the early 1990s. A workshop was organized to apply the I- Space model to analyze the locations and trajectories of BPX's technology-based knowledge assets.

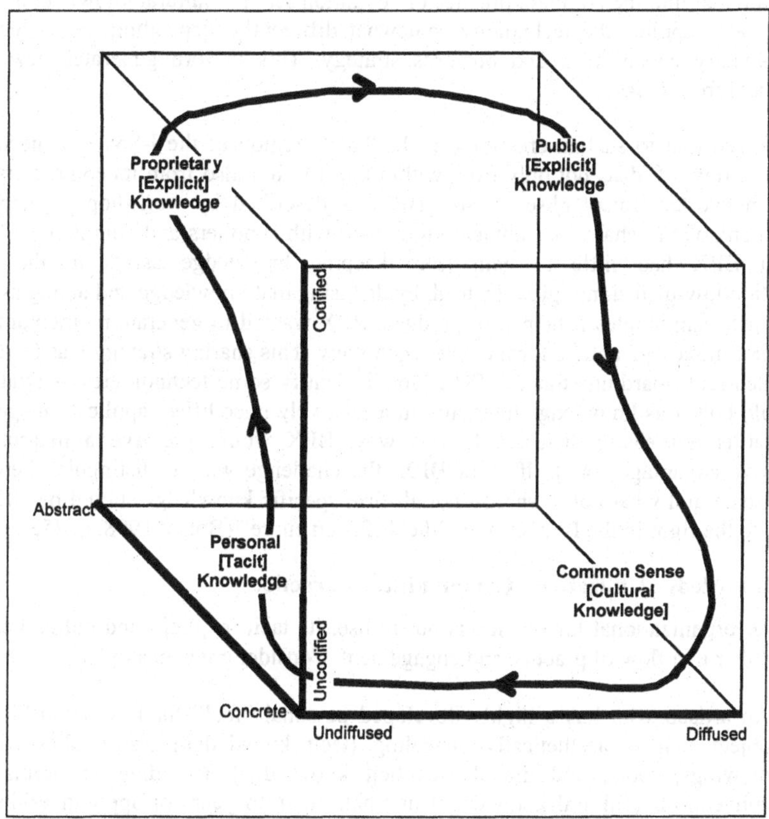

Figure 2.4 Knowledge Diffusion: Information Space Model (Adapted from Boisot 1998, p. 59)

The use of the I-Space model led BPX to a re-interpretation of the firm's technology strategy as follows. (1) First, BPX produces novel approaches to technical problems and establishes a "proof of concept" that demonstrates the feasibility and viability of the solution. Thus, BPX was an important generator of technology in its own right. When the firm plotted its technology assets in I-Space, most of them were in the low-codification and low-diffusion region, where the knowledge is tacit or internal to the firm or its members. (2) Further development of the new approach is outsourced to one or more external contractors or suppliers. Outsourcing and collaboration moves the new technology's knowledge trajectory from the tacit to the explicit region of the I-Space. (3) BPX underwrites contractors' development risk by being the "lead user" of the new solution. By promoting development and application, BPX was increasing the diffusibility and usability of the new technology. Indeed, BPX was happy to see the new solutions diffuse to competitors, as this helps to establish the new technology as an industry standard. The hope is for the new knowledge to become widely available and applied. (4) Over time, the use of the technology becomes increasingly taken-for-granted and assimilated into the common practice or "common sense" (cultural knowledge). Each company also applies the technology somewhat differently, depending on its history, complementary capabilities, and business strategy. This in turn generates new tacit insights and fresh ideas.

BPX realized that to sustain creativity in the "tacit" region of the I-Space, it needed a continuous flow of ideas not only from within the firm but also from its contractors and external networks. Boisot observes that BPX, as described by workshop participants, appeared anxious to share its technical know-how with suppliers and competitors. They felt that BPX had little to gain from keeping knowledge assets in the low-codification/low-diffusion region. Instead, by diffusing that knowledge and acting as lead user for the technologies it helped to produce, BPX wanted to generate momentum and accrue first-mover advantage for the new technology. This sharing strategy was balanced by a concurrent hoarding strategy. BPX would identify some technologies as strategic, and would hold this knowledge internally in a relatively uncodified, application-specific form that is not easily diffused. In this way, BPX would preserve a measure of competitive advantage for itself. "For BPX, the challenge was to distinguish between what to share and what not to share—not all firm-specific knowledge should be allowed to travel to the right in the I-Space along the diffusion curve" (Boisot 1998, p. 253).

2.3.3 Knowledge Utilization: Communities of Practice

Whenever organizational knowledge is put in use, its tacit, explicit, and cultural facets bind together in a flow of practice and engagement. Consider a few examples:

- An artisan who has a highly developed personal "feel" for how to fashion an object that is aesthetically appealing (tacit knowledge) also makes use of drawings, tools, and models (explicit knowledge) according to norms and conventions (cultural knowledge) internalized from years of apprenticeship and membership in a guild.

- A librarian who has extensive explicit knowledge about reference sources also exercises tacit judgment in interpreting a client's information needs in order to locate relevant information, all the while observing professional rules and practices (cultural knowledge) that protect the client's interests.

- Members of a grassroots organization strongly believe in the group's goals and values (cultural knowledge) which then serve as a framework for selecting and activating known channels of influence (explicit knowledge), the use of which often requires exercising creativity and resourcefulness (tacit knowledge) in order to overcome obstacles.

As was noted before, the tighter the integration between all three types of knowledge, the more unique the advantage that is derived from possessing and practicing that knowledge.

Given that organizational knowledge is a tightly bundled package of the tacit, the explicit, and the cultural, how could newcomers to an organization assimilate this knowledge effectively? Lave and Wenger (1991) suggest a process of "legitimate peripheral participation." The process emphasizes that learning takes place through active participation, but that this participation needs to be modified to enhance peripherality and legitimacy. Thus, the novice starts by staying safely on the periphery of practice as a participant observer. Peripherality provides an approximation of full participation that allows learners to engage fully in the actual practice, while at the same lowering the intensity, the risk, cost of error, stress levels, and the need for close supervision. When she feels sufficiently comfortable or when the mentor feels she is ready, the learner can move from the periphery to the center to engage the task, and then move back out again. In this sense the learner is also a legitimate participant who can move to the center of practice from time to time. Legitimacy gives new learners enough authority to be treated as potential members. Legitimacy can take many forms, for example: being sponsored, being useful, being the right kind of person, having the birth right. Being legitimately on the periphery also means that learners have access to the various modes of communication used by the competent practitioner (mail, meetings, stories, reports) so that they can pick up valuable know-how on technique and nuance.

Work practices are social activities that link people through mutual engagement. Work groups form around these practices, creating communities of practice (Lave and Wenger 1991, Wenger 1998). Communities of practice emerge of their own accord and tend to self-organize: people join and stay because they have something to learn and to contribute. By sharing and jointly developing practice, communities of practice evolve patterns of relating and interacting with one another. Over time, they develop a common understanding of the meaning and value of their work, as well as a shared repertory of resources that include both the tacit ("war stories," workarounds, heuristics) and the explicit (notebooks, tools, communication devices). Communities of practice therefore constitute historical and social settings that embrace all three categories of organizational knowledge (cultural, tacit, explicit):

> "It [a community of practice] includes what is said and what is left unsaid; what is represented and what is assumed. It includes the language, tools, documents, images, symbols, well-defined roles, specified criteria, codified procedures, regulations, and contracts that various practices make explicit for a variety of purposes. But it also includes all the implicit relations, tacit conventions, subtle cues, untold rules of thumb, recognizable intuitions, specific perceptions, well-tuned sensitivities, embodied understandings, underlying assumptions, and shared world views. Most of these may never be articulated, yet they are unmistakable signs of membership in communities of practice and are crucial to the success of their enterprise." (Wenger 1998, p. 47)

Within such communities, knowledge is shared and applied through learning in practice that is composed of the processes of: (1) evolving mutual engagement, (2) understanding the nature of the joint enterprise, and (3) developing a shared repertoire (Figure 2.5). Wenger enumerates the elements of each of these processes:

- "Evolving forms of mutual engagement: discovering how to engage, what helps and what hinders; developing mutual relationships; defining identities, establishing who is who, who is good at what, who knows what, who is easy or hard to get along with.
- Understanding and tuning their [the joint] enterprise: aligning their engagement with it, and learning to become and hold each other accountable to it; struggling to define the enterprise and reconciling conflicting interpretations of what the enterprise is about.
- Developing their [the shared] repertoire, styles, and discourses: renegotiating the meaning of various elements; producing or adopting tools, artifacts, representations; recording and recalling events; inventing new terms and redefining or abandoning old ones; telling and retelling stories; creating and breaking routines." (Wenger 1998, p. 95)

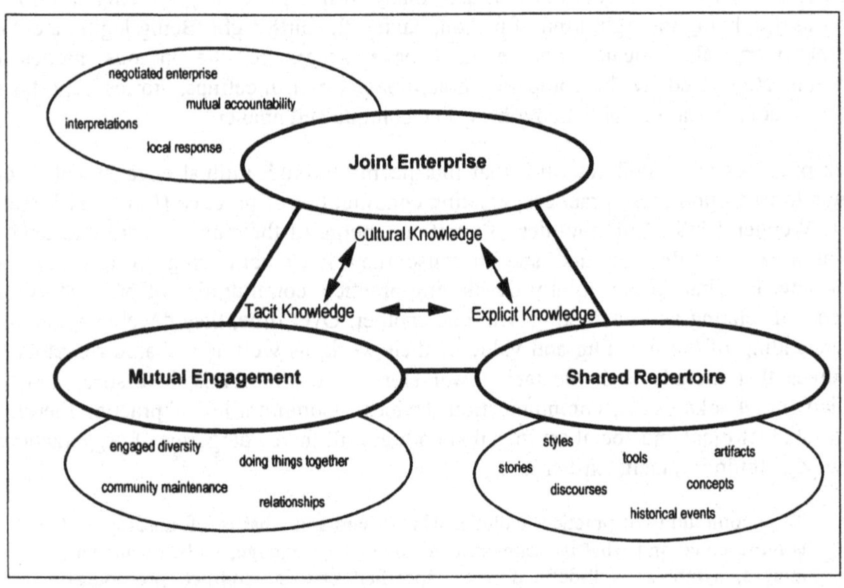

Figure 2.5 Knowledge-in-Use: Communities of Practice (Adapted from Wenger 1998, p. 73, fig. 2.1)

Notice how cultural, explicit and tactical knowledge are blended in these processes. In mutual engagement, a form of group-based tacit knowledge emerges as each member of a community of practice contributes not only his or her own competence, but also involves the competence of others (Wenger 1998, p. 76). These competences may be complementary (as when different members of a team have different roles) or overlapping (as when members have some knowledge of each other's work). When the collective capabilities of a group depends on the interaction between multiple sets of competencies possessed by its members, it becomes more important for members to know how to give and receive help than to try to know everything.

In understanding their joint enterprise, cultural knowledge plays an important role. Communities of practice are not self-contained entities: "they develop in larger contexts—historical, social, cultural, institutional—with specific resources and constraints" (Wenger 1998, p. 79). Members define their enterprise by taking into account their position within a broader industry or job system, and the influence of the institution that employs them. The enterprise of a community of practice also establishes relations of accountability that answer questions on

> "what matters and what does not, what is important and why it is important, what to do and not to do, what to pay attention and what to ignore, what to talk and what to leave unsaid, what to justify and what to take for granted, what to display and what to withhold, when actions and artifacts are good enough and when they need improvement or refinement." (Wenger 1998, p. 81)

In developing a shared repertoire, explicit knowledge becomes a source of coherence for a community of practice. The repertoire of a community of practice includes routines, tools, and concepts, that Wenger describes as "shared" in order to stress its rehearsed character and its availability for further engagement in practice. Thus, routines and artifacts reflect and encode a history of learning and practice, and so provide "recognizable histories of interpretation and usage" that facilitate communication and coordination. At the same time, the shared repertoire of a community of practice also includes stories, symbols, gestures, and ways of doing things. Members use these resources to retain and re-introduce ambiguity in the process of negotiating new meanings and creating new practices. Explicit knowledge therefore has a dual function: it encodes past learning and serves as initial material for the production of new understanding.

Wenger (1998) describes a community of practice that he studied in a medical claims processing center operated by a large US insurance company. Medical claims processing is based on well-structured procedures. Claims processors follow sequences of steps, and make use of work objects such as forms, worksheets, computer screens, and manuals. They learn these procedures through formal as well as on-the-job training. However, their learning to use the knowledge embodied in procedures also embraces much more:

> "What claims processors learn cannot easily be categorized into discrete skills and pieces of information that are useful or harmful, functional or dysfunctional. Learning their jobs, they also learn how much they are to make sense of what they do or encounter. They learn how not learn and how to live with the ignorance they deem appropriate. They learn to keep their shoulders bent and their fingers busy, to follow the rules and to ignore the rules. They learn how to engage and disengage, accept and resist, as well as how to keep a sense of themselves in spite of the status of their occupation. They learn to weave together their work and their private lives. They learn how to find little joys and how to deal with being depressed. What they learn and don't learn makes sense only as

> part of an identity, which is as big as the world and as small as their computer screens, and which subsumes the skills they acquire and gives them meaning. They *become* claims processors." (Wenger 1998, p. 41)

Although the claims processors appear to work individually following set procedures, these explicit policies, metrics, training programs, and system designs are often in conflict with the reality of their work. In order to make it possible to meet the demands of the organization, claims processors collectively construct a local practice that allows them to invent and maintain ways of reconciling institutional requirements with the shifting contingencies of actual work situations. The claims processors create a community of practice that functions by: (1) resolving contradictions between explicit, institutionalized knowledge and personal, situated actions; (2) supporting a communal memory so that individuals can do their work without having to know everything; (3) helping newcomers to join the community; (4) creating a cultural environment in which the monotonous aspects of the work become part of the rituals, customs, and rhythms of community life.

2.4 The Integration of Organizational Knowledge

An organization may be perceived as a repository of capabilities, capabilities that are "determined by the social knowledge embedded in enduring individual relationships structured by organizing principles" (Kogut and Zander 1992, p. 396). These organizing principles establish a common language and set of mechanisms through which people in an organization cooperate, share and transfer knowledge. They enable sets of functional expertise to be communicated and combined so that the organization as a whole can exist as integrated communities. However, the stability of these relationships and principles induces inertia in the organization's capabilities, making it difficult for the organization to switch to new capabilities. Instead, the organization learns new skills by recombining its current capabilities, by synthesizing and applying its current and acquired knowledge:

> "Creating new knowledge does not occur in abstraction from current abilities. Rather, new learning, such as innovations, are products of a firm's **combinative capabilities** to generate new applications from existing knowledge. By combinative capabilities, we mean the intersection of the capability of the firm to exploit its knowledge and the unexplored potential of the technology..." (Kogut and Zander 1992)

This perspective is in line with Schumpeter's (1934) thesis that innovations generally are combinations of existing knowledge and incremental learning. Kogut and Zander (1992) suggest that the main reason why organizations tend to learn in areas that are cognate to their existing practice is because the introduction and exploitation of innovations occur by building on the social relationships that currently exist in the organization, since "a firm's capabilities cannot be separated from how it is currently organized" (p. 392).

Grant (1996b) sees organizational capability as the outcome of knowledge integration—the result of the organization's ability to coordinate and integrate the knowledge of many individual specialists. In Grant's view, knowledge creation is an individual activity, and this means that the primary role of an organization is to apply knowledge rather than to create it. More specifically, the organization exists as an institution that "can create conditions under which multiple individuals can integrate their specialist knowledge" (Grant 1996a, p. 112). The fundamental task of an organization is to integrate the knowledge and coordinate the efforts of its many specialized individuals. Whereas Nonaka and Takeuchi (1995) and Wenger (1998) emphasize the movement and transfer of knowledge, Grant (1996a) maintains that transferring knowledge is not an efficient approach to integrating knowledge. The key to efficiency here is to achieve effective integration while minimizing knowledge transfer: that is, to develop modes of communication that integrate knowledge while reducing the time and effort required to transfer knowledge between collaborators.

Grant identifies four mechanisms for integrating specialized knowledge that economize on communication and coordination: rules and directives; sequencing; routines; and group problem solving and decision making. Rules and directives regulate the actions between individuals, and can provide a means by which tacit knowledge is converted into readily comprehensible explicit knowledge:

> "it is highly inefficient for a quality engineer to teach every production worker all that he knows about quality control. A more efficient means of integrating this knowledge into the production process is for him to establish a set of procedures and rules for quality control." (Grant 1996a, p. 115)

Sequencing organizes production activities in a time sequence so that each specialist's input occurs independently in a pre-assigned time slot. Routines can support relatively complex patterns of behaviors and interactions between individuals without the need to specify rules and directives. Organizational routines may be designed to be flexible, permitting individuals to vary their responses and interactions. Group problem solving and decision making, in contrast with the other mechanisms, rely on high levels of communication and non-standard coordination methods to deal with problems that are high in task complexity and task uncertainty. All four mechanisms depend upon the existence of common knowledge for their operation. Common knowledge may take the form of: a common language between organizational members; commonality in the individuals' specialized knowledge; shared meanings and understandings between individuals; and awareness and recognition of the individuals' knowledge domains (Grant 1996a).

While Kogut and Zander (1992), Grant (1996a,b), and others regard organizations as institutions for combining and integrating knowledge, Tsoukas (1996) suggests that there may be limits to the extent that organizational knowledge may be integrated. As we have noted earlier, an organization's knowledge is distributed over time, physical and social space, as well as over different groups and individuals. Tsoukas (1996) carries the conceptualization of the firm as a distributed knowledge system further by using a constructionist approach. Organizations are analyzed as "distributed knowledge systems in a strong sense: they are de-centered systems. A firm's knowledge cannot be surveyed as a whole: it is not self-contained; it is inherently indeterminate and continually reconfiguring" (Tsoukas 1996, p. 13). The utilization of organizational knowledge cannot be known by a single agent—no single individual or agent can fully specify in advance what kind of knowledge is going to be relevant, when and where. There is no "master control room" where knowledge may be centrally managed.

Instead, organizational knowledge is continually constituted and reconstituted through the activities undertaken within the organization. Knowledge is the emergent outcome of engaging in work as social practices that consist of three dimensions: role-related normative expectations; personal dispositions; and local interactions with particular situations (Mouzelis 1995, Bourdieu 1988). First, there are the normative expectations that are associated with the carrying out of an organizational role. Second, personal dispositions are the mental patterns of perception, thought and action acquired by an individual through past socializations and experiences. Third, local interactions with particular situations arise when normative expectations and personal dispositions interact with specific features and circumstances of the work situation. Whereas an organization may have some control over role-related normative expectations, it has little or no control over members' dispositions or how these dispositions and role expectations play out in particular situations. An organization's knowledge is therefore always emergent and contingent. Moreover, expectations, dispositions, and situations are rarely congruent, so that three elements are separated by gaps. To close these gaps, practitioners exercise their judgment by selecting what they consider to be relevant features from each of the three dimensions, and attempting to fit them together.

Viewing the organization as a distributed knowledge system thus refines our perspectives of what knowledge management needs to entail:

> "Organizations are seen as being in constant flux, out of which the potential for the emergence of novel practices is never exhausted—human action is inherently creative. Organizational members do follow rules but how they do so is an inescapably contingent-cum-local matter. In organizations, both rule-bound action and novelty are present, as are continuity and change, regularity and creativity. Management, therefore, can be seen as an open-ended process of coordinating purposeful individuals, whose actions stem from applying their unique interpretations to the local circumstances confronting them. ... Given the distributed character of organizational knowledge, the key to achieving coordinated action does not so much depend on those 'higher up' collecting more and more knowledge, as on those 'lower down' finding more and more ways of getting connected and interrelating the knowledge each one has. A necessary condition for this to happen is to appreciate the character of a firm as a discursive practice: a form of life, a community, in which individuals come to share an unarticulated background of common understandings. Sustaining a discursive practice is just as important as finding ways of integrating distributed knowledge." (Tsoukas 1996, p. 22-23)

2.5 Organizational Knowledge and Sensemaking, Decision Making

The capacity to create, diffuse, and utilize knowledge is distributed over a larger canvas of processes by which an organization engages and processes information. An organization uses information in three arenas: to make sense of its environment, to create new knowledge, and to make decisions (Choo 1998). Sensemaking creates a framework of shared meanings and purpose that give identity and value to the activities of the organization. Sensemaking frames the perception of problems or opportunities that the organization needs to work on. Dealing with problems and opportunities often become occasions for decision making, and when the problems are complex and novel, they may require the creation of new knowledge. An organization possesses three categories of knowledge: tacit knowledge cultivated through the experience and expertise of individuals; explicit knowledge codified as artifacts, rules and routines; and cultural knowledge expressed as assumptions, beliefs, and values. The creation of new knowledge depends on the conversion, sharing and combination of these three forms of organizational knowledge. The results of knowledge creation are new innovations or an expansion of the organization's capabilities. Decision making is structured by rules and routines, and guided by preferences that are based on a shared understanding of the purpose and goals of the organization. Where new capabilities or innovations are available, they introduce new alternatives and enlarge the problem search space. Decision making selects a course of action that is expected to perform well (or well enough) along the dimensions of organizational goals and preferences.

Thus, the capacity to develop organizational knowledge is distributed over a network of information processes and participants who construct meanings about the organization's identity and actions; create, discover, and apply new knowledge; and initiate patterns of behavior through search, evaluation, and selection of alternatives. Rather than being centrally controlled and coordinated, the capacity to develop knowledge emerges from the complex, unpredictable patchwork of processes and participants who enact and negotiate their own meanings of what is going on; stumble upon and wrestle with new knowledge to make it work; creatively improvise and bend rules and routines to deal with specific problems.

As shown in Figure 2.6, sensemaking is precipitated by the perception of signals indicating changes in the organization's environment. Weick (1995) described how people enact or actively construct the environment that they attend to, by bracketing experience, and by creating new features in the environment. Beliefs form expectations and act as initial nodes of meaning from which to grow larger structures of understanding. By selecting and overlaying past meanings over current equivocal data, a plausible interpretation is enacted and retained for future sensemaking. Through sensemaking, organizational members create and negotiate beliefs and interpretations to construct shared meanings and common goals. Shared meanings and purpose are the outcome of sensemaking, and they compose the framework for explaining observed reality, and for determining saliency and appropriateness. Shared meanings and purpose help to establish a shared organizational agenda, a set of issues that people in the organization agree on as being important to the well-being of the organization. While they may not agree about the content of a particular issue, and may adopt diverse positions on how it should be resolved, nevertheless there is collective recognition that these issues are vital to the organization. Shared meanings and purpose also help to shape a collective organizational identity, or perhaps more accurately, a set of multiple identities, since an organization assumes different identities in different situations. Defining an organizational identity establishes norms and expectations about the propriety, accountability, and legitimacy of the organization's choices and behaviors. A framework of shared meanings and purpose is therefore used by organizational members to assess consequentiality and appropriateness, and to reduce information ambiguity and uncertainty to a level that enables dialogue, choice and action making.

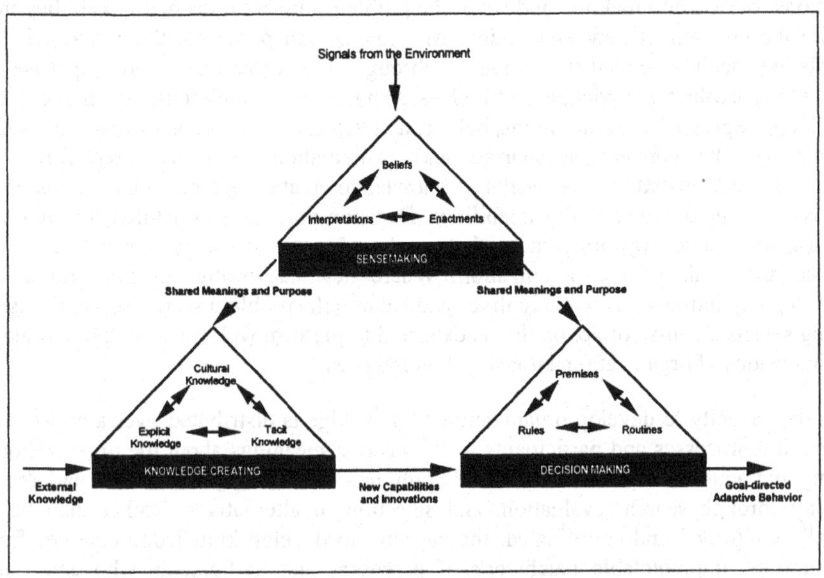

Figure 2.6 Sensemaking, Knowledge Creating, and Decision Making (Adapted from Choo 1998, p. 241, fig. 6.9). Arrows in figure suggest interaction and interdependence, not causality or sequence.

Within the framework of its constructed meaning, agenda, and identity, the organization exploits current specializations or develops new capabilities in order to move towards its vision and goals. Movement may be blocked by gaps in the knowledge needed to bridge meaning and action. When the organization experiences gaps in its existing knowledge or limitations in its current capabilities, it initiates knowledge seeking and creating, guided by boundaries and directions derived from an interpretation of the organization's goals, agendas, and priorities.

As we have discussed in this chapter, organizational members individually and collectively fabricate new knowledge by converting, sharing and combining their tacit, explicit, and cultural knowledge, as well as by cross-linking knowledge from outside. The fruits of knowledge creation are new capabilities and innovations that enhance existing competencies or build new ones; develop new products, services, or processes; or extend the range of viable organizational responses to a problem situation. While it enables new forms of action, new knowledge also introduces new forms of uncertainty: novel innovations are untested in the market; budding capabilities are unexercised. New knowledge represents a potential for action, and it is through the decision making process that the organization chooses whether to convert this potential into a commitment for action.

Shared meanings and purposes, as well as new knowledge and capabilities converge on decision making as the activity leading to the selection and initiation of action. Shared meanings, agendas and identities (the results of sensemaking) select the premises, rules, and routines that structure decision making. New knowledge and capabilities make available new alternatives and outcomes. By structuring choice behavior through premises, rules and routines, the organization simplifies decision making, codifies and transmits past learning, and proclaims competence and accountability (Simon 1997, March & Simon 1993, Cyert & March 1963/1992). Rules and routines specify 'rational' criteria for the evaluation of alternatives, 'legitimate' methods for the allocation of resources, and 'objective' conditions for distinguishing between predictability and uncertainty.

Over time, the organization has learned and codified a large number of rules and routines, so that choosing which rules to activate for a specific choice situation is itself problematic. Shared meanings and understandings about the nature and needs of a particular situation are used to guide rule activation. Shared interpretations help select which rules to apply by answering the questions "What kind of situation is this?" and "What rules do we have for dealing with this type of situation?" Shared interpretations may also select rules according to the criterion of appropriateness: "What kind of organization are we? What would be appropriate behavior for an organization like ours in a situation like this one?" (March 1994). Occasionally, shared interpretations indicate that the situation is unfamiliar, where none of the learned rules seem to apply. When rules break down, the organization attempts to make new meaning in time to initiate action, effectively prototyping new rules to prompt choice making. The end result of this interaction between shared meaning (in interpretations and understandings) and shared learning (in rules and routines) is the execution of a pattern of actions that simultaneously constitutes the organization's attempt to move towards current goals and maintain current identity, as well as its attempt to adapt to changed conditions in the environment. In this sense, the outcome of decision making is behavior that is both goal-directed and adaptive.

While each organization adjusts its behavior to perceived changes in the environment, its responses are diluted and diffracted by the concurrent actions of other actors that participate in the same arena. Thus each organization is reacting to the actions of other organizations that are also reacting to it. The resultant meshwork of interactions configure new patterns and new conditions that pose fresh ambiguities and uncertainties. A continuous stream of new events and equivocal cues necessitates iterative cycles of information processing. Where meanings or purpose change as a result of reinterpreting the environment, or where rules or routines are altered as a result of acquiring knowledge and understanding, the organization is adapting to variation and feedback in its environment.

An organization maintains a background of stable definitions of identity, renderings of reality, and patterns of behavior. Against this background, there is a foreground where individuals are capable of creating meanings, discovering knowledge, and making choices. It is this interplay between a sturdy, orderly background and a vigorous, surprising foreground that animates organizational learning and adaptation. An organization thus constructs knowledge across three planes. It constructs knowledge as shared meanings about what the organization can perceive as reality; it constructs knowledge as expanded competencies about what the organization can do; and it constructs knowledge as learned behaviors about what the organization can achieve.

2.6 Summary

This chapter began with an analysis of the relationship between data, information, and knowledge. The transformation of data into information, and information into knowledge is achieved by increasing the level of physical, cognitive, and belief-based structuring. This structuring requires progressively greater amounts of human effort to sense, select, construct meaning, and form beliefs. Knowledge in organizations is learned and acquired through observation, experience, and practice. Although epistemology defines knowledge as justified true belief, the justification of organizational knowledge is problematic because justification is often based on informal evidence, non-rigorous methods, or public, social processes where power and interests are brought into play.

Structurally, organizational knowledge may be categorized into tacit, explicit, and cultural knowledge. Tacit knowledge is personal knowledge that is rooted in hands-on experience and revealed through skillful practice. Explicit knowledge is codified knowledge that has been written down, embodied in artifacts, or articulated in organizational rules and routines. Cultural knowledge consists of assumptions, beliefs, and values that are used to construct reality and to assign significance to new information and knowledge. Differentiating knowledge categories in this way bring out the differences and dependencies between aspects of organizational knowledge that we otherwise cannot easily analyze.

Knowledge is never static, but continuously in motion. The dynamics of organizational knowledge is examined by looking at knowledge creation, knowledge diffusion, and knowledge utilization. The creation of knowledge leverages tacit knowledge by converting it into new explicit knowledge (Nonaka and Takeuchi 1995). Through operationalization and dissemination, the new explicit knowledge is re-experienced and re-internalized as cultural knowledge. The diffusion of organizational knowledge is increased and accelerated by the codification and abstraction of personal knowledge into public knowledge. The trajectory of knowledge diffusion may be mapped to trace its evolution from concrete, tacit knowledge to proprietary and public explicit knowledge, and then to the common sense of cultural knowledge (Boisot 1998). Knowledge utilization is examined as active, ongoing cycles of learning and adaptation that take place in communities of practice (Wenger 1998). In these natural communities, tacit, explicit and cultural knowledge bind to form a social context where members jointly construct purpose and identity, and negotiate the meanings of objects, actions, and events.

Knowledge is assimilated and converted into meaningful practice, and new knowledge emerges through constant renewal and reconstruction.

The chapter concludes with two approaches in presenting a holistic view of how organizations create and use information. Kogut and Zander (1992) and Grant (1996a,b) emphasize the role of the organization in generating new capabilities by combining its existing knowledge and integrating the knowledge of its specialized individuals. Choo (1998) views organizational learning and adaptation as the emergent outcome of a network of information processes that connects knowledge creation to sensemaking and decision making.

Section II: Knowledge Work on Intranets

Chapter 3: The Intranet as Infrastructure for Knowledge Work

In the previous section of this monograph, we illustrated and described two predominant themes. The first examined information seeking as a human activity consisting of primarily three social processes: the experiencing of information needs, the seeking of information, and the using of information. The second explored the nature of organizational knowledge and the social processes by which organizational knowledge is created and shared. In this chapter, we bring these perspectives closer together by exploring how many organizations today are bridging these two areas of interest by introducing and implementing intranets in their corporations. We argue that intranets can promote information seeking and knowledge work by functioning as IT infrastructures that stimulate and foster organizational knowledge and intelligence.

To elaborate our position, we start with a detailed description of intranets, examining the major components of their underlying technology and the architectures that comprise a typical intranet implementation. We discuss the potential benefits intranets offer organizations and the challenges that inhibit their adoption and use. From there, we expand on the intranet's capacity to serve as an information technology infrastructure for organizational learning by devising a trilateral model, one which portrays the intranet as a shared information space consisting of distinct information content, communications, and collaboration spaces. To illustrate the barriers affecting the adoption and use of intranets in corporations and the organizational changes that can result in implementing an intranet infrastructure, we look to the lessons learned from the field of Computer Supported Cooperative Work (CSCW). Last, we briefly profile a selected number of "early-adopter" organizations which have embarked on this technology by examining their intranet applications.

3.1 What are Intranets?

In short, intranets are private, internal networks based on internet standards. In terms of access, intranets are restricted to organizational participants only; firewalls prevent access from external internet users and allow information to be securely managed inside an organization (Hinrich 1997). Abraham (1998) defines an intranet as a set of applications built on an internet-enabled infrastructure meant for internal use only by employees of a single organization. In this way, intranets refer not only to the underlying network but also to the information content, services, and applications built on top of that network infrastructure.

In an attempt to consolidate various departmental intranets across the enterprise, organizations are constructing "corporate intranets" or "portals" which function as home pages to departmental intranet sites and external internet resources (Detlor, 2000). Corporate portals differ from departmental intranets in that a portal's primary function is to provide a transparent directory of information already available elsewhere, not act as a separate source of information itself. Recently, industry trend-watchers have forecasted the rise of portal development in corporations. For instance, Gartner Group predicts with 80% probability that more than half of all major companies by the end of the year 2001 will implement corporate portals as the primary method for organizing and discovering corporate resources (Verity, 1999). Likewise, the Delphi Group found that 55% of Fortune 500 companies currently have corporate portal projects in progress; further, Merrill Lynch estimates that the market for portal tools and services will be worth upwards of $14.8 billion (US) by the year 2002 (Roberts-Witt, 1999).

The excitement over corporate portals is due in large part to the success Yahoo! had with its 1996 launch of a personalized portal service called MyYahoo!, which allowed users to customize their own Web interfaces to filter and provide information that was relevant and meaningful to them (Plumtree, 1999). Organizations were quick to notice the success of this product in terms of its adoption and use by the general public and started to investigate ways to develop a similar view of corporate information. Overall, corporate portals are following a similar trajectory as consumer portals, though over much shorter time frames. First version portals containing referential links to information plus a search engine are quickly evolving into more complex, interactive gateways that embed applications to enhance personal and work group productivity, all within time periods as short as 12 months (Eckerson, 1999). Common elements contained within corporate portal designs include an enterprise taxonomy or classification of information categories that help organize information for easy retrieval; a search engine to facilitate more specific and exact information requests; and links to both internal and external Web sites and information sources.

Together, both corporate and departmental intranets provide organizations with an internet-enabled infrastructure that offers a means of reducing the complexity of accessing information distributed across the enterprise. For instance, intranets allow organizational participants to utilize browsers, such as Netscape Navigator or Microsoft Internet Explorer, to retrieve files scattered throughout the organization, opening and displaying them as part of the request. These files may contain hyperlinks or pointers to other files which allow users to navigate corporate information using a point-and-click interface. These files appear to users as standard displayed documents called pages. Basically, there are two specific types: content pages, which contain information of value created by individual employees; and broker pages, which are used to help people find content pages (Telleen 1996a). To help employees "find their way", many organizations provide users with a corporate home page as a starting point or launch pad. Usually, this page has links to departmental home pages and provides a mechanism for users to read current business announcements.

In the last few years, there has been considerable growth in the use of intranets in organizations (Abraham 1998; Haynal 1996). The reason for this growth lies in the promise of intranet technology to alleviate the difficulty and complexity of accessing information stored in traditional computer-based information systems across a multitude of organizational departments and divisions (Wolesky 1996). Cortese (1996) describes how intranets can do what computer and software makers have frequently promised to do, but never actually delivered—the ability to pull together all the various computer, software, and database technologies that dot the corporate landscape into a single system which enables employees to find information wherever it resides. The platform independent nature of this new technology makes it possible for any computer to display documents created for the intranet, no matter what software application was used to create it, and eliminates the need for employees to be concerned about where information is physically stored (Sprout and Coxeter 1995).

This surge of interest in intranet technology is recognized by some as a turning point in the history of computing in organizations. Telleen (1996b, chapter 6) notes that intranets are having an analogous effect on information management to what the invention of solid state electronics and microprocessors had on computer hardware. Others point out the parallel of the adoption of intranet technology in organizations to the PC revolution of the 1980's (James 1996; Strom 1995), where grassroots user demand for better control and access to information created a shift away from a centralized control approach to information management in mainframe computing environments to a more distributed model of information available from the employee desktop.

3.1.1 Intranet Technology

In terms of technology, intranets are based on the same underlying HTTP (HyperText Transfer Protocol) communication and HTML (HyperText Markup Language) document publishing protocols as the World Wide Web (WWW), developed in 1991 to link physicists and engineers at remote sites to share ideas and aspects of a common project (Berners-Lee et al. 1994). As such, intranets operate on a client/server model of computing—an information technology architecture, popular in organizational settings since the mid-1980s, where centralized servers or computing machines handle information requests across a distributed network of client computers or processes.

Figure 3.1 illustrates the basic workings of the traditional web client/server model. The diagram shows how web browsers send information requests to web servers, which retrieve the required information from a variety of platforms across the organization such as files, legacy systems and databases, and pass it back to the appropriate requesting client.

To invoke an information request, a web browser sends an HTTP request command to the web server that contains the particular piece of information being sought. Restrictions may prevent access to information on servers to specific users and/or machines. As information can be stored in any format, it is the server's responsibility to inform the client as to the format of the requested information so that the client can handle it accordingly. When the server returns an HTTP response command back to the client, the response consists of two portions: the header which identifies the type of data it is, and the body which contains the information requested.

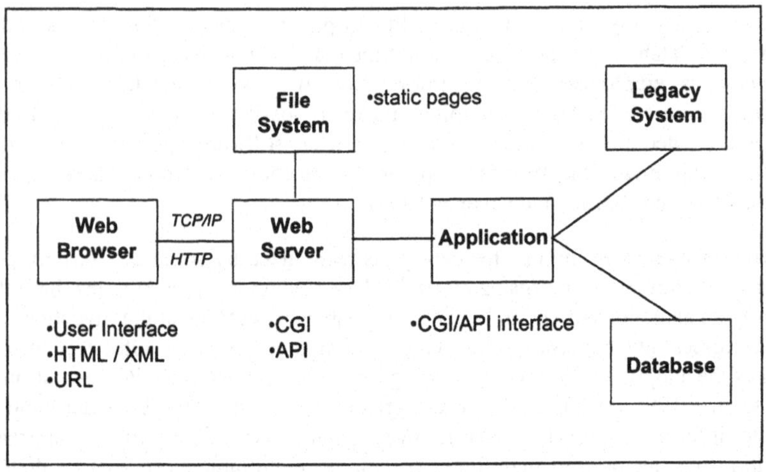

Figure 3.1 Basic workings of the web client/server model

HTTP is a lightweight stateless networking protocol that uses minimal network bandwidth (Bentley et. al. 1997b). According to Fielding, Irvine, Gettys, Mogul, Frystyk, and Berners-Lee (1997), the Hypertext Transfer Protocol is

> "an application-level protocol for distributed, collaborative, hypermedia information systems. It is a generic, stateless object-oriented protocol which can be used for many tasks, such as name servers and distributed object management systems through extension of its request methods. A feature of HTTP is the typing and negotiation of data representation, allowing systems to be built independently of the data being transferred." (p. 1)

Designed as a simple request-response protocol, the commands of HTTP are used to request particular services from a web server. The most frequently used are: the GET command, used to request information such as an HTML page or sound clip; the POST command, used to transmit HTML form data to a server; and the HEAD command, used to request header information only contained in an information entity. Less supported commands are PUT and DELETE which send and remove documents from a server respectively. HTTP is stateless in that it handles each request as an independent transaction. In this sense, HTTP does not support "sessions" in that each command sent to a server must contain the name and password of the user issuing the request. One of the strengths of the HTTP protocol is its independence from the format of the transmitted data; it is the responsibility of servers and browsers to handle new data formats.

HTTP runs over TCP/IP, which is the basis of Web communication services and increasingly the de facto standard for corporate networks. TCP/IP is a suite of networking protocols used to transmit and receive information packets between host computers; the three major protocols in this suite are IP, the Internet Protocol; TCP, the Transmission Control Protocol; and UDP, the User Datagram Protocol (Liu et. al. 1994). The basic underpinning of TCP/IP is that every computing machine on the network is labeled with a unique identifier or address generally expressed as ###.###.###.###. When a client makes an information request to a server, the request or message (also called a packet) is fragmented into smaller frames and transmitted over the network. Each frame has a header containing a fragment number and the address of the computer to which the fragment is being sent. The fragment is retransmitted across servers until it is received at the appropriate destination. As fragments may be received in any order, it is the responsibility of the destination host to unpackage the fragments and re-order them in proper sequence using the unique fragment numbers as guides.

As such, the web browser is the portion of the web client/server model with which the user "sees" and interacts. It is the interface running on the user's desktop through which all requests for information stored on the intranet are made and presented. As a result, its design and functionality become crucial elements in determining the extent to which the intranet is adopted and used.

In terms of information presentation, the web browser typically displays HTML pages of text and graphics. HTML is a simple subset of SGML, the Standard Generalized Markup Language which describes the logical structure of a document. HTML transforms a plain text document into a hypertext structure by using simple mark-up tags. Here, authors of documents use tags to indicate which sections of the document are links to other information entities and specify the web address or URL (Uniform Resource Locator) the client should send as part of the HTTP request to the server if the user clicks on that section. In this way, numerous HTML pages residing on possibly different servers can be linked together to form a single hypertext structure. The advantage of HTML is its simplicity of use for both web page authors, who create such documents, and for browsers, which must interpret them in turn.

More recently, XML (Extensible Markup Language) has been approved as a W3C (World Wide Web Consortium) Recommendation (http://www.w3.org/TR/REC-xml). XML is a subset of SGML that specifies a set of rules for describing the content and structure of documents on the Web. Unlike HTML, XML describes the content and context (meanings and relationships) of elements in the document but it does not describe their formatting. Like SGML, XML is a metalanguage that allows users to create their own tags to describe document elements and attributes (example XML tags might be <customer-name>, <company>, <order-number>), as well as define the relationships between these elements. If applications agree on their use of these extended tag definitions, then they are able to understand the meaning and context of the text exchanged between them. XML's growing importance comes from its potential to enable emerging Web-based applications in electronic commerce, enterprise content management, information discovery, application integration, and knowledge sharing. Some areas where XML is expected to have an impact are:

(1) Domain-specific markup languages

Examples include the Mathematical Markup Language for representing mathematical formulae; Chemical Markup Language for describing molecular structure; Bioinformatic Sequence Markup Language for encoding DNA, RNA and protein sequence information; and Open Financial Exchange for transferring financial documents.

(2) Data interchange between applications

XML provides a solution for EDI (Electronic Data Interchange) over the Internet. XML may be used to define a standardized, machine-readable data format that maintains content and structure, but separates the business rules from the data. Thus each trading partner can apply its own business rules to the data.

(3) Metadata and resource description frameworks

Resource Description Framework (RDF) will be an XML document type for metadata just as XML is at the document level. This means that RDF documents will be able to describe new relations and develop new relational vocabularies between documents, images and other Web resources.

(4) Online information searching and sharing

The searching, browsing, discovering, and sharing of information online may be made significantly more flexible (and more precise) by taking advantage of tags and features in XML documents, and by using supporting XML technologies such as extended linking.

As a means to extend web browsers to handle different types of data, most *web servers* provide APIs (Application Programming Interfaces) for extending the server with new functionality. An API describes how an application service can be invoked from another application. It is through APIs that web servers can communicate efficiently with databases and legacy applications to make requests for complex information structures. A CGI (Common Gateway Interface) offers comparable functionality to that of an API—the difference being that an API is part of an application which serves as an interface, while a CGI is predominantly a script or developer-supplied program serving as an interface between a server and other applications. With CGIs, scripts are configured to the server to handle certain HTTP requests. CGI specifies the request information that is needed to process the command and returns a reply back to the client that requested the information. This is usually in the form of a HTML page. The most common scripting languages include C, C++, JavaScript, Microsoft VBScript, and PERL.

There are various ways in which the elements of the web client/server model can be arranged to suit the needs of an organization. Guengerich et. al. (1997) describe five common intranet architectures: content distribution; DBMS direct integration; traditional client/server; non-traditional client/server; and collaborative. Each of these are variations of the web client/server model described above. Content distribution is the basic infrastructure that can be used and is usually the first to be implemented. It consists solely of clients and web servers, where clients request static HTML pages off web servers. DBMS direct integration refers to direct database access from a web server. Traditional and non-traditional client/servers are variations of the web client/server model that include an intermediary application service layer between the web server and the information being sought. Here, the terms "traditional" and "non-traditional" differentiate those instances when the information being sought resides on typical versus non-typical computing platforms such as transaction-oriented relational database systems (traditional) and document management systems (non-traditional). The collaborative architecture refers to access to communication-type devices, such as an e-mail server, directly from a web server.

Figure 3.2 helps clarify the workings of the web client/server model by demonstrating the internal actions that occur for an intranet database request. Specifically, the diagram illustrates the sequence of actions that typically occur when a user makes a request over the intranet to retrieve information stored in a centralized data repository. This repository may be any type of data storage medium, such as a relational database, data warehouse, or data mart. For our example, it is assumed that the organization maintains a centralized repository of customer information and the user is making a request to retrieve profile information from this repository for a particular customer. Though the user perceives this as a simple desktop operation, in actuality this interaction consists of a series of coordinated events that occur across the intranet's component parts.

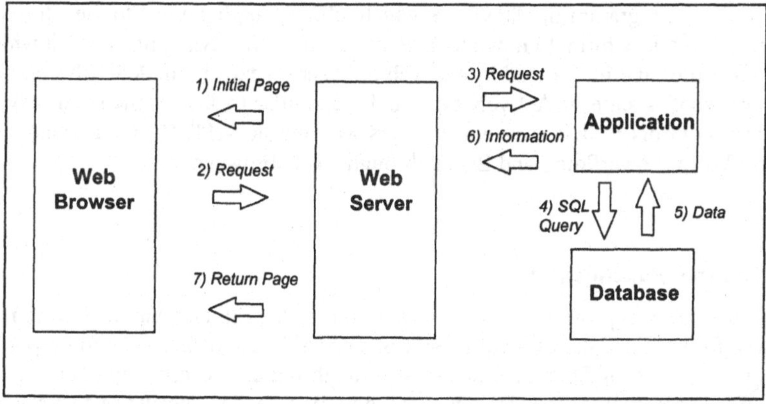

Figure 3.2 Process for obtaining database information over an intranet

As Figure 3.2 shows, the first step involves the loading of an initial page from the web server onto the user's desktop. Typically, this involves the use of a form which allows organizational participants to enter information in a pre-defined format. In step two, the browser packages the user's input into an HTTP request and sends it to the web server. In step three, the server recognizes that the request is to be processed by a back-end application program. The server, through an API or CGI, sets up the application program and forwards the request to it. In step four, the application must parse and validate the user's request for information. The application then formulates the proper syntax for an SQL (Structured Query Language) query to the database which contains the user's request. In step five, the requested customer data is passed back from the database to the application program. From there, the application program dynamically reformats the data, typically into an HTML web page. In step six, the web page is forwarded to the web server. It is the responsibility of the web server in step seven to transmit the formatted customer information back to the web browser from which the original request was generated.

As the example illustrates, the majority of the functionality required to service a user's request for information resides on the backend of the client/server model. Though such an architecture frees the web client to perform other services, this is not always a desirable state. One problem is that the overall system performance degrades as the server is handling the majority of the work. Another is that the resulting dynamically-generated HTML page returned to the client is limited in terms of how it can be presented and displayed. To overcome this inadequacy, new web application tools have been developed to increase the functionality offered in web client pages. These include Java applets and ActiveX controls.

Java applets and ActiveX controls are executable code fragments embedded in a web page and downloaded to client-side browsers for execution. They can be used to enhance the interface of an HTML page by providing additional functionality within the web browser. Java applets are small Java programs integrated into an HTML page. Java is an object-oriented programming language which allows applications to be stored in a platform independent format known as byte code. As such, Java applets are downloaded as byte-code files and interpreted by the web browser on execution. ActiveX controls are part of Microsoft's suite of ActiveX tools and are similar to Java applets. An advantage of ActiveX controls is that they enable users to view non-HTML documents, such as Microsoft Word, PowerPoint, and Excel, through a web browser.

3.1.2 Intranet Functionality

Though our customer profile example focuses on how the intranet can be used to retrieve database information, data retrieval is only one possible use of intranets in corporations. In fact, a wide array of functionalities exist through intranet technology (Telleen 1996b, chapter 6). These include services such as e-mail, threaded discussions, newsgroups, shared electronic white boards, and work flow systems, all which support two-way dialogue and help provide a means by which participants can easily feedback comments to one another in unstructured formats. Electronic mail and threaded discussions enable organizational participants to discuss and share ideas with one another. Newsgroups allow organizational employees to exchange information directly with other members of the corporation. As the posting of this information is made available to others, the use of newsgroups results in a "corporate knowledge base" available to all members of the organization. Shared electronic white boards facilitate organizational collaboration. They allow the same web page to appear and be updated on multiple computers. Participants can make changes to shared intranet pages as well as see changes to these pages as they are made. Workflow systems, commonly used for project management purposes, typically involve a system of integrated mail and web pages to help coordinate work requests, action items, and resources across the enterprise.

Despite this wide and varied set of functionalities, intranets are being used in most organizations today primarily for basic information access purposes, namely the retrieval of corporate documents. The more predominant uses of intranets in organizations support the dissemination of information in sales and marketing, product development, customer service and support, and human resources. Typically the information found on organizational intranets includes competitive sales information, human resources and employee benefits statements, corporate directories, policy guides, and company newsletters. As such, most corporations use the intranet primarily for information dissemination purposes.

However, in the future, it is expected that organizations will start capitalizing on the more interactive features of the intranet. Organizations are just starting to use the intranet more frequently to let employees fill out forms, query databases, or hold virtual conferences over private webs. Telleen (1996b) calls for more robust usage of intranets in organizations other than document access. He states that much of the material on corporate home pages consists of traditional collateral translated to Web standards. According to Telleen, the technology has not been incorporated into the business infrastructure where it has the most potential to transform the way the enterprise manages itself.

3.2 Benefits and Challenges of Intranets

There are many benefits offered through the adoption and use of intranets in organizations. One of the more significant is the ability of intranets to facilitate organizational knowledge work. Here, knowledge work is defined as the acquisition, creation, packaging, application, and reuse of knowledge—activities characterized by variety and exception rather than routine, and performed by professional or technical workers with a high level of skill and expertise (Davenport, Jarvenpaa, and Beers 1996). According to Davenport et al. (p. 61), intranets support the three primary redesign strategies for knowledge work processes: intranets change knowledge by reducing it to a unit that workers can reuse and access; intranets reduce the geographic distance between workers by providing access to information regardless of its physical location; and intranets create knowledge bases and enable telecommunications infrastructures to bolster knowledge work.

Interestingly, in recent years, intranets have been making headway in providing organizations with an infrastructure for delivering knowledge management solutions. Davenport and Prusak (1998, p. 131) declare both Lotus Notes and intranet-based webs as the leading toolsets for managing knowledge repositories today. Likewise, Ginsburg and Duliba (1997) state that many of the same capabilities offered through Lotus Notes are replicable with intranet-based solutions in that both technologies are flexible groupware applications which permit asynchronous interaction between widely physically-distributed organizational participants. In their analysis of several case study sites of organizations which implemented Notes, Ginsburg and Duliba describe Notes' ability to leverage organizational knowledge, specifically through the capture, dissemination, and reuse of knowledge. The authors give a rich description of how organizations use Notes as repositories to capture organizational memory which could "be built just as easily using Intranet technology" (p. 216).

Another appealing benefit of intranets is their ability to promote organizational communications. Due to their underlying network understructure, intranets can encourage both cross-organizational and hierarchical communications (Gonzalez 1997). Further, geographic restrictions are few as intranets can provide access for employees in locations that span the globe. In fact, intranets may serve as bridges between branch and home offices, as well as domestic and foreign divisions, which is an important consideration for widely dispersed corporations.

As such, intranets can increase the volume and quality of electronic communications between employees. Sproull (1991b) discusses the benefits of increased electronic connections between organizational participants. Receiving information allows users to learn from others and to "discover similarities they share with people who have different jobs and are located in different places" (p. 81). Likewise, sending information gives users the opportunity to have a voice in their work group and with their superiors. In this sense, electronic communications in the workplace give organizational participants a "window on the world" and a "voice for the voiceless". Additionally electronic connections bring peripheral employees who are physically isolated from other organizational members back into the fold, increase employee emotional commitment to the company, and promote information connections between organizational participants through communication of sincere, unsolicited messages which cut across organizational boundaries. Similarly, Finholt and Sproull (1990) remark on the ability of electronic groups in the workplace to cut across organizational boundaries of geography and work unit, to tap and pool expertise of individual employees regardless of their physical location, and to provide a means by which employees can discover others with similar interests.

Another benefit of intranets is their ability to support group collaboration. In fact, it is argued by many that the WWW is an enabling technology for cooperative work (Bentley et al. 1997a, 1997b; Dix 1997; Grasso et al. 1997). This same argument can apply to intranets. Intranets give users the capability of browsing and searching for both structured and unstructured information to help formulate new understandings or stimulate innovation. They provide a means for organizational participants to gather others' experiences and negotiate a shared consensus towards common goals and ideas. The intranet's hypertext structure allows users to browse information created by fellow employees more easily; this encourages intranet users to become aware of other employees in the organization and their availability for cooperative action.

In a sense, intranets are a new form of groupware. The term groupware, coined by Peter and Trudy Johnson-Lenz (1982, p. 47), refers to a category of computer-based systems designed to support groups of people engaged in common tasks or goals through the provision of an interface to a shared environment (Ellis, Gibbs, and Rein 1991, p. 40). Viewing intranets in this manner, and not merely as simple information dissemination tools, helps enrich our understanding of intranets for collaborative work.

Despite these benefits, certain challenges commonly arise in the introduction of intranet technology in the workplace. These include the need to introduce some form of security within the corporate infrastructure to restrict access to intranet pages on a user or group basis and to establish measures to prevent the invasion of privacy (INET 1996). For example, Bannon and Schmidt (1991), recognizing the political nature of organizations and the desire of organizational participants not to share or reveal information to one other, cautions that discretionary access to shared information spaces must be made. He states that controls are required to regulate the dissemination of information pertaining to a worker's decision-making. A similar argument for the need to create regionalized communication spaces to support "real world" negotiations between organizational actors is made by Clement and Wagner (1995). Such a concept is also supported by Schatz (1991-1992) who recommends a mechanism for controlling "levels of privacy" in an electronic community system for scientists sharing research; here each member of the community is permitted to control who has access to his/her material.

Another challenge that many corporations must face is how to establish the layout or "look and feel" of their intranet web pages. Basically, organizations can position between two opposing extremes: one of planned control; the other of natural growth. Companies can either have top management dictate a consistent format to organizational web pages or grant freedom to employees to create web pages as they see fit (Thyfault 1996). A middle ground approach would be to force departmental web pages to follow corporate guidelines and allow individual employee home pages to be formatted as desired. Other social issues for organizations to address include whether to allow employees to chat on-line anonymously and whether to restrict conversations on the intranet to predefined communities.

Steve Telleen, a specialist in intranet implementation, notes the challenge of understanding the organizational context surrounding intranets:

> "Talking to companies that have implemented Intranets, the toughest issues are not the technology but the people issues... The technology is exciting, the tools more amazing everyday. But without an understanding of the organizational and management implications of this technology the implementer risks becoming part of the road rather than part of the steam-roller creating it." (1996b, preface)

Telleen (1996b, chapter 2), in his on-line book on the organizational impacts and issues surrounding intranet technology, outlines the need for organizations to balance structure and looseness in managing any distributed system such as the intranet. On the one hand, he states that "without some standards organizations lose their ability to communicate effectively and coordinate their activities" and that "without some level of support, knowledge workers become too involved in low level maintenance activities at the expense of the higher level functions that most benefit the enterprise". On the other, he recognizes the need for looseness as a means to enable independent decision and action. The challenge in managing these technologies, according to Telleen, is "meeting the needs for coordination and efficiency without destroying the independence of decision making and action that makes enterprises strong and flexible".

In response, Telleen (1996a) identifies the need for creating a management infrastructure which supports content creation, maintenance and use in a distributed decision-making environment. Specifically, he states that the traditional focus on technology and information content in intranet development projects in organizations needs to be balanced with an effective management infrastructure. In his approach, he describes management as consisting of the various roles, policies and processes necessary to manage the life cycle of information content on the intranet. These roles include web administrators who manage the web content (as opposed to webmasters who oversee the technical infrastructure), publishers, editors, and authors. Telleen's framework recognizes the traditional approaches to intranet development that focus on technology and information content, and calls attention for the need for better management of these two components.

3.3 The Intranet as IT Infrastructure

Though intranet implementations may pose certain organizational challenges, we suggest that the benefits intranets offer corporations can exceed interim costs. In terms of their potential, intranets can help facilitate group collaboration, organizational communication, and improve access to information content across the enterprise. As such, intranets can provide organizations with a sound information technology (IT) infrastructure upon which to cultivate organizational knowledge and intelligence.

Based on an extensive analysis of more than fifty multidivisional firms in the financial services, manufacturing, petroleum, retail, and telecommunications industries, Broadbent and Weill (1997) describe how IT infrastructures can provide firms with the necessary foundation upon which to build business applications that align with the strategic context of the organization. Such infrastructures, usually managed by an information systems group or department, comprise three layers: hardware and software components; shared information technology services; and staff who help bind the hardware and software components into a set of reliable, shared, information technology services.

According to the authors (pp. 85-86), there are four ways in which an organization can choose to implement an IT infrastructure: none, utility, dependent, and enabling. A none view occurs when a company decides to forgo any firm-wide synergy of information technology investment across its departments or groups. A utility view is one where the organization views expenditures on IT infrastructure as a way to lower costs through rationalization of shared expenses; in general, organizations that adopt a utility view have a lower than average firm-wide IT infrastructure investment. A dependent view occurs when investments in infrastructure primarily respond to specific current strategies as a means of balancing the desire to obtain lower costs and greater flexibility; firms adopting this approach typically have an average investment in IT infrastructure. An enabling view is one when the firm's desire to achieve greater flexibility in reaching its long-term goals results in a larger than average investment in IT infrastructure in terms of current needs; by focusing on strategic flexibility, firms adopting the enabling view provide extensive infrastructure services in a highly centralized way.

In terms of promoting organizational intelligence, we suggest the dependent and enabling views of IT infrastructures may be more appropriate for organizations to adopt in that they place greater emphasis on achieving organizational flexibility. In today's marketplace, flexibility is a must for organizations that wish to grow and adapt in a dynamic, uncertain world. Corporations need to adapt and respond quickly to external and internal environmental changes. As such, organizations need flexible IT infrastructures which help organizational members gather, share, use, and store information quickly and creatively as possible if they are to respond successfully to the environmental changes that constantly occur around them.

We argue that intranets can help greatly in this regard. Due to their underlying network-centric nature, they offer organizational participants the ability to break free from many of the communication barriers commonly found in traditional organizational hierarchies. By connecting people cross-organizationally, intranets remove the need for employees to rely on information intermediaries or gatekeepers who are required in traditional organizational hierarchies to filter communications up and down stove-pipe reporting structures. In this way, intranets can help companies shorten learning cycles and respond faster to environmental changes through improved information access and use.

To implement an enabling or dependent information technology infrastructure, Broadbent and Weill (1997) find empirical evidence to link infrastructure and organizational strategy closely together, an approach they label "management by maxim". In this approach, the essence and challenge of making an investment decision on information technology is to choose an infrastructure that will readily enable the necessary business applications in the future. To do this, the authors map out a three-step process. The first is to derive strategic statements or business maxims which capture the essence of a firm's future direction from the company's overall strategic context. The second is to use these business maxims to identify the information strategy of the organization or IT maxims in terms of the IT resources and access to information required. The third is to use these IT maxims to decide on the IT infrastructure services that should be delivered.

Broadbent and Weill point out that the "management by maxim" approach is not the only approach for organizations to take when implementing an IT infrastructure. Another option is "management by deals" where decisions on infrastructure are based more on immediate needs of the business and through negotiations between an organization's various business units. Though organizations are free to adopt either of these routes, the authors find evidence for the need to follow the "management by maxim" approach to create enabling or dependent views of IT infrastructure. It seems that the pressure of costs and emphasis on current rather than long-term strategies in the deals route prohibits the establishment of flexible IT infrastructures. Further to this finding, the authors observe that top management support is required to establish enabling views. It appears that the creation of flexible firm-wide IT infrastructures that offer extensive services requires the political weight and backing of executive management.

These findings may have important implications for organizations that want to establish intranets for the use of cultivating organizational knowledge and intelligence. First, they suggest that if intranets are to offer flexibility and a variety of services that help users access and utilize information quickly, then the design of intranets needs to be based on an analysis of the strategic context of the organization. Second, they imply that senior management must support and promote the intranet initiative as a means of facilitating its adoption and use. There are various ways this can be done. One is to obtain senior management buy-in at the start of an intranet initiative. Another is to achieve executive support at some point later in the diffusion process of this technology across the enterprise. For example, a workable scenario may be for an organization first to follow a grassroots approach where a single department or business unit launches its own local intranet as a means of demonstrating the benefits of intranet technology to top management and generating sufficient senior-level enthusiasm prior to the roll-out of the intranet to other departments in the organization.

However, at this point, such simplified guidelines for intranet implementations should remain tentative. Though workable and promising, more empirical validation is required before any general rules of thumb regarding infrastructure implementation can be accepted wholeheartedly. For example, Ciborra (1998), in his exploratory study of the deployment and use of infrastructures in six large multinational companies, finds preliminary evidence of a contingency approach to infrastructure implementation that suggests a more complex relationship between top management buy-in and the success to which an infrastructure enables higher-level knowledge processes. Ciborra observes that infrastructure can be established either through top-down, fragmented, or grass-root implementation processes, and that various levels of knowledge processes, such as routine, recombination, and emergent knowledge, can be supported or enabled by the infrastructure as a result.

Though there may be many various ways in which organizations can choose to implement IT infrastructures, we consider intranets appropriate technological platforms for many organizations to adopt. We believe intranets can provide firms with flexible, enabling IT infrastructures that support the growth of organizational knowledge and intelligence. Our claim is based on the proposition that intranets can offer organizations the improved ability to access and share information throughout the enterprise. By helping organizational participants acquire, distribute, interpret, store, and retrieve information from both internal and external information sources, we suggest that intranets can function as rich information-processing mediums that support and foster the way organizations learn.

Huber (1996), in his analysis of organizational learning constructs, describes four information-based processes associated with organizational learning: knowledge acquisition, information distribution, information interpretation, and organizational memory. Intranets can help in each of these areas. In terms of knowledge acquisition, intranets can provide organizational participants with search and browsing tools to find information stored in various locations both within and outside the company. In information distribution, intranets can act as communications networks that cut across traditional hierarchical organizational structures. In terms of information interpretation, intranets can support dialogue and discourse through the provision of chat groups and discussion forums. With respect to organizational memory, intranets can serve as knowledge repositories which house information content from a variety of sources throughout the enterprise. We argue that by supporting these various information processes, intranets can help facilitate the creation and exchange of knowledge in organizations.

Nonaka and Takeuchi (1995) present a description of organizational knowledge creation that may offer help in understanding the role intranets can play in helping organizations learn. The authors define knowledge creation as "the capability of a company as a whole to create new knowledge, disseminate it throughout the organization, and embody it in products, services, and systems" (1995, p. 3). According to Nonaka and Takeuchi, creating knowledge is "not simply a matter of learning from others or acquiring knowledge from the outside" but rather a process requiring frequent "intensive and laborious interaction among members of the organization" (1995, p. 10). Of relevance is their call for both the formal retention of organizational know-how in a knowledge base and the use of this structure to support sense-making activities that occur during communication among project teams. We suggest that intranets provide such a supporting infrastructure for organizational creation and use.

Recall from earlier chapters how Nonaka and Takeuchi distinguish between two types of knowledge: explicit knowledge, that which can be expressed in formal, systematic language and transmitted to individuals easily, and tacit knowledge, that which is personal, context-specific, and difficult to articulate formally. Specifically, Nonaka and Takeuchi describe four major modes of knowledge creation which involve the interaction between tacit and explicit knowledge and the individual and the organization. The first mode, socialization, is the process of sharing experiences and represents tacit-to-tacit knowledge exchange. The second mode, externalization, is the process of articulating this tacit knowledge into explicit concepts. The third mode, combination, is an explicit-to-explicit exchange of knowledge where concepts are systematized into a knowledge system. The fourth mode, internalization, is the process of converting this explicit knowledge back into tacit knowledge. (1995, pp. 62-70)

Using these modes, Nonaka and Takeuchi (pp. 84-89) formulate a five-phase process of organizational knowledge creation: sharing tacit knowledge, creating concepts, justifying concepts, building archetypes, and cross-leveling knowledge. To illustrate these five processes at work, Nonaka and Takeuchi propose a model called the hypertext organization that "enables an organization to create knowledge efficiently and continuously" (p. 160). In this model, organizations "acquire, create, exploit, and accumulate new knowledge... repeatedly in a cyclical process" (p. 166). Here, the hypertext organization consists of several interconnected layers: the business-system, the project-team, and the knowledge-base. The business-system layer refers to the context in which formal information processing routines are carried out. The project-team layer refers to the context in which groups of organizational participants working in teams engage in knowledge-creating activities. The knowledge-base layer refers to the context in which the organizational knowledge generated in the other two layers are re-categorized (p. 167).

What is interesting about the hypertext organization is that these three layers coexist simultaneously within the same organization. Organizational participants move easily among the different layers as they deal with changing situations inside and outside the company. As a result of this movement, knowledge is transferred among the three layers. That is, knowledge is used and incorporated back into the knowledge-base from either of the other two layers. For instance, project team members can tap existing organizational knowledge from the knowledge-base layer to help formulate new knowledge creating activities. Likewise, new knowledge from the project-team layer can be incorporated back into the knowledge-base layer. From there, this same knowledge can be used by routine operating practices in the business-system layer. In this way, the hypertext model supports the generation and use of new knowledge (Nonaka and Takeuchi 1995).

3.4 Intranets as Shared Information Work Spaces

By their recognition of sensemaking activities to build knowledge and the use of routines and procedures to tap a shared knowledge base, Nonaka and Takeuchi's hypertext model adds support to our call for intranets to function as IT infrastructures for facilitating organizational knowledge creation and use. Their model describes the need for both knowledge bases and communication spaces. Intranets can function well in this regard by providing organizations with a rich and complex shared information work space for the creation, exchange, retention, and reuse of knowledge.

To elaborate this position, we present a new, information-based model of the intranet in terms of its ability to help cultivate organizational knowledge and intelligence. Figure 3.3 illustrates the various components of the model which comprise our view of an intranet's shared information work space: a content space to facilitate information access and retrieval; a communication space to negotiate collective interpretations and shared meanings; and a collaboration space to support cooperative work action. We suggest that the provision of shared information work spaces in intranet designs may offer great benefits to organizations in that they can help organizational participants acquire, distribute, interpret, store, and retrieve information in their daily work practice and support the way organizations learn.

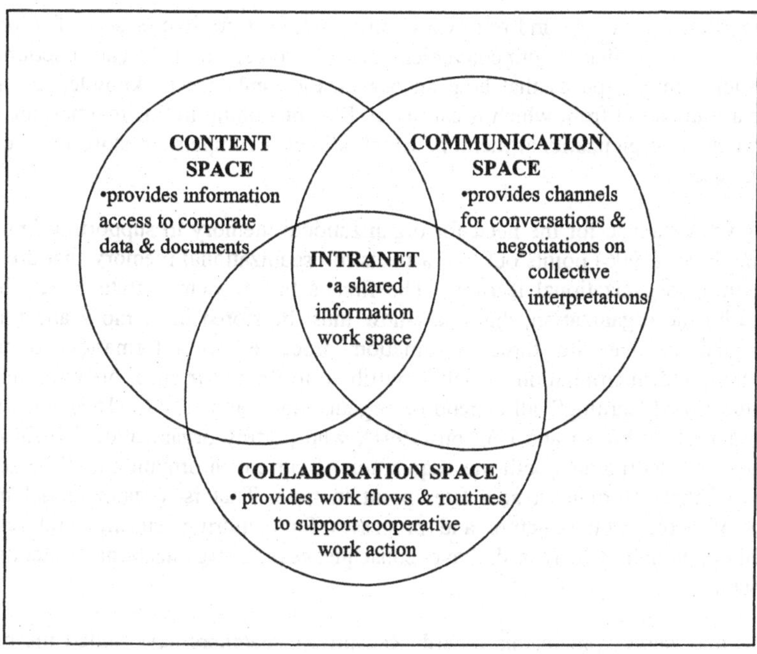

Figure 3.3 The intranet as a shared information work space

3.4.1 Intranets as Content Spaces

In terms of improved information storage and retrieval, intranets can help organizations by functioning as information content spaces.

Due to their platform independent nature, intranets can provide organizations with increased access to a wide variety of information sources, such as databases, legacy systems, and web file servers, that reside both within and outside the company. The information obtained from these sources can vary considerably, ranging from hard, quantitative data typically found in most database application systems to more soft, unstructured information located in a multitude of organizational documents and procedure guides.

Further, access to this diverse set of information sources is in a convenient form as intranets allow users to search and browse for information directly from individual desktops. This convenience can promote the acquisition and use of information throughout the entire organization as individuals tend to use information characterized by high accessibility (Allen 1977; O'Reilly 1982). This is an important consideration for the promotion of organizational knowledge and intelligence as the utilization of a wide and varied number of information sources can increase the success of both information retrieval efforts and learning by individuals and organizational units (Huber 1996).

By supporting the storage and retrieval of information from diverse sets of information sources in a manner that is both convenient and easy to use, intranets can function as rich information content spaces that help an organization enhance its knowledge base and provide a foundation from which it can learn. By functioning in this manner, an intranet can serve as an organizational memory which allows a company to store its knowledge for future use.

Huber gives evidence for the need for organizational memory in supporting knowledge creation. Huber (1996) points out two aspects of organizational memory that are critical in supporting organizational learning. The first is that to demonstrate or use learning acquired by the organization, this know-how must be stored in memory and retrieved. The second is that the three information processes of information acquisition, distribution, and interpretation, which "contribute to the occurrence, breadth, and depth of organizational learning", all depend on organizational memory (p. 150). This view is also supported by Walsh and Ungson (1991), who portray organizational memory as a construct that incorporates both the acquisition of current information and the retention and use of that information at a later point in time. That is, organizational memory consists of a retention structure and processes for acquiring, storing, and retrieving information, which, when used, have consequences on organizational outcomes and performance.

Intranets may serve well in this regard. Recently, researchers have called the need for technology to support organizational memory for the purpose of achieving increased levels of organizational effectiveness. For example, Stein and Zwass (1995) recommend the adoption of information technology as a means of facilitating organizational memory. Huber (1990) argues that the availability of advanced information technologies and related procedures can encourage the use of expert systems and databases as components of organizational memory. Davenport (1996, pp. 61-64) suggests systems applications create and manage knowledge as reusable objects so that information can be captured and stored in ways to promote knowledge sharing.

3.4.2 Intranets as Communication Spaces

As described by Nonaka and Takeuchi, to facilitate knowledge creation and use, organizational participants need more than just access to a repository of explicit knowledge. Employees must also be able to use this information as a base from which to engage in conversations with other organizational actors to share interpretations and perspectives gained by the organization so far. In this way, new perspectives and innovation can result and be stored back into the knowledge base for later use.

Thus intranets, if they are to foster organizational knowledge and intelligence, also need to function as communication spaces that provide channels through which conversations and negotiations can occur. Here, organizational knowledge is interpreted as "a fluid mix of framed experience, values, contextual information, and expert insight that provides a framework for evaluating and incorporating new experiences and information. It originates in the minds of knowers." (Davenport and Prusak 1998, p. 5). As such, knowledge creation is viewed as inherently a social process, where people engage in discourse and dialogue to learn to make sense of each other's interpretations and experiences.

This social constructionist approach to knowledge creation assumes knowledge is built on what has been learned so far and is a point of departure for further learning. Here, "organizational learning occurs through shared insights, knowledge and mental models... (and) builds on past knowledge and experience" (Stata 1989, p. 64) and on collective memory, a construct which refers to the social process of articulating, exchanging, and sharing information leading to shared interpretations (Halbwachs 1980). Organizational learning refers to "the capacity of an organization to learn how to do what it does, where what it learns is possessed not by individual members of the organization but by the aggregate itself" (Cook and Yanow 1996, p. 438). This occurs when a group acquires the know-how associated with its ability to carry out its collective activities. Huber (1996, pp. 126-127) furthers this understanding in his description of four attributes of organizational learning: in terms of existence, organizations learn if any of its units acquires knowledge that it recognizes as potentially useful; in terms of breadth, more organizational learning occurs when more units obtain this knowledge and recognize it as useful; in terms of elaborateness, more organizational learning occurs when more varied interpretations are developed; and, in terms of thoroughness, more organizational learning occurs when more units develop uniform comprehensions of the various interpretations.

This approach to organizational learning is similar to Lave and Wenger's (1995) view of learning as situated activity. As discussed briefly in Chapter 2, the central defining characteristic of this approach is a process of legitimate peripheral participation which describes how newcomers become part of a larger community of practice through participation that is at first legitimately peripheral but gradually increases in engagement and complexity. A person's intention to learn is configured in the process of becoming a full participant in sociocultural practice; learners are viewed as socially part of a community of practitioners and that "mastery of knowledge and skill requires newcomers to move toward full participation in the sociocultural practices of a community" (p. 29). In accordance with the interpretive perspective, Lave and Wenger reject the traditional view of learning as the reception of factual knowledge or information (p. 33). Rather they present learning as being situated in action and with the world, where "agent, activity, and the world mutually constitute each other" (p. 33). Learning is an integral and inseparable aspect of social practice, which takes place in a "participation framework, not in an individual mind" (p. 15).

Therefore, there is a need for intranets to provide organizational participants with a medium through which discussions about individual interpretations of the environment can take place, for it is through such dialogue and discourse that organizational members are able to negotiate collective interpretations and shared meanings. In this respect, we suggest that intranets tolerate a certain amount of chaos and redundancy of information as this would help organizational members express their feelings and communicate their tacit understandings. Though "messy" work, such informal communication in group work is extremely effective in helping organizational participants make sense of one another's interpretations, more so than formal channels (Kraut et al. 1990). Such dialogue calls for rich communication channels to help users overcome different frames of reference, resolve differences in opinion, and enact shared meanings (Huber and Daft 1987, p. 153).

Intranets can help facilitate both information distribution and information interpretation, which according to Huber (1996) are important elements in supporting how organizations learn. Information distribution is the process by which information from different sources is shared and used to gain new understanding or insights across the enterprise; such activity can lead to more broadly based organizational learning (pp. 141-142). Information interpretation is the process by which common understandings are obtained through the sharing and discussion of information from various sources; Huber argues that more learning occurs when more varied interpretations have been developed and when more organizational units understand the nature of the various interpretations held by others (p. 143).

3.4.3 Intranets as Collaboration Spaces

Besides functioning as content and communication spaces, intranets can provide organizations with collaboration spaces that help organizational participants utilize knowledge in their daily work practice.

As collaboration spaces, intranets can give organizational participants the ability to coordinate the flow of information necessary for cooperative action between various organizational units. To do this, organizational participants need functionality in their intranet designs which help automate information work flows and/or co-ordinate work routines. Further, intranet features are required which support the awareness of others in the organization and their availability for cooperative action.

In this regard, intranets may be viewed as a new form of groupware. The similar phrase "computer supported cooperative work"(CSCW), christened by Irene Greif and Paul Cashman in a call for participation for a workshop in 1984, refers to a new field of research that developed originally out of a need to design software to help groups increase their competence in working together; the field has since grown to incorporate and emphasize the social aspects of cooperative work settings (Bannon and Schmidt 1991; Kuutti 1996; Robinson 1991a). Viewing intranets in this manner enriches our understanding of the potential of this new technology in supporting knowledge utilization and the coordination of work tasks.

As collaboration spaces, intranets would provide the necessary context for articulation work (Robinson 1991a, p. 71), tasks beyond those described by formal procedures which are required to coordinate "real" work activities and keep them running, such as scheduling, organizing, negotiating, making ad hoc decisions, recovering from errors, and assembling resources (Gerson and Star 1986; Kuutti 1996, p. 183; Robinson 1991a, p. 69). Further, these spaces would help incorporate both formal and cultural levels of communication involved in work practice. Robinson (1991b) suggests collaborative systems provide the ability for users to interact over two "levels of language" as a means of helping users negotiate between formal plans and task articulation. Here, the formal level corresponds to plans and represents a sort of external world that can be pointed at, and whose behavior is rule governed and predictable; the cultural level is an interweaving of subjectivities, involves interpretation and viewpoint, and is the channel where articulation work occurs. According to Robinson, both levels are required as the formal level is meaningless without interpretation, and the cultural level is vacuous without being grounded.

Others have noted the benefits in utilizing electronic technology for collaborative work. For example, Finholt and Sproull (1990) remark on the ability of electronic groups in the workplace to cut across organizational boundaries of geography and work unit, to tap and pool expertise of individual employees regardless of their physical location, and to provide a means by which employees can discover others with similar interests. Likewise, Malone et al. (1989) extol the benefits of electronic systems in organizations in their description of their experience with their own e-mail based system called the Information Lens which facilitates the exchange of semi-structured messages across an organization. In their discussion, the authors describe the system's ability to help people "filter, sort, and prioritize messages that are already addressed to them, and... find useful messages they would not otherwise have received" (p. 66). Here, the tool's facility to help aid the filtering and distribution of messages increased information sharing and coordination across the enterprise.

3.4.4 Supporting *Ba* Through Intranets

Our information-based model of intranets as shared information work space is in line with Nonaka and Konno's (1998) suggestion that organizations need to create a shared space or "*Ba*" as a foundation for organizational knowledge creation. In their writings, the authors utilize the Japanese concept of *Ba*, which roughly translates into the English word "place", to describe the necessary context in which individual and collective knowledge creation can occur. Here, *Ba* is both a physical and mental space, and cannot be considered as something external to individuals but rather something of which they are a part.

Nonaka and Konno identify four types of *Ba* that correspond to the four stages of Nonaka and Takeuchi's (1995) knowledge creation cycle described earlier in Chapter 2: socialization (tacit to tacit knowledge exchange); externalization (explicit to explicit knowledge exchange); combination (explicit to explicit knowledge exchange); and internalization (explicit to tacit exchange).

The first type, Originating *Ba*, describes the world where individuals share feelings, emotions, experiences, and mental models. It is the place where the knowledge creation starts and represents the socialization phase. A major component of this space is the sharing and exploration of ideas that generate new ideas which is typically characterized through physical, face-to-face contact between organizational participants. The second type, Interacting *Ba*, is the place tacit knowledge is made explicit and is facilitated through dialogue and the extensive use of metaphor. In this space, individuals develop common understanding of terms and concepts. The third type, Cyber *Ba*, is the place where new explicit knowledge is combined with existing explicit knowledge and is organized, shared, and stored throughout the organization. This space is most efficiently supported in collaborative environment utilizing information technology, such as corporate intranets. The fourth type, Exercising *Ba*, is the place where explicit knowledge is reincorporated back into tacit knowledge through the active use of this knowledge in work practice.

Though Nonaka and Konno visualize the primary role of information technology as supporting Cyber *Ba*, we take a broader view in the role that information technology, namely intranets, can play in supporting all four types of *Ba*. As Nonaka and Konno suggest, intranets can support the explicit to explicit exchange of new to existing knowledge by functioning as a content space. That is, intranets can provide organizational participants with the means to add, update, organize, and share new explicit know-how and insights into existing data and documents residing on the intranet. However, as stated earlier, rather than utilizing intranets just as a publishing medium for explicit knowledge, we argue that intranets can also be used to support organizational communication and collaboration. These expanded uses of intranets reflect more closely the other types of *Ba* that Nonaka and Konno discuss. For example, as a communication space, intranets can support Originating and Interacting *Ba* by facilitating the dialogue and exchange of ideas between organizational participants. Also, as a collaboration space, intranets can support Exercising *Ba* by providing work flows and routines that habituate the practice and active use of explicit knowledge by organizational participants.

In this way, we suggest a more holistic understanding of intranets as a shared information work space that facilitates information access and retrieval, the negotiation of collective interpretations and shared meanings, and cooperative work action. Doing so can help create a shared space or *Ba* that functions as a foundation for organizational knowledge creation.

3.5 Lessons Learned from CSCW

As described in section 3.4.3, intranets may be viewed as a new form of groupware. In this regard, we suggest that intranet designers look to the lessons learned from the field of CSCW to become aware of the organizational barriers to the adoption and use of groupware systems. Such lessons can be valuable to corporations that plan to implement intranet infrastructures in their organizations.

There have been few success stories in the last decade with respect to the development of organizational groupware systems; many describe the obstacles in introducing groupware into organizational settings (Bowers 1994; Conklin 1992; Grudin 1994; Harper 1992; Orlikowski 1992; Perrin 1991; Rogers 1994; Zuboff 1988).

Grudin (1990; 1994) discusses eight reasons why groupware systems typically fail. Some of the more pertinent reasons are that: they require some people to do additional work who often are not the ones who perceive a direct benefit from use of the groupware application; they call for a critical mass of users to adopt the system; they lead to activity which may disrupt social processes, such as violations of social taboos, threats against existing political structures, or demotivations to crucial users; and they are hampered by poor developer intuition on multi-user needs. To address these problems, Grudin suggests several solutions. For example, he recommends: designers try to ensure that everyone benefits from groupware; there are incentives for use; there is flexibility and tailorability built into design; there is an understanding of current work practice; that groupware features are added to an already successful application; and that users get involved in design.

Similarly, Bowers (1994) identifies the impact groupware has on current work practice and points out the difficulty in getting users to "trust" the system, share data, and be held accountable in their electronic communications to a larger community. In addition to the many barriers to implementing groupware, Bowers mentions that a change in mindset from traditional ways of working is required to support user collaboration and adoption of new concepts such as the writing down of one's ideas in posterity for everyone to see.

In addition to the observations made by Grudin, Rogers (1994) notes the effect organizational culture may have in the acceptance of groupware systems. Likewise, Perrin (1991) suggests that social and cultural factors may inhibit the adoption and use of groupware in organizations and cautions developers of groupware applications to address this issue to improve the successfulness of organizational groupware implementation. Harper (1992) agrees and notes the impact of organizational structure in influencing the acceptability of technology in her study of the use of active badges in two research laboratories.

A similar observation is made by Zuboff (1988, p. 363) in her description of a company where management felt threatened by employee use of a electronic communications system for "access to information, thoughtful dialogue, and social banter" when the system's supposedly closed conversations were made public; this resulted in the demise of the system as its use for discourse and dialogue by more innovative participants was curtailed by management's critical and punitive attitude.

In a discussion of a new technological infrastructure to support organizational memory, Conklin (1992) states that a technological solution alone is insufficient to remedy the problems organizations have in remembering and learning from the past. What is also required is a supporting organizational culture which is committed to the use of the technology. However, Conklin states that getting such organizational commitment is often the most challenging component in implementing any technological strategy to support organizational memory (p. 136).

Likewise, Orlikowski (1992) notes the influence a competitive organizational culture may have on preventing acceptance of groupware which attempts to engender cooperation among users of the system. Interestingly, this study showed how members of a competitive culture were reluctant to use a newly implemented groupware system, while those of a subgroup, who were not part of the competitive culture of the company, were eager to share information and experiences with one another using the new technology. The different reactions by these two groups demonstrates the importance of organizational context on the successful adoption and use of new technology in the workplace.

To aid the successful implementation of organizational groupware, Orlikowski elaborates on the need to educate people on the benefits of new technology so that their personal cognitions or mental models can be enhanced to interpret or understand the collaborative nature of such technologies. She also stresses the need to change organizational structural properties to induce norms or incentives for cooperating or sharing expertise to encourage the adoption and use of groupware systems. She concludes by emphasizing the need for developers, researchers, and practitioners of groupware to anticipate how new technology will be received in the workplace by understanding current work practice and social interaction. In a later study, Orlikowski (1995) describes the planned and emergent changes that occurred in an organization which adopted use of groupware technology; there, she suggests organizations can benefit from this technology if they are accepting of the ideas of collaboration and group sharing, and if they are willing to make changes to adapt the technology to their needs.

In addition to the organizational barriers mentioned above, intranet designers also need to be aware how the introduction of groupware in an organization in turn can affect the structure, culture, and work practices of the enterprise.

In 1995, Orlikowski analysed the organizational changes resulting from an implementation of Notes in a customer support department to track problems in a shared database. Foremost was the change in work practice for the department; here the nature of support work changed from primarily one of problem-solving to one of problem-solving and documentation. Customer support representatives used Notes to document the resolution of incoming problem calls. Essentially, this documentation became the department's knowledge base. It offered managers a full audit trail of the work accomplished on all calls and gave customer support representatives the ability to scan for insights in how to solve particular problems. It also facilitated spontaneous forms of help-giving as participants could use the knowledge base to obtain a shared group view of the work load across the department. Another major finding of the study was that the organization adapted itself to the technology. The company made a number of structural adjustments in response to use of the groupware. For example, it divided customer support work among junior, intermediate and senior positions, and developed a series of new innovations including the use of the knowledge base as a training tool, the integration of customer support work with that of overseas offices, and the dissemination of filtered versions of knowledge from the repository to the rest of the organization and customers.

Orlikowski found that there were social repercussions resulting from implementation of the groupware technology. For example, the more junior participants had difficulty negotiating the assignment of work to more senior colleagues, and some participants felt uneasy with their work becoming "visible" to others as it made them feel scrutinized and vulnerable. However, Orlikowski stresses that once the system became established and norms for use of the knowledge base were developed, most organizational participants became accustomed to the shared knowledge base being observed and worked on by many others. A large part of this acceptance was due to the cooperative culture, and the open and collegial respect members of the customer support department had for each other. Similar findings are reported by Ginsburg and Duliba (1997). Here, the successfulness of the adoption and use of Lotus Notes technology was in large part due to a change in the culture of the firm to "a more open and information sharing environment" which induced people to share more information with one another than ever before (p. 218).

Sproull and Kiesler (1991a) comment on the effects technology has on work practice in their description of how electronic interactions between workers profoundly affect the organizational structure and the conduct of work itself. During a series of experiments at Carnegie Mellon University, Sproull and Kiesler compared how small groups of people made decisions over electronic networks versus face-to-face meetings and found that electronic interactions induced people to talk more frankly, more equally, and generate more proposals for action. However, they also noted a degradation in time to make decisions as the inability to interrupt conversations over electronic networks slowed decision-making and increased conflict as some people tried to dominate control over the conversation. They also found that people using electronic channels for communication were more likely to vent anger more openly (known as flaming). In terms of work structure, Sproull and Kiesler (1991a) note that organizations adopting computer networks become more flexible and less hierarchical. Furthermore, they state that the use of electronic communications could significantly change patterns of information sharing through the increased exchange of informal, personal information across the enterprise; in the past, such communication was restricted by physical proximity and social acquaintance. The authors state that networks seem to encourage discretionary information sharing between people who do not know one another because the cost of responding to an information request is extremely low and respondents feel that replying to such requests enhances the overall electronic community and leads to a richer information environment.

Likewise, Francik et al. (1995) note that new technologies create work pattern changes. Developers need to be aware of the potential effects of technology on people and their interactions as "a sensitivity to this dimension can make the difference between a groupware system which is accepted and used regularly within an organization, and one that is rejected" (Ellis, Gibbs, and Rein 1991, p. 47).

In response to the unsuccessful adoption of technology in the work place, Bannon and Schmidt (1991, p. 12) stress the need to adapt technology to the organization and vice versa. Here, designing computer-based systems for cooperative work is like "writing in water" as the introduction of a system into the organizational setting induces a change in work practice for which the system itself was designed to support. Thus, gaining insights into the future use of systems is important as understanding how current work practice affects design.

Similar comments have been made by others in the CSCW field. For example, according to Grudin (1994, p. 101), "developers who understand the work environment well enough to design successfully will be in a good position to help design strategies for supporting adoption as well." Likewise, Rogers (1994, p. 67) comments on the increased difficulty of "how to tailor a new CSCW system to fit in with existing work practices, whilst also changing the organization to adapt to the new system". In her paper, she explores the co-evolution process involved in tailoring a CSCW application to fit into current work environments while adapting organizational work practice to adjust to the new system. Specifically, she notes the complexity of introducing CSCW systems into organizations. She describes the different perspectives and work practices which need to be recognized and dealt with prior to groupware implementation. For instance, she describes the effect of distributed knock-on viscosity which occurs when group members fail to understand the use situations of all members of the group and make decisions on design which enables one group of users while constraining others. She also comments on the notion of gradient of resistance in systems design where the more radical proposals to changes in established work practices in organizations proposed by a CSCW system are met with higher degrees of resistance.

These examples from the CSCW field illustrate the difficulty in designing groupware systems to fit organizational structure, culture, and work practice. The design of intranets as an IT infrastructure may follow suit. Intranet designers need to obtain a better understanding of the effects of technology on user information behavior and the changes required at the organizational level to promote the adoption and use of this technology. Paying attention to the lessons learned from CSCW may help increase the success of introducing intranets in organizations as an IT infrastructure for organizational knowledge work.

3.6 Intranet Case Studies

To understand better how intranet infrastructures can be implemented successfully in organizations, we turn our attention to a few select intranet case studies, namely Coopers and Lybrand, Maritz, and US West. These companies offer intranet designs that are innovative and help improve the gathering, sharing, and creation of knowledge across the enterprise. Each organization is recognized by industry observers for having developed and implemented intranets which have added significant value to the organizations they support. As such, these case studies can serve as exemplars for other organizations to follow by demonstrating ways in which to implement intranet designs that support users and their information needs.

Coopers & Lybrand (C&L), a professional services firm, has an award-winning intranet system, called KnowledgeCurve, that helps employees find and access the information they need to do their jobs (CIO Communications 1998b). Originally designed to serve C&L's 19,000 employees, this number has jumped to over 140,000 users worldwide with C&L's recent merger with Price Waterhouse. With such an exponential increase in numbers, the ability to coordinate work and share information quickly with others has never been more critical for Coopers & Lybrand. This is especially true with fast-paced consultancy firms where the business of the day is centered around the acquisition and selling of knowledge. In fact, among the consulting services firms, Coopers & Lybrand has been one of the most aggressive in using internet technologies to link to customers as well as to share information within its own organization (Ryan Garcia 1997).

Central to KnowledgeCurve's success is its emphasis on providing all organizational participants with direct access to both internal and external information sources (Mullich 1997). This strategy is in marked contrast to most intranet implementations in other organizations which tend to focus on the delivery of internal information sources only. In fact, the most popular component of KnowledgeCurve is an area called CyberLYB that gives C&L professionals seamless access to external information sources. One reason for the interest in this area is that CyberLYB is maintained and kept up-to-date by an internal group of information professionals who decide what external third-party information to provide and what set of external internet links are required to support the information needs of the organization. It is this dual combination of direct access and the pre-filtering of external information that has helped employees quickly find and stay abreast of the knowledge they need to do their work.

To implement their intranet design, a team of developers at Coopers & Lybrand conducted personal surveys with a diverse set of 500 end users to determine the information content required and the ways to categorize this information in a manner that users expect to find it. From the surveys, the need for external information sources quickly became evident. This required changes by information providers such as Dow Jones and Knight Ridder Information Inc. to not only modify their information provision pricing strategies but also their user interfaces to allow C&L employees seamless access through a single universal authentication (Mullich 1997). With a seamless interface, users do not need separate log-in ids and passwords that are typically required when accessing fee-based information off the internet. In fact, Coopers and Lybrand was among the first organizations to create a seamless approach to data gathering for its staff; for example, the firm was the first corporate customer of Dow Jones Interactive in November, 1997.

Overall, KnowledgeCurve offers employees five essential services: 1) it synthesizes world-class external research; 2) it broadcasts real-time news; 3) it provides discussion groups for its employees; 4) it offers access to internal information sources; and 5) it functions as a repository of up-to-date, relevant business-related URL links (CMP Media 1998). An important feature of KnowledgeCurve is that it gives employees the ability to create their own personal home pages which contain biographical information as well as descriptions of their individual areas of expertise. This component helps organizational participants learn more about each other, increases interaction with others across the organization, and fosters areas of expertise by bringing people with related interests together.

By incorporating such features into its design, KnowledgeCurve helps cultivate organizational knowledge and intelligence. It does this by providing a rich information content space where employees can expect to find the best up-to-date, accurate information, as well as a virtual home in which organizational participants can "ask colleagues for help, offer an opinion of their own, learn about new initiatives, get administrative paperwork or just stop by to hear about what their peers are doing" (PricewaterhouseCoopers 1998).

Maritz Inc., a privately held personal services company with about 2,200 employees and sales of 700 million dollars, has developed its own intranet called "Let's Talk!" for gathering intelligence and facilitating corporate communications. Ottenlips et. al. (1997) conducted over 45 personal interviews with Maritz individuals to determine how that company utilized their intranet. In their award-winning Society for Information Management report, Ottenlips et. al. describe Let's Talk! as "a great starting point to gather corporate intelligence concerning performance improvement programs and improved communications across the entire enterprise".

Maritz provides over 150 professional services to its clients; in a typical year these services are custom designed to fit about 300 unique performance programs. Globalization has placed an increased demand on developing quicker solutions for a larger client base. To face the challenges of a global market, Maritz responded with the development of a corporate intranet as a means to provide employees with information access 24 hours a day, seven days a week. In this way, the intranet was devised to help share knowledge across the enterprise, keep everyone up-to-date, and prevent the re-creation of existing ideas time and time again.

A key component of Maritz' intranet was the development of a shared content space to house an electronic file cabinet for each of the 150 services the company offers. This solution was devised to address the problem of sales representatives not having current, accurate information on the products and services they were selling. In the electronic file cabinet, each service has three areas. The first is a guide which contains 10 to 40 pages of textual, non-structured information on the service in question. The guide allows the author of the document the freedom to record all his/her thoughts and not be restricted by print and postage costs, the ease of correcting and updating the materials, and the ability for easy access to this information by the sales staff. Included in the guide area is a section of Frequently Asked Questions (FAQs) for sales representatives to reference. The second area is a collection of sales brochures for each service that sales representatives can peruse and distribute to clients. This area ensures that accurate and up-to-date brochures are always available and reduces the cost of printing unwanted and unneeded brochures. The third area is a collection of PowerPoint presentations on particular services that sales representatives could use and tailor to customize their own sales pitches to meet individual client needs. Included with the presentations are the original authors' comments on how they would alter the presentation if they had to do it over again.

Another component of Let's Talk! was the establishment of an organizational memory of past case histories. This area is responsible for housing the context surrounding past client solutions. It allows sales representatives to search case histories of the results that other clients have achieved that used Maritz' services in the past.

A third component of Maritz' intranet was the creation of a people space which contained searchable profiles of all Maritz' employees. Each profile includes a digital colour photo and a business biography. Organizational participants are granted freedom to tailor their profiles to emphasize their unique areas of expertise and personal identities. This tool allows others in the organization to become familiar with colleagues they might not otherwise know, and to locate experts within the organization in various knowledge areas who may be ready for cooperative action on certain projects. To facilitate such collaboration, Let's Talk offers several communication vehicles; this includes on-line company phone directories, World Wide Web access, and chat rooms/bulletin boards which are used to foster a sense of community and build relationships across the organization.

US West, a relative veteran of intranet technology use, has developed intranet-based applications to improve communications and streamline processes since 1993 (CIO Communications 1998a). The company provides telecommunication services to more than 25 million customers in 14 U.S. states and offers an integrated package of telephony, data, cellular, and entertainment services to its customers. What is interesting about the history of intranet development at US West is that it started out as a grassroots initiative which swept the company by storm. By delivering a few key applications at reasonable costs, upper management quickly realized the potential impact intranets could make in helping the organization better facilitate communication and collaboration, and distribute information across the enterprise (Gonzalez 1997).

US West's intranet, internally referred to as the "Global Village", has now become an integral part of the company's business strategy. The intranet offers several key application areas. The first is in the area of business computing. The intranet allows customer service representatives to access the information they need to do their jobs. For example, the "Global Village" is used by sales representatives to determine if the necessary telephone facilities are physically available prior to making installation commitments to customers. Prior to this solution, sales representatives had difficulty locating and deciphering this information which was embedded in a mainframe database; in fact the mainframe interface was so complicated and poorly formatted that it took three weeks to learn how to use, and even then only a handful of people could understand the information that was obtained (CIO Communications 1998a). The intranet changed all that by providing the information that was needed in an accessible, easy-to-read format. This is in turn led to reduced missed commitments and customer complaints.

The second is the provision of shared information resources. With the "Global Village", employees have on-line access to a Life Situations database of employee benefit information, daily corporate newspapers and advisories, as well as a directory containing employees' names, e-mail, fax, pager, and physical addresses.

The third is the creation of a communication and collaboration space, aptly referenced as the "Rumor Mill". It is a forum in which employees are free to ask questions, raise issues or concerns with others in the organization. Answers and responses are posted back on the Rumor Mill for everyone to review. This feature has provided the corporation with an effective and efficient way to communicate in a timely manner with employees across the company about current issues and concerns.

In summary, these brief reviews of the three case studies from Coopers & Lybrand, Maritz, and US West highlight the potential intranets offers corporations in terms of their ability to provide shared information content, communication, and collaboration spaces. Organizations can learn from these examples and consider new and better ways to create functionalities in their own intranet designs which help improve knowledge acquisition and creation across the enterprise.

3.7 Conclusion

It has been the goal of this chapter to provide a better understanding of intranets and their potential to stimulate organizational knowledge and intelligence. We suggest that by being aware of the many challenges and difficulties that may jeopardize any intranet initiative, one can be better prepared to deliver intranet solutions that serve the enterprise. We also indicate that intranets can be more effective as knowledge infrastructures when they are designed and utilized as shared information work environments that act simultaneously and seamlessly as spaces for content access, communication, and collaboration.

In the next chapter, we shift our focus away from the benefits and challenges of intranet adoption and use towards intranet design. By focusing on the need to adopt a user-centered perspective on intranet development, we argue that intranets may be better positioned to support organizational knowledge acquisition and use.

Chapter 4: Designing Intranets to Support Knowledge Work

The last chapter presented an overview of the potential of intranets as an IT infrastructure to support knowledge work. As a means to foster the design of intranets for this purpose, we now operationalize some of the concepts discussed in the first section of this book on information needs and uses and the context and manner in which organizations create, diffuse, and utilize organizational knowledge. Central to our approach is the need for intranet developers to analyze the contexts in which organizational actors access, search, collect, create, store, and use information as a prerequisite for developing and enhancing the features and functions of the intranet which facilitate and foster the sharing and re-use of knowledge.

This chapter begins with a description of the traditional system development approach towards intranet design, one that primarily subscribes to a publishing paradigm. We examine the limitations of such an orientation and suggest that intranet development be based on the information context in which organizational participants utilize information in their work practice. A review of the major research analyzing the structure of organizational information environments is then presented. Common elements are identified and a new framework for the development of intranets is proposed, one which concentrates on the information needs and behaviors of organizational actors in their work settings. The viability of the framework is then discussed and related approaches are compared.

4.1 Intranet System Development

In general, most organizations move through several common phases during the adoption and implementation of intranets (Telleen 1996c). The first phase typically involves a pilot project for a subgroup or department within the organization. Usually, the pilot generates enthusiasm and interest in other areas of the company. This leads to the second phase, where the organization embarks on a strategy for rolling out the technology to other parts of the enterprise. Abraham (1998), in his dissertation on the business value of intranets, confirms this typical development cycle. In his investigation of various intranet designs from 17 different companies, Abraham acknowledges the predominance of intranet initiatives in large corporations stemming from grassroots efforts. However, he notes a recent change in this trend towards involvement of top management and MIS departments from the start of an intranet project.

This involvement is evident in many intranet case studies. For example, system developers at Coopers & Lybrand, prior to their intranet design, first conducted an extensive survey of more than 500 users from clerks to partners, asking questions like "what information do you need?" and "with what frequency do you use that information?". They then distributed the same survey to librarians and other information professionals in the company to identify what information was used most often by employees. Putting the results of these two surveys together, the design team was able to decide what information to include on the company's intranet web pages. A similar strategy was used at Xerox to determine the content and layout of that corporation's intranet. Here, a dozen focus sessions were held and a survey of 1,500 employees was conducted to gains insights on how employees "thought about, prioritized and categorized information" prior to that corporation's intranet design (Hildebrand 1997).

In his research, Abraham observes that most companies start their initial intranet designs with only a few publishing applications. These are later expanded and furthered with ones which support a broader collection of intranet functionalities. More specifically, Abraham states that organizations generally tend to progress in a linear fashion across four distinct intranet categorizations. The first and most common is the Publishing Intranet; its primary purpose is to keep organizational participants informed and to foster internal communications. The next stage is the Knowledge Intranet, which concentrates on the provision of information access and creation tools to help organizational participants share information and experiences with one another. The following category is the Collaboration Intranet; its purpose is to help teams work together on specific tasks. The last and final stage of intranet design is the Business Intranet, which unlike the others, focuses on improvements in workflow rather than on helping users per se.

Of interest is Abraham's observation that this linear progression of intranet functionality is starting to change as better intranet development tools and platforms become available in the marketplace. Abraham indicates that though most companies may still start with a Publishing Intranet, companies are more likely to skip the knowledge and collaboration phases and go directly into the development of intranet business applications. Thus, according to Abraham, there is no "finishing line" or "highest level" of development for intranet design. Rather, intranets develop and evolve continuously, expanding in cycles and focusing on different kinds of applications in no particular order. In fact, Abraham posits that shortly after the new millennium, most intranets likely will become a collection of applications from all four categories of the publication, knowledge, collaboration, and business process intranet models.

However, most companies today still launch and maintain intranet development initiatives under the traditional publishing paradigm as a means to help organizations reduce internal information publishing costs and enhance corporate information distribution (Cortese 1996; Rice 1996; Thyfault 1996). We suggest that this scenario may have direct implications on how corporations perceive and foster intranet development. For example, in the publishing paradigm, organizations may tend to view intranets as systems which support the capture, retention, and retrieval of enterprise-wide information in the sense that HTML pages are created and stored on a variety of web servers and retrieved through the use of search engines. As a result, system developers may over-emphasize the identification and organization of information content and the incorporation of technological tools and features in intranet designs that best support information retrieval, rather than ones that foster knowledge creation, ideas, or group collaboration.

To further the development of intranets, we need to temper the predominant focus on information content and technology concerns with an awareness of the information needs and uses of organizational participants. To do this, we suggest that priority in intranet design be placed on people—understanding the work contexts in which they are situated, the problems they typically face, and the ways they use information to help resolve their problems.

In this sense, intranets are better conceptualized as socio-technical systems in which information seeking and use take place, rather than as systems that merely support the retrieval of information. As voiced by Marchionini (1995) in his discussion of information seeking in electronic environments,

> "*information seeking* is preferred to *information retrieval* because it is more human oriented and open ended. Retrieval implies that the object must have been 'known' at some point; most often, those people who 'knew' it organized it for later 'knowing' by themselves or someone else. Seeking connotes the process of acquiring knowledge; it is more problem oriented as the solution may or may not be found." (pp. 5-6).

Designers need to understand the work related problems and contexts that draw people to use intranets and the ways in which information must be packaged and presented to make it meaningful to them. Designers can no longer assume that employees approach an intranet knowing what information they want and that they can search for it directly. People often use the intranet not to find a specific answer, but to help them make sense of their environment, learn new ideas, or resolve their problems. By viewing intranets in this way, intranets may be better designed to deliver functionalities which support the information needs and uses of employees.

This perspective of intranets as information seeking systems is a less technocratic and more human-centered one. It aligns itself closely to the human-centered models of information seeking behavior proposed by Dervin (1977), Belkin, Oddy & Brooks (1982a; 1982b), and Kuhlthau (1991) that "share perspectives on information seeking as a problem-solving activity that depend on communication acts... but has only begun to influence designers and engineers who implement electronic retrieval systems" (Marchionini 1995, pp. 29-30).

4.2 Basing Design on the Analysis of the Information Environment

The argument to ground design on an understanding of the information environment is similar to one prevalent in the Computer Support for Co-operative Work (CSCW) and Participatory Design (PD) literatures for system designers to understand the contexts in which users work (Schuler and Namioka 1993). For example, Grudin (1990) calls "for better understanding of work environments and for corresponding adjustments by developers", which requires "better knowledge of the intended users' workplace" (1994, p. 94). Similarly, Kling calls for an understanding of people and their relationships in support of work when designing information systems. He provides an extensive overview of the social processes and contexts that drive and shape computerization in organizations

(1996a) and highlights how the success in the adoption and use of a new technology depends not only on technical choices, but social ones as well (1996b, p. 294).

Drawing upon decades of research in information needs and uses, Taylor (1986) presents a framework for analyzing the organizational information environment of different groups of users. Specifically, Taylor proposes that major input to the design of information systems must come from an analysis of the information environment of users (1986, p. 3) and offers a user-driven model to system design, an approach he labels the value-added model. According to Taylor (1986, p. 204), the "principal strength of the value-added model lies in its stress on the user and on the needs and dimensions of the information environment as a major element in the design and evaluation of systems".

Underlying Taylor's (1986) argument for the value-added model is the belief that an information message carries only the potential for value. There is no inherent value carried by an information message; rather, a message has value only in context and is given value by the person who uses it. By defining the value of information in this way, Taylor suggests that system designers should "make estimates as to the probable utility of certain kinds of information, the preferred modes of access, and the kinds of enhancements or signals the system can provide so that use can be facilitated in that particular context" (Taylor 1986, p. 5).

Taylor defines an information system as a series of formal, value-adding processes whose purpose is to enhance the potential usefulness of information messages. These systems may be machine or human based, or more likely a combination of the two (p. 10). The primary purpose of an information system is to help users make choices and clarify problems (pp. 5-6). In fact, the merit of an information system is determined by its success in signaling the potential value of information, in helping to address or clarify particular problems, and in providing sufficient flexibility to adapt to individual needs (p. 203).

Value-added processes serve the dual purpose of signaling the potential value of information messages and relating this potential to a specific problem in a specific environment (p. 17). These activities can take several general forms which vary in importance across different types of information systems. Such activities include: selecting input; storing and organizing for physical access; describing and labeling for retrieval; analyzing, evaluating, and comparing for quality; combining and interpreting; and, responding and adapting to specific user problems (p. 202).

Taylor's value-added model is comprised of three basic components: 1) a formal information system comprised of specific processes which add value to information messages being processed; 2) a user or set of users who, because they sit in particular information environments, have certain problems which establish the criteria for judging the utility of system outputs; and, 3) an interface or negotiation space between system and users where the system displays its value-added output to assist users in making choices (pp. 201-202). For a schematic overview of the major components of the model, refer to Figure 4.1.

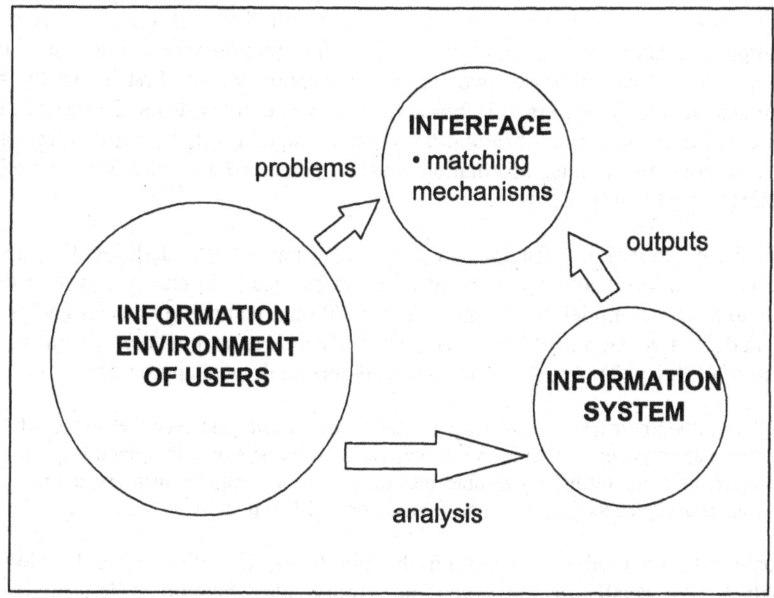

Figure 4.1 Taylor's (1986) value-added approach to information systems

Figure 4.1 shows how the design and operation of formal systems is based largely on an analysis of the context in which users find themselves. Such an analysis requires that the organization, its people, and their problems be described in sufficient detail to obtain an understanding of the design requirements of the information system and of the negotiating space between system and human. (p. 25).

Taylor presents several steps for the design and operation of an information system based on an analysis of the information environment. For the purposes of this chapter, these are summarized into three major steps. The first is to perform an analysis of the information environment of users. This analysis must inform system designers not only of the magnitude of the information requirements but also of the types, structure and display of information required to help users perform "current and anticipated tasks, responsibilities, decisions, and problems in a particular environment" (p. 26). The second step uses this analysis to create value-added processes for the information system. Once operational, the products and services of the system produce outputs. They are what the users "see". Moreover, they are what the users work with to solve problems and answer questions (p. 33). The third step involves judging the merit of the value-added processes by determining how well the outputs of the system help users solve their problems. This is done through an analysis of the negotiating space where attempts are made to match the outputs of the system with the problems users face in their work contexts.

Taylor recognizes the need for empirical validation of his model and suggests that the model remains tentative. He explains that it is "an early attempt to organize what we seem to know about the environments within which different types of users seek information and make choices about the utility of information available to them" (1991, p. 219). Further, Taylor proposes two limits to his approach. The first is that the model concentrates on groups of users of information, rather than individuals. The second is that his model is limited to formal information which is "sought in the context of recognized problems or concerns, that is, information which is perceived and intended to be relevant to a particular problem (p. 220).

Despite these limitations, Taylor's value-added approach underlines the need to investigate the information environment of users as means to enhance system design. Taylor's user-driven model complements the traditional technology-driven and content-driven models of development "which are presently the major inputs to systems thinking and design" (1986, p. 3). According to Taylor, the technological approach:

> "basically prescribes the size, shape, function, dynamism, and even the content of information systems. That is to say, what is and can be stored in a book (report, paper, or other formal retrievable message) or in a computer memory defines what is accepted as knowledge or information." (1991, p. 218)

The content-driven model is based on the traditional classification and ordering of information, "especially as reflected in library classification schemes, indexing constructs, and such mechanisms as thesauri and data dictionaries" (1991, p. 218). The problem with such content-based structures is that they tend to become viewed in the minds of users as reality itself, instead of merely being considered as representations of knowledge, of which they truly are. As observed by Taylor (1986, pp. 3-4)

> "It is not that these content-driven and technology-driven models are poor. It is rather that they are no longer enough in our information-rich world. They need to be tempered and informed by a frame of reference that begins to get at the uses and utility of information and ultimately to fundamental concerns of the value of information."

Taylor suggests that current design approaches could be improved by an approach which focuses on the user and attempts to understand the criteria by which information will be judged to be valuable. He states that users and their environments are critical and necessary ingredients to the understanding and improvement of systems. Taylor's value-added model makes clear the need to be able to describe user environments and translate those descriptions into useful parameters for system design (1986, p. 202). That is, to look

> "...at the *user and the uses of information*, and the contexts within which those users make choices about what information is useful to them at particular times. These choices are based, not only on subject matter, but on other elements of the context within which a user lives and works." (1991, p. 218)

4.3 The Structure of the Organizational Information Environment

To increase our understanding of information environments and their relationship to information behaviors, four major works in this area are examined: Taylor (1991); Katzer & Fletcher (1992); Rosenbaum (1996); and Davenport (1997). Common elements are then identified and compared.

4.3.1 Taylor's (1991) Information Use Environment

Taylor (1991) defines the information use environment (IUE) as "the set of those elements that (a) affect the flow and use of information messages into, within, and out of any definable entity; and (b) determine the criteria by which the value of information messages will be judged" (1986, pp. 3-4). Moreover, Taylor describes four categories of the IUE: sets of people, their problems, typical settings, and problem resolutions (1991, p. 221).

For the first category, sets of people, Taylor identifies four dividing classes: professions (e.g. engineers, lawyers, and managers); entrepreneurs (e.g. farmers, small business persons); special interest groups (e.g. consumers, citizen groups); and special socioeconomic groups (e.g. the information-poor, minorities). For these sets of people, Taylor recommends the identification of those demographic variables which help define the information environment and information behavior; specifically, he suggests education and socioeconomic status as demographic variables preferable to those such as age, sex, and marital status. Among non-demographic terms, Taylor recommends the following variables as being more important: media use; social networks; and, attitudes toward education, new technology, risk taking, and innovation (1991, pp. 222-224).

For the second category, the structure and thrust of problems sets of people typically face, Taylor states that each definable IUE has its own discrete class of problems and that these change over time. More importantly, problems have certain characteristics, beyond specific subject matter, called problem dimensions, "that establish the criteria for judging the relevance of information to a problem or to a class of problems" (MacMullin and Taylor 1984, p. 103; Taylor 1986, p. 42). According to Taylor, this criteria can be used to assess the usefulness of information to a user's situation.

As outlined in Table 1.2, MacMullin & Taylor (1984) identify 22 distinct types of problem dimensions, presented as a list of 11 dichotomous categories: 1) well structured vs. ill structured; 2) complex vs. simple; 3) assumptions agreed upon vs. not agreed upon; 4) familiar vs. new patterns; 5) design vs. discovery; 6) specific vs. amorphous goals; 7) initial state understood vs. not understood; 8) assumptions explicit vs. not explicit; 9) magnitude of risk great vs. not great; 10) susceptible to empirical analysis vs. not susceptible; and, 11) internal vs. external imposition. Furthermore, these dimensions are not independent of each other nor do they apply in all situations. Additionally, the authors caution that their list of dimensions is based on conceptual analysis only and that the problem dimensions may not be complete. However, an empirical investigation by Fletcher (1991) substantiates the existence of problem dimensions and finds support for 18 broad categories, ten of which match those described by MacMullin & Taylor. In her study of 26 managers in the public and private sectors, Fletcher set out to find empirical evidence of MacMullin & Taylor's list of 11 problem dichotomies and to examine the characteristics of situations experienced by users as they seek and use information to resolve problems. Her schema of 18 broad categories were organized further into 67 subcategories and 26 sub-subcategories. The problem dimensions of "assumptions agreed upon" and "assumptions not agreed upon" did not emerge. Interestingly, she found evidence of problem dimensions changing over time, but could not conclude any discernible pattern from her data.

For the third category of the IUE, typical settings, Taylor (1991, p. 226) highlights the importance of the physical context and describes how that context affects the way people work and live, and the way they seek and make use of information. Taylor elaborates on four general influences of setting which affect user information behavior in organizations: 1) the structure and style of the organization in terms of its attitude toward information and the causal effect of this attitude on employee information behavior; 2) the domain of interest of the unit of concern (i.e. the type of information people need to do their work); 3) the accessibility to information (i.e. physical or psychological barriers that may inhibit information access); and, 4) the history and experience of the organization (i.e. the tendency of the organization to become bureaucratic thus reducing the effect of new information).

For the fourth and last category, resolution of problems, Taylor (1991, pp. 228-231) describes the need to understand the way sets of people typically anticipate solutions to their problems. There are two components to this. The first is the way sets of people typically use information to solve their problems. In this regard, Taylor identifies eight classes of information use (refer to Section 1.3): 1) enlightenment (i.e. the desire for context information or ideas to make sense of a situation); 2) problem understanding (i.e. better comprehension of particular problems); 3) instrumental (i.e. finding out what to do and how to do something); 4) factual (i.e. the need and consequent provision of precise data); 5) confirmational (i.e. the need to verify a piece of information); 6) projective (i.e. concerned with estimates and probabilities); 7) motivational (i.e. personal involvement); and, 8) personal or political (i.e. relationships, status, reputation, personal fulfillment).

The second is a concern over how information should be identified and presented to help people discover resolutions to their problems. Such information traits are "the special attributes that can be used to define the ways that information can be identified and presented. More importantly, these traits can be related directly to the dimensions of a problem" (MacMullin and Taylor 1984, p. 98).

In terms of information traits, MacMullin & Taylor (pp. 99-102) identify nine continuums: 1) quantitative continuum (i.e. from quantitative to qualitative); 2) data continuum (i.e. from hard to soft data); 3) temporal continuum (i.e. from historical to forecasting); 4) solution continuum (i.e. from single to multiple solutions); 5) focus continuum (i.e. from factual to diffuse information); 6) specificity of use continuum (i.e. from applied to theoretical); 7) substantive continuum (i.e. from operational to descriptive); 8) aggregation continuum (i.e. from clinical to aggregated information); and,

9) casual/diagnostic continuum (i.e. from why to what is happening). The authors define these traits as "characteristic of stored information as are subject descriptions" (p. 101).

4.3.2 Katzer & Fletcher's (1992) Information Environment of Managers

An elaborated model of the information environment of managers explicitly based on Taylor's concept of the IUE is presented by Katzer & Fletcher (1992). Using the context and the person as two fairly fixed starting points (1992, p. 231), the authors formulate a model based on the characteristics of Taylor's IUE, namely people (i.e. managers), their organizational settings, their typical problems, and their range of acceptable resolutions.

Central to the model is the notion that managers, as they attend to their information environments, are confronted with problematic situations. Here, a problematic situation is

> "a personally defined subset of the endless and murky stream of events and meanings that continuously 'flow through' a person's life. By identifying selected parts of that stream, by putting a fuzzy boundary around those parts, and by labeling those parts as a single entity that requires attention and possible action, the person creates a problematic situation. A problematic situation can be thought of as an 'agenda item' that will require cognitive and perhaps behavioral action in order for it to be taken off that person's agenda and be considered resolved. Although a problematic situation is created and defined by a single individual, it is also shaped by the features of the setting." (Katzer and Fletcher 1992, p. 231)

Thus, it is through the concept of problematic situations that the IUE and information behaviors are linked together.

According to the model, during the resolution of problematic situations, managers exhibit information behaviors, which are actions that contribute to the usefulness of information. In doing so, managers determine

> "whether or not to seek information, what information to seek, where to seek it, how to seek it, how much to seek, how to interpret it, how to assess it, and how to use it. The person's responses to questions such as these produce information behaviors." (Katzer and Fletcher 1992, p. 233)

Furthermore, as managers exhibit information behaviors, problematic situations change over time. That is,

> "new uncertainties and concerns may emerge, different activities or roles become dominant, and other dimensions increase in importance. As long as the (revised) problematic situation remains unresolved, additional information behaviors will emerge. These, in turn, are influenced by the manager's current definition of the situation and current 'choice' of activities, roles, and dimensions. This process continues until the problematic situation becomes resolved... in the mind of the manager." (Katzer and Fletcher 1992, p. 233)

The significance of this model is that it attempts to explain the dynamics and processes by which the IUE influences information behavior, a topic largely left ambiguous in

Taylor's writings (Rosenbaum 1996). It does this through the concept of problematic situations which provides a mechanism for relating the organizational setting to managerial information behaviors. Though the model suggests "one-directional causal relationships" between the IUE and information behaviors, Katzer & Fletcher caution that this is "an oversimplification; most likely some of the links are bi-directional" (1992, p. 231).

4.3.3 Rosenbaum's (1996) Structurationally Informed Value-Added Model

Recent work by Rosenbaum (1993; 1996) extends Taylor's value-added model by clarifying the relationship between the IUE and information behavior. In his doctoral research, Rosenbaum develops and verifies a new framework for describing the information needs and uses of managers in a public sector organization. There, he commends Taylor's (1986; 1991) development of the information use environment as an attempt to side-step the recent debate in the Library and Information Science literature over user-centered and system-centered approaches to determining information needs and uses (Dervin and Nilan 1986; Hewins 1990). However, Rosenbaum states that Taylor's constructs are ambiguous and that the relationship between the IUE and information behaviors needs clarification.

Rosenbaum (1996, p. 81) rejects "the determinative and generative powers... attributed to IUEs, including the abilities to generate problems, create information needs, and produce information behaviors". As well, Rosenbaum refutes Taylor's (1991, p. 221) definition of information behavior as being a product of the four elements of the IUE (i.e. set of users, problems, settings, and problem resolutions) in that it suggests a unidirectional influence of structure over behavior, and does not recognize a possible counter-influencing effect of information behavior on the IUE. Further, Rosenbaum does not agree with the inclusion of sets of people in the IUE itself (1996, p. 81).

To strengthen Taylor's model, Rosenbaum looks to Giddens' theory of structuration (1984), a theory which bridges the debate in the field of Sociology on whether society shapes the individual or the individual shapes society. According to Giddens, both are true; individuals actively shape the world in which they live as the world simultaneously shapes them.

There are three primary components of Giddens' theory of structuration which Rosenbaum draws upon to enhance Taylor's model: interaction, structure, and the duality of structure. Interaction comprises the action of two or more people. Here only people can act and as they do they generate social life. People are assumed to be knowledgeable actors having both discursive and practical knowledge. The former refers to knowledge that people can articulate while the latter refers to people's tacit knowledge. There is also mutual knowledge—procedural and normative rules of social interaction found in people's consciousness and invoked tacitly in interaction. As people interact they use these different kinds of knowledge resulting in social practice; recurring social practices are called social systems.

Structure, on the other hand, are the rules and resources implicated in the production and reproduction of social systems. These rules and resources have temporal and possibly material existence, but only when they are instantiated in action. According to Giddens, structure is reproduced in social interaction as people engage in routine social practices.

The duality of structure is the process by which structure and interaction interrelate. Structure provides the rules and resources that influence people as they interact. Though free to determine alternate rules and resources, by and large people do not. Instead, they act in same past ways, unintentionally re-verifying the rules and resources of structure and replicating social practice across time and space. There is a bi-directionality in the relationship between structure and interaction as each depends on the other for its existence.

Using Giddens' theory of structuration, Rosenbaum identifies Taylor's concept of the IUE as a structural component and information behaviors as an action-oriented one. Specifically, he develops a structurationally informed value-added approach to describe the information needs and use of managers.

In Rosenbaum's framework, the IUE is structural in nature and comprised of rules, resources, problems, and problem resolutions. Here, the IUE "has virtual existence until instantiated in action" and is "routinely produced and reproduced through the social practices or information behaviors of users" (1996, p. 112).

Information behaviors are depicted as action-oriented, existing outside of the structure of the IUE. They "can be grouped together and seen as social practices which exist in the world" (p. 112). Additionally, "information behaviors are not generated or produced by an IUE, although they can certainly be constrained, shaped, and enabled by an IUE." (p. 113).

Furthermore, there is a bi-directionality in the relationship between the IUE and information behaviors as each is shown to influence the other. That is, "the presence of each makes the other possible; neither has meaning without the other" (p. 112).

In his field study, Rosenbaum finds supporting evidence for his model. He also identifies a range of information behaviors exhibited by the managers in his study which include information producing, gathering, filtering, and sharing. Furthermore, he notes tensions among the elements of the IUE as different managers used conflicting rules, resources, and assumptions about problems and problem resolutions.

An interesting aspect of Rosenbaum's framework is that it offers an explanation for the persistence of information behavior in organizations over time. This happens as users attempt to solve problem situations and engage in information behaviors; they draw upon the rules, resources, problems and assumptions of problem resolutions of the IUE. Though users can choose not to be influenced by the components of the IUE, they tend not to, and, as a result, end up unintentionally re-verifying the structure of the IUE. This explains how the same information behaviors of managers, namely the producing, gathering, filtering, and sharing of information, are replicated across time and space in organizations.

Rosenbaum's framework extends Taylor's value-added approach. As stated by Rosenbaum, the structurationally informed value-added framework

> "does not seem to violate any assumptions or principles of the value-added approach, in fact, it seems to strengthen the approach by firmly grounding it in a theory of social action. When integrated into the structuration approach, the information use environment and information behaviors are linked through the duality of structure. There is no priority assigned to either; as users interact, they draw upon the structure of the IUE, and, in doing so, reproduce the IUE as they simultaneously constitute the conditions which make their interactions possible. This move resolves, at a theoretical level, the fundamental ambiguity found in Taylor's formulation of the IUE and information behaviors." (1996, p. 114)

Rosenbaum's framework advances Taylor's value-added model in two significant ways: 1) it clarifies the relationship between the IUE and information behavior; and 2) it emphasizes the bi-directional influence of these two constructs on one another. The framework also "is a valuable conceptual framework that can be used in information science to conduct research on information in organizations" (Rosenbaum 1993, p. 243). It also offers "a theoretical approach that may prove to be a useful way to learn about the ways in which people in a wide variety of settings engage in information behaviors, creating and recreating their information use environments over time" (Rosenbaum 1996, p. 487).

4.3.4 Davenport's (1997) Information Ecology Model

Davenport (1994; 1997) underlines the need to understand organizational information environments and the way people use information in their work settings. He critiques traditional information management efforts, such as those which overemphasize the use of technology or suggest information be managed like other valuable corporate resource in organizations like capital and labour (Horton 1979). Rather, Davenport (1997) states that traditional approaches to information management no longer fit our information-rich world. Instead, he suggests a new, holistic approach, labelled information ecology, which emphasizes "*how* people create, distribute, understand, and use information" (p. 5).

Davenport suggests that information providers not concern themselves just with the production and distribution of information but also with what recipients do upon receiving this information. There is a need to "pay attention to people and what they do" (p. 33). Only by knowing how "individuals workers seek, share, structure, and make sense of information" (p. 32) can information providers facilitate its effective use.

To help organizations better manage information, Davenport proposes an ecological model for information management that consists of three nested environments: the information environment, the organizational environment, and the business environment.

Davenport places the information environment within the constructs of the external and organizational environments. The external environment consists of business, technology, and information markets outside of an organization which have a bearing on the company's information needs and uses. The organizational environment, on the other hand, consists of internal factors such as the corporation's overall business situation, existing technology investment, and physical arrangement; all these can affect a company's information environment as well. (pp. 37-39).

The information environment is at "the core of an ecological management approach... and encompasses the six most critical components of information ecology— strategy, politics, behavior/culture, staff, processes, and architecture" (p. 34).

The first component, information strategy, refers to the high-level information intent of an organization concerning items such as information content, common information, information processes, and new information markets. Davenport, in line with his views on ecological change, states that an information strategy must be flexible. Developing a set of basic principles, rather than fixed specific intentions, is a better vehicle for expressing an organization's information strategy (p. 35).

The second component, information politics, "involves the power information provides and the governance responsibilities for its management and use" (p. 35). In an earlier work, Davenport et al. (1992) describe how attempts to create information-based organizations or launch information management initiatives often end in failure due to a lack of awareness of human politics. Their study identifies five political models of information management: 1) technocratic utopianism, a belief that technology can solve all problems of information governance; 2) anarchy, where individuals manage their own information, often at their own peril; 3) feudalism, where business units define their own information needs and report limited information back to the corporation; 4) monarchy, where a central person dictates information management policies on behalf of everyone else; and 5) federalism, where there is consensus and negotiation among business units on the use of information. Davenport (1997, pp. 68-69) prefers federalism because of its awareness to the existence of politics and its need for rational negotiation; however, he notes that such an approach is not appropriate for all organizations.

The third component, information behavior and culture, are two related factors that "may matter most in creating a successful information environment" (p. 35). An information culture is made up of an organization's information behaviors, whether these are good or bad. According to Davenport (p. 35), "particular information cultures determine how much those involved value information, share it across organizational boundaries, disclose it internally and externally, and capitalize on it in their businesses."

Furthermore, Davenport identifies three specific types of information behavior critical to the improvement of a company's information environment. The first is information sharing, "the voluntary act of making information available to others" (p. 87), which Davenport contends is "almost an unnatural act" (p. 90) and requires the active removal of various political, emotional, and technological barriers by management. The second is handling information overload. Here, Davenport calls for engagement, a term used to describe the need to communicate information in compelling ways to encourage the right people to recognize and use the right information. According to Davenport, "we almost always filter information when we successfully engage with it" (p. 91), and it is this filtering that helps people handle information overload.

Davenport recognizes the difficulty in trying to promote information engagement. Most information is presented to users at the low end of a hierarchy of an information engagements scale, namely in read/view mode when the user receives information passively. "Even when providers try to make information more engaging—with appealing graphics, say, or a bulleted outline—the user generally only notices certain attributes of it" (p. 92). Presenting information in this manner "has little chance of affecting anyone's behavior" (p. 92). To address this problem, Davenport recommends the use of higher level tactics on the information engagement scale; these are, in ascending order, acting on/discussing information, arguing/defending information, presenting/teaching information, and simulating/living information (p. 93). Further, Davenport lists secondary attributes that improve engagement as well. These are content, source, and situational attributes, such as emotional interest, originality, and perceived expertise of the information provider, all which help enhance the transfer of information and thus reduce the effects of information overload.

The third and last type of information behavior critical to the improvement of a company's information environment is dealing with multiple meanings. Davenport suggests that having multiple meanings for terms used in an organization is not always a bad thing; rather it suggests an interest in an information item. However, he does mention that there are times when multiple meanings have to be controlled, but adds that this requires consensus and cooperation among employees close to the terms (pp. 95-97).

The fourth component of the information environment, information staff, refers to the people in an organization needed to provide and interpret information to others in the company. These people do not just include technology professionals, but also content specialists, such as librarians and market researchers, and information guides who help users identify their information needs and access multiple types of information. The primary goal of such staff is to make information meaningful. Davenport recommends that information staff do this by providing information that is accurate, timely, accessible, engaging, applicable, and rare. Further, he encourages information staff to perform a new set of tasks that increases the value of information: pruning information, adding to its context, enhancing its format, and choosing the right medium for it (pp. 108-127).

The fifth component, information processes, "concerns how information work gets done" and consists of "all those activities performed by information workers" (p. 36). Such activities includes the determination of information requirements, the capturing of information, its distribution, and use. Here, designers of information processes need to focus on user problems and current situations.

The sixth and last component of the information environment referred to by Davenport is information architecture. He defines this component as "simply a guide to the structure and location of information within an organization" (p. 36). This can either be descriptive, such as a map of the current information environment, or prescriptive, as in the creation of a future model of the information environment. Furthermore, the architecture should be readable by all organizational participants, incorporate both computer and non-computer based information sources including pointers to people, and influence information behavior and culture (pp. 156-174).

Davenport's ecological approach to information management provides a detailed description of the components of the information environment. It brings awareness to the importance of user information behavior and offers insight into the rich and complex context in which users work.

4.3.5 Common Elements

The review of these four models of information environments illustrates a steady progression in the understanding of this conceptual construct. MacMullin & Taylor's (1984) initial call for the need to match user problem dimensions with proper information traits is amplified by Taylor's (1991) and Katzer & Fletcher's (1992) description of the structure of user information environments. Likewise, Rosenbaum's dissertation helps clarify the relationship between information behavior and the environment itself. Davenport's (1997) model broadens this further by acknowledging the complexity of the information environment and the influence organizational factors have in shaping its structure. For an overview of the main points of each of the four models, refer to Table 4.1.

A scan of the major tenets of these four models reveals several recurring themes in the structure of the information environment and its relationship to user information behaviors.

First, all four models describe how problem situations constitute a central component of the information environment construct. Taylor declares problems as dynamic, characterized by problem dimensions, and distinct to each IUE. Katzer & Fletcher posit problematic situations as the linking mechanism between the IUE and information behaviors. Rosenbaum positions problems as part of the make up of the IUE itself. Davenport stresses the need to focus on user problems and current situations as a means of understanding information processes.

Second, all four models, especially those by Rosenbaum and Davenport, emphasize the importance of analyzing information behaviors. Rosenbaum gives equal weight to information behaviors and information environments, while Davenport emphasizes the need to understand user information behavior as a prerequisite to the management of information in organizations. Both identify information filtering and information sharing as key information behavior activities.

Third, all four models note a relationship between the information environment and information behaviors, though the description of this relationship varies from model to model. Taylor describes how information is used to resolve problems; his model suggests a unidirectional influence of structure over behavior. Katzer & Fletcher, through the concept of problematic situations, describe the IUE as influencing information behavior though the authors recognize the possibility of a counter-influence. Rosenbaum clearly positions information behavior outside of the construct of the IUE and notes the bi-directional relationship between the two. Davenport defines information behavior as one of the primary components of the information environment in organizations.

Author	Major Tenets
Taylor (1991)	• The IUE consists of: 1) sets of people; 2) problems, characterized by problem dimensions; 3) settings; 4) problem resolutions, concerned with information use and information traits.
Katzer & Fletcher (1992)	• The IUE and information behaviors are linked through problematic situations.
Rosenbaum (1996)	• The IUE consists of rules, resources, problems, and problem resolutions; • Information behaviors include information producing, gathering, filtering, and sharing; • There is a bi-directional relationship between the IUE and information behaviors.
Davenport (1997)	• The information environment lies within the constructs of the external and organizational environments; • The information environment consists of six primary components: 1) information strategy; 2) information politics; 3) information behavior/culture; 4) information staff; 5) information processes; 6) information architecture.

Table 4.1 Major tenets of the four models of the information environment

Fourth, both Taylor and Davenport discuss the need to present information in engaging ways to help people solve their problems. Taylor, in his comments on information traits, encourages the display and presentation of information to help signal the potential value of information messages to users. Similarly, Davenport stresses the need to present information at the higher end of the information engagement scale as a means to reduce information overload and promote information filtering.

Fifth, to varying degrees, all four models discuss the influence organizational setting and culture have on information environments. Taylor and Davenport illustrate this best. Taylor, in his description of typical settings, explains the effect organizational structure and style have on an organization's attitude toward information, its domain of information interest, its tendency to bureaucratize information processes, and on employee information behavior and the flow and sharing of information across the enterprise. These are the same traits identified by Davenport in his information ecology model describing how an organization's information culture, information architecture, and information processes constitute and define the information environment of organizations.

4.4 A Behavioral-Ecological Framework for Intranet Design

One of the motifs of this book is to explore how intranets may be designed as an open infrastructure that supports the creation, sharing, and use of knowledge. Our review of the research literature suggests that pursuing a dual design approach based on the information behaviors of groups and individuals as well as the information ecology of the organization as a whole may be a fruitful enterprise. This section extends a conceptual framework originally proposed by Detlor (1998b) for the design of organizational intranets to facilitate information access and use. That framework combined Taylor's value-added model with common elements of the four models of the information environment outlined above.

In the modified framework, designing an intranet to support knowledge work embraces three nested layers: information ecology; information needs and uses; and value-added processes (Figure 4.2). The design activity begins with a simultaneous analysis of the organization's information ecology and users' information behaviors. As described earlier, information ecology refers to the information environment of an organization. The internal information environment comprises many interdependent and interacting social and cultural subsystems that influence the creation, flow, and use of information. Information behaviors refer to the practices of individuals and groups as they go about obtaining and using information to resolve their work-related problem situations.

A detailed understanding of the general information ecology and the particular information practices will help underpin the design of intranet content and services as value-added processes (Taylor 1986) that signal and amplify the value of information. The following sections examine each of the three design layers.

4.4.1 Information Ecology

The information ecology is an organization's information environment, and consists of the numerous interacting and interdependent social, cultural, and political subsystems that shape the creation, flow and use of information in the organization. Thus an organization's information ecology influences what information is produced and stored, what information is made available and to whom, and what information is required and valued in task performance. Typically, an organization's ecological subsystems coexist in a fragile balance, so that altering one component necessarily induces changes in the others.

Extending the framework proposed by Davenport (1997), we suggest that in analyzing an organization's information ecology to guide intranet design, the following eight elements would need to be examined: the organization's mission; the intranet's goals; information management plans; information culture; information politics; physical setting; information staff; and information handling.

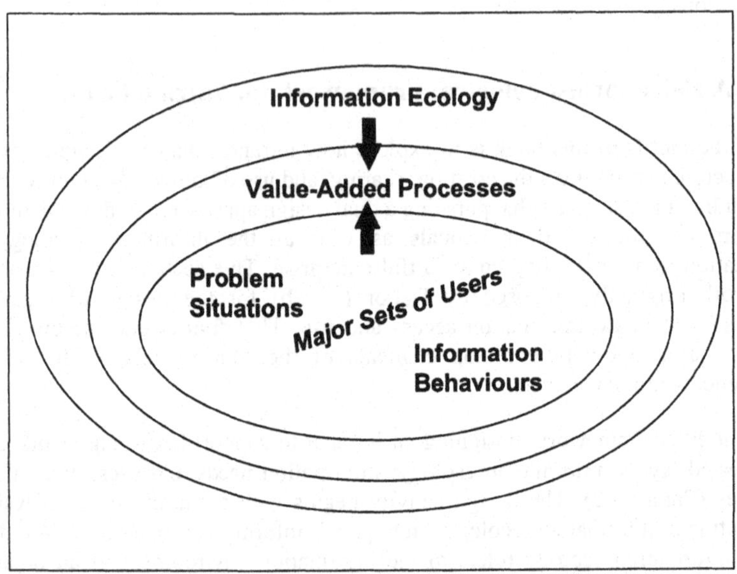

Figure 4.2 A Behavioral-Ecological Framework for Intranet Design

The organization's mission is described by the overarching goals and activities of the organization that define its identity and purpose. An analysis of the organization's mission should also elaborate the role that information plays, the contribution of its information resources and services, as well as the differences between actual situations and intended scenarios.

This logically leads to the second element, an articulation of the intranet's goals in relation to the organizational purpose, that is, the ways in which the intranet would help the organization accomplish its mission.

The third element, information management plans, are the formal plans, policies and standards that the organization has established to structure control, coordination, and roles in the management of information resources and services.

Information culture is indicated by the attitudes and norms that the organization's participants hold about issues such as the ownership and sharing of information, and the amount and intensity of information gathering and analysis that is appropriate or expected in the organization.

Information politics often obstruct the movement of information across departmental boundaries and can lead to unproductive information hiding and hoarding. Davenport, Eccles and Prusak (1992) identify common political structures, and assess their consequences for information sharing and management.

An organization's physical setting can also impose particular constraints and requirements. For example, an organization that is dispersed over multiple locations, or whose employees spend most of their time in the field, would need to address issues such as information access, remote communications, data currency, and so on.

Although information staff are clearly vital players in the information ecology, they are surprisingly often overlooked in intranet design projects. The level and modus of their participation need to be clarified: Are the information staff formally trained? What are their organizational roles (do they act as intermediaries, support staff, or as members of work teams)? What are their relationships with line staff and top management?

Finally, an organization may have set in place information handling rules and routines for the management of records and archives, and the maintenance of institutional memory. These routines are important because they allow the organization to encode and transfer past learning, and to present an accountable trace of its actions. In evaluating the various elements that constitute an organization's information ecology, we are constantly asking to what extent each element is harming or helping the organization's efforts to attain its goals.

4.4.2 Information Needs and Uses

Human information needs and uses are complex phenomena, and perhaps the best hope of gaining a fair representation of them is to observe and learn directly from users in their natural work settings. The framework takes this analysis in three steps. First, we develop a clear understanding of who the users are in terms of their information needs and information seeking characteristics. Second, we investigate and understand the structure of the work-related problem situations that they typically face. Third, we chronicle and examine the information behaviors and practices that they employ to resolve problem situations.

4.4.2.1 Information Users

Information becomes valuable when it enables actions. Information enables action only after it is given meaning and significance in the minds of human actors. Unfortunately, information does not announce its meaning or significance. It is people who endow data and information with salience and suggestion. Through their acts of social and mental construction, people transform information from bloodless artifacts into goals and reasons for action. A first step in designing an intranet as information infrastructure would therefore be to understand who the major sets of users are, what work they perform, and how they require, acquire and use information in the course of engaging this work. As presented earlier, Taylor (1991) helpfully identifies demographic and non-demographic variables that affect the information use patterns of sets of users. "Non-demographic" attributes such as users' professional or work experience, social networks, preferences for media, and attitudes towards innovation and risk taking seem likely to be important variables. We next examine how an intranet's users perceive their information needs, look for and adjudge information, and choose to use or not use information they encounter.

4.4.2.2 Problem situations

We are concerned with users' information behaviors as they go about resolving their work-related problem situations. In particular, we seek to understand how users perceive their work problem situations; how they locate and obtain information; as well as how they then select from and make use of information to resolve their task problems. At first glance, work problem situations appear to span a limitless range that defies classification. MacMullin and Taylor (1984) propose that beneath this variety is an underlying structure which may be used to describe task-related problem situations in informational terms. They identify eleven dimensions that they believe could adequately define the information attributes of most work problem situations. These dimensions are discussed in an earlier section, and include such categories as "design/discovery," "well/ill-structured," "specific/amorphous goals." It may be helpful to recall that an analysis of problem situations serves two important purposes: (1) they provide a rich representation of users' information needs; and (2) they establish the criteria by which users determine the value or helpfulness of the information they meet.

4.4.2.3 Information Behaviors

Based on the perceptions of their work problem situations, users seek and prefer information in ways that fit well with the specific contingencies imposed by the situational problem dimensions. Again, MacMullin and Taylor (1984) have proposed a generalized list of information traits by which information is recognized and evaluated. These traits go beyond subject relevance (what is this message about?) to situational relevance (how can this message help me in my work situation?). The denouement of information seeking and selection is information use, and here, drawing upon the earlier field studies of Dervin and others, Taylor (1991) suggests eight generic ways in which individuals use information. In summary, an analysis structured by the constructs of problem dimensions, information traits, and information uses, could produce a fine-grained representation of the information needs, information seeking, and information use patterns of a community of intranet users.

4.4.3 Value-Added Processes

Findings from the analysis of an organization's information ecology and users' information behaviors converge as we design intranet-based resources and services. These applications are developed as value-added processes that signal, amplify and extend the value of information to the organization and its users. Within the framework of the concepts presented in this monograph, we highlight five value-adding design approaches.

First, at the task level, intranet applications may be designed so that they directly support the information behaviors of users as they resolve their work-related problem situations. This requires a reasonably accurate and complete description of these information behaviors. We propose that the constructs presented here—problem dimensions, information traits, and information use patterns—can characterize information behaviors with enough true detail to guide design. For example, field investigations may show users handling a task with problem dimensions of "discovery, ill-structure, and amorphous goals," by seeking and valuing information with traits that are high on the "qualitative, soft, and diagnostic continua," and then using the information in certain recurrent patterns or categories. Each of these sets of dimensions, traits, and categories then serve as design parameters which describe the types of information and the forms of information seeking and use practices that intranet applications can be designed to support.

Second, at the organizational level, intranet applications and services may be designed to fit or improve the organization's information ecology. Where properties of the ecology contribute positively to the attainment of organizational goals (for example, an information-sharing culture, skilled information staff, well-developed information handling procedures), these features may be enhanced and leveraged by applications and services on the intranet. Where aspects of the ecology block or reduce organizational effectiveness (for example, geographically dispersed work units, information feudalism, and information overload), the intranet might be designed to compensate for or attenuate these negative effects.

Third, as presented in an earlier chapter, the intranet provides a unified information space in which users can move seamlessly between accessing content, engaging in communications, and collaborating with others. For content, intranets provide single points of access to internal and external information. Internal information may comprise current data that describe recent conditions, or historical data that facilitate reflection and learning from experience. For communications, intranets allow many design options in the choice of topology (one-to-one; one-to-many; and many-to-many), timing (asynchronous or synchronous), and media (text, voice, or video). For collaboration, intranets make it easier to co-locate issues, participants, and information resources and tools, and thereby promote shared problem ownership and shared problem solving.

Fourth, intranets may add value by facilitating the sharing, conversion, and combined use of the organization's tacit, explicit, and cultural knowledge. Tacit knowledge is personal knowledge that is activated through discourse and interaction during shared problem solving. Explicit knowledge is codified knowledge where the requirement is for just the right amount of knowledge to be available just in time to the persons who need it. Cultural knowledge consists of the assumptions and beliefs that define what is important and valuable for the organization, and thus supply the context for the exercise of tacit and explicit knowledge. Intranets may facilitate the simultaneous use of all three forms of knowledge. For example, they can create shared problem-solving spaces that include: electronic communication venues for finding and sharing tacit knowledge; access tools for searching or browsing codified explicit knowledge; and news feeds about developments in the organization's community (people, products, projects) which animate its cultural identity.

Fifth, intranet applications and services may add value by supporting the organization's sense making, knowledge creating, and decision making processes. In sense making, intranets can constitute part of the discourse infrastructure in which participants are involved in meaning construction through enactment, dialog and negotiation. The intranet's extended reach and multiple communication channels can give voice to a greater number and a greater diversity of information sources and points-of-view, thus enriching the sense making process. In knowledge creating, as described in an earlier chapter, work performed through the intranet allows the knowledge created or utilized in that work to be textualized and contextualized. When work-related problem situations are resolved using electronic media such as the intranet, the problem solving conversations may be recorded as narrative—text that also encapsulates part of the context surrounding each task experience. In decision making, intranets can be deployed to structure choice processes according to rules and routines. This may be accomplished by applying tools as simple as online forms, or as complex as workflow and document management systems. At the same time, intranet applications can also be designed to render decision premises and assumptions more visible and therefore more discussable, to promote wider participation, to broaden information search, and to increase the amount and timeliness of feedback.

Since sense, knowledge, and decision making are all linked as a network of information processes that enable feedback, innovation, and organizational adaptation, intranet designers must build in flexibility and openness into an infrastructure that is continuously evolving through the experimentation and creativity of its users.

4.4.4 Summary

The behavioral-ecological framework presented in this section embodies a number of beliefs and principles about the design of intranets. Our starting position is that intranets are a new breed of information systems whose design needs to be driven not just by data or flows of data, but also by a full appreciation of the organizational and human processes that are being supported. The framework maintains that information culture, politics, and ecology are all components of the design environment, and that a close analysis of these elements is an essential step in the design activity. The framework is also firmly user-centered, since it places at its core an understanding of the situated information practices by which participants recognize and characterize problem situations, experience information needs; seek and select information according to its fit and merit, and use information to respond to particular task and social contingencies. The framework proposes a dual-track design process that is simultaneously top-down and bottom-up: it is top-down because it underscores an alignment with organizational purpose and aspirations, and it is bottom-up because it is built upon the information behaviors and practices of individuals and groups whose work turn these aspirations into actuality. Ultimately, the framework is an attempt to help realize the promise that intranets hold out as a viable platform for supporting knowledge work—that the openness and flexibility of intranets can augment knowledge acquisition, creating, organizing, sharing and use to a greater extent than is possible with traditional data processing systems.

It is suggested that by using such a layered approach for design, intranets may better support the information ecology and information behaviors of organizational participants. Table 4.2 summarizes the steps intranet designers should follow.

Intranet Design Principles
1) Analyze the organization's information ecology.
2) Identify the typical problems and associated problem dimensions experienced by major sets of users.
3) Analyze the information behaviors of these sets of users by concentrating on typical problem resolutions in terms of the information sources used and the information traits more likely valued.
4) Create value-added processes in the intranet design that foster and enhance the information ecology of the organization and help users resolve their typical problems.

Table 4.2 Design principles for intranets

4.5 Empirical Testing of the Behavioral-Ecological Framework

To test the usefulness of the framework, Detlor (1998a) instructed project teams of graduate students to utilize the steps outlined in Table 4.2 to develop intranet designs for local organizations. The designs were analysed in terms of their ability to match the organization's information environment and information behaviors of users. This analysis served to answer two broad research questions. The first is to investigate the viability of the approach in creating intranet designs that matched the information context and behavior of organizational participants. The second is to identify the components of the approach that were more frequently utilized in the creation of value-added processes.

The project teams comprised 31 graduate students of a one-semester intranet design course. Each project team consisted of two or three members, who recorded the experiences of their use of the approach in a project workbook. The first section of the workbook dealt with information ecology. This section asked team members to describe the organization's mission statement, physical setting, intranet goals, and the six ecological components identified by Davenport (1997): information strategy, information politics, information culture, information staff, information processes, and information architecture.

The second section of the workbook dealt with information behaviors. It asked project members to identify major sets of users for the intranet and to discuss their typical work-related problems and tasks, specifically their problem dimensions and their problem resolutions in terms of information sources, information uses, and information traits. To do this, project members rated each problem according to the 11 dichotomous categories of problem dimensions identified by MacMullin and Taylor (1984) and each information source typically used to resolve these problems in terms of MacMullin and Taylor's

(1984) nine continuums of information traits and Taylor's (1991) eight classes of information use.

The third section of the workbook dealt with functional design. Team members were asked to include an intranet site map, a print-out of the intranet's entry page, a print-out of one of the intranet's second-level pages, and a description of one partially-implemented functional feature.

The last section of the workbook dealt with value-added processes. This section asked project members to describe the major value-added processes offered by the intranet design that helped users resolve their typical problems and that fit or improved the organizational information ecology. Specifically, team members were asked to describe how the value-added processes addressed the information ecology, problem dimensions, and information traits identified in the earlier sections of the workbook.

In total, 11 intranet designs were developed using the approach. All project teams each made a 45 minute presentation in which they described their experiences using the framework, the types of organizations they studied, the major sets of users, and their typical problems and problem resolutions. Each presentation included an online demonstration of the team's intranet prototype and example applications.

Each team's workbook was collected and analysed. An Excel spreadsheet was created to help identify trends and patterns across the various designs. Rows of the spreadsheet corresponded to individual projects; columns corresponded to the various categories and questions of the workbook itself. To investigate the degree to which the approach aided team members in creating their intranet designs, the teams' descriptions of how each of their value-added processes helped people solve their problems and helped fit the information ecology were coded using the nine information ecology components, 11 problem dimension dichotomies, and nine information trait continuums discussed above as coding categories. Condensing the contents of the project workbooks in this way enabled the analysis and comparison of workbook categories across projects.

The organizations studied varied considerably between project teams. Some were large organizations with global operations; others were much smaller with all organizational participants inhabiting the same physical location. The types of organizations studied included bank departments, philanthropic agencies, financial & career placement services, and public & academic libraries. On average, the project teams identified two or three major sets of users per organization. For each of these sets, one or two significant information problems were described, as well as one or two information sources typically used to help resolve each problem. Of the 43 different information sources used by the various project teams, almost half (48.8%) were identified as being used predominantly for instrumental reasons, that is, to find out what to do or how to do something.

In terms of information ecology, most project teams deemed the purpose of the intranet was to support the organization's mission statement and, more specifically, to improve information access, sharing, and use throughout the enterprise. Most viewed intranets as a medium by which to foster group collaboration, knowledge creation, and organizational communication.

Of the 11 organizations studied, 6 had no formal information management plans. All teams indicated an aspiration towards a federalistic approach to managing information through shared consensus and negotiation, though 5 teams stated that a feudalistic approach was most representative where individual departments managed their own information needs. Interestingly, 4 teams indicated that anarchy prevailed to some extent in terms of the information politics of the organization.

Though the organizations varied greatly in terms of their structure and size, 10 of the 11 project teams reported that the physical setting restricted access to information in the organizations that were studied. In terms of information culture, 6 teams indicated that even though their organizations strived to value and share information, the prevailing information culture was characterized by either information hoarding and/or information overload. Three sites had no formal information staff available to organizational participants to help manage the information assets of the enterprise or act as information intermediaries. The information processes of the organizations studied were considerably varied. In terms of information architecture, only half of the organizations had some sort of information mapping tool or guide available to help organizational participants understand the location of information in the company.

In total, 42 value-added processes were created and described in the workbooks. Though the designs varied considerably across project teams, the two most commonly implemented value-added processes were discussion areas, which provided a forum for organizational participants to communicate and share interpretations, and knowledge repositories, which allowed organizational participants to access databases containing items such as best practices, frequently-asked questions, meeting minutes, task force updates, case studies, and company profiles. Less commonly implemented value-added processes were ones that provided access to corporate documents such as staff directories and company policies.

For each value-added process, project teams identified components of the approach used in the formation of value-added processes. Tables 4.3, 4.4, and 4.5 provide a summary of the information ecology, problem dimension, and information trait components utilized in the creation of value-added processes in the intranet designs.

Rank	Component	Number of value-added processes created that used this component	Percentage of value-added processes created that used this component (N=42)
1	Physical Setting	25	59.5%
2	Information Culture	18	42.3%
3	Information Politics	11	26.2%
4	Information Strategy	5	11.9%
5	Organizational Mission	4	9.5%
6/7	Information Staff	3	7.1%
6/7	Information Processes	3	7.1%
8	Information Architecture	2	4.8%
9	Intranet Goals	0	0.0%

Table 4.3 Frequency of Information Ecology Components Used in the Creation of Value-Added Processes

Rank	Component	Number of value-added processes created that used this component	Percentage of value-added processes created that used this component (N=42)
1	Design/Discovery	9	21.4%
2/3/4	Well/Ill Structured	4	9.5%
2/3/4	Complex/Simple	4	9.5%
2/3/4	Specific/Amorphous Goals	4	9.5%
5/6	Initial State Understood/Not Understood	3	7.1%
5/6	Familiar/New Pattern	3	7.1%
7	Internal/External Imposition	2	4.8%
8/9/10	Assumptions Agree Upon/Not Agreed Upon	1	2.4%
8/9/10	Assumptions Explicit/Not Explicit	1	2.4%
8/9/10	Susceptible/Not Susceptible to Empirical Analysis	1	2.4%
11	Magnitude of Risk Great/Not Great	0	0.0%

Table 4.4: Frequency of Problem Dimension Components Used in the Creation of Value-Added Processes

Rank	Component	Number of value-added processes created that used this component	Percentage of value-added processes created that used this component (N=42)
1	Historical/Forecasting	13	31.0%
2	Factual/Diffuse	12	28.6%
3/4	Quantitative/Qualitative	7	16.7%
3/4	Clinical/Aggregated	7	16.7%
5	Applied/Theoretical	5	11.9%
6/7	Hard/Soft Data	4	9.5%
6/7	Operational/Descriptive	4	9.5%
8/9	Single/Multiple Solutions	1	2.4%
8/9	Casual/Diagnostic	1	2.4%

Table 4.5: Frequency of Information Trait Components Used in the Creation of Value-Added Processes

The framework for intranet design presented in this chapter seems viable to the extent that it led to the development of feasible intranet designs. That is, the designs produced by the project teams offered practical solutions through the creation of value-added processes which provide information in ways that help organizational participants resolve their typical problems. In fact, one project team indicated that the organization they studied had implemented their intranet design in practice.

In terms of the components of the approach more frequently utilized, most team members had little difficulty turning knowledge of the organization's information ecology, typical problems, information sources, and information uses into ideas for value-added processes. Most members used these components reasonably well. However, the low frequency counts of problem dimensions and information traits used in the creation of value-added processes suggest that project teams experienced difficulty utilizing these lower-level components to devise value-added processes. The reason for this may not necessarily reflect the potential utility of problem dimensions and information traits but rather a lack of understanding of these constructs by team members. Despite this lower usage, the analysis of the workbook descriptions showed evidence of problem dimensions and information traits as beneficial in terms of helping team members gain clarity on the nature of the typical problems faced and the information behaviors exhibited by organizational participants.

Though many useful value-added processes were created by the project teams, the approach did not prevent the inclusion of processes that did not address the typical problems faced or information behaviors exhibited by major sets of users. For example, some project members imposed design solutions that appeared to them as being useful, despite the fact that these solutions did not meet an expressed or observed information need of the people being studied. It should be noted that these instances comprised only a small minority of the processes created.

Another observation was that the approach led to the development of technical solutions only. All project teams devised value-added processes in their intranet designs; none developed recommendations for management to remove organizational barriers that deter or prevent information overload and information sharing. In this respect, project members suffered from technocratic utopianism, a term which describes the underlying assumption of technology's ability to solve all problems of information governance (Davenport 1997, pg. 77). Most project teams were idealistic towards the potential benefits of their technological solutions. The creation of value-added processes may be better served to include recommendations for social incentives which encourage organizational participants to use intranets in ways they were intended. Doing so may facilitate intranet adoption and use.

In terms of limitations, the lack of system design experience by members of the design teams was probably an influencing factor in the quality of designs produced. The inclusion of more experienced designers in the study likely would have led to the development of different types of value-added processes or the use of different components of the approach. Another limitation was the lack of familiarity with the approach by the design team members.

Despite these concerns, the study was useful in that it provided initial support for the viability of a new approach to intranet design, one based on an understanding of the organizational information environment and user information behavior.

4.6 Other Complementary Research

Allen (1996) presents a user-centered approach to information system development that describes the need to adopt a problem-solving perspective to the construction of information systems. Similar to Taylor's (1986) value-added approach, Allen (p.1) recommends that the information needs of users play a more influential role in system design than data or technology.

Specifically, Allen outlines a user-centered approach to information system development that describes the need to adopt a problem-solving perspective to the construction of systems. His six steps are as follows: 1) identify a user population; 2) investigate the information needs of each user group; 3) discover the tasks that users accomplish as they meet these user needs; 4) investigate the resources that users require to complete these tasks; 5) package the preceding steps into user profiles; and 6) create system features that augment the resources of users and enable them to complete the tasks to meet their information needs.

Allen's approach appears to support the framework for intranet design sketched in this chapter. It emphasizes the investigation of information needs through the identification of user problems, the discovery of information tasks (i.e. behaviors) that users accomplish as they attempt to meet these needs, and the creation of value-added processes in the system design that promote usability.

As for intranet studies, a team of researchers from the University of Washington's Graduate School of Library and Information Science recently undertook an in-depth investigation at Boeing on how its employees use the company's intranet. The research team conducted first-hand observations and interviews with a group of Boeing engineers to learn more about how they go about seeking information off the company's intranet to find answers to questions. To carry out their study, the research team utilized a theoretical framework for work environments developed by Annelise Mark Pejtersen of Risø Labs Denmark, which bears resemblance to the framework for intranet design presented in this chapter in that both call for an analysis of the larger work context in which users are situated as well as an understanding of lower-level information needs and uses of major sets of users.

Pejtersen proposes an approach for work systems evaluation that involves the analysis of well-defined levels or boundaries of user-workplace interaction (Pejtersen 1996; Pejtersen and Rasmussen 1997; Rasmussen, Pejtersen, and Goodstein 1994). Her model depicts the evaluation of information systems as a series of concentric levels, with the inner-most levels representing more user-related characteristics in terms of the design of the user interface and the understanding of various user mental models, and the outer-most levels representing broader work-related concepts such as the tasks situations facing users and the work environments in which users are situated.

Each level represents a "boundary" in the organizational work context of users which require both analytical and empirical evaluation. For example, the inner-most level involves an analysis of user characteristics such as their cognitive resources and value criteria. The next level concentrates on identifying and understanding specific user task situations. The next broader level of circles involves understanding the division of work tasks in terms of the roles users perform and how work is coordinated throughout the organization. The outermost level analyzes the work environment in terms of its physical configuration and the goals, constraints, and productive resources within which the information system must operate.

Pejtersen calls for a non-sequential analysis of the various boundaries or levels. That is, work analysis does not proceed in any orderly top-down or bottom-up procession of the perspectives described above. Rather, the analysis is iterative across boundaries in that frequent iterations among the perspectives are necessary. This is similar to the framework for intranet design presented in this chapter which suggests an iterative evaluation of the major components of the framework: the information ecology; groups of information users, their problem situations, and associated information behaviors.

4.7 Conclusion

In this chapter, we have sketched a new framework for intranet design based on an analysis of the organizational information environment. Our underlying assumption is that the current emphasis on information content and technology in intranet design needs to be balanced with a focus on user, especially the behaviors, practices, and contexts in which information is utilized. We suggest that doing so may lead to improved and more useful intranet designs. By more fully addressing information needs, information behaviors, and information ecology of organizational participants system developers can create richer and more robust intranet designs that go beyond the current publishing paradigm towards a flexible infrastructure that supports the creation and sharing of knowledge throughout the enterprise.

Section III: Information Seeking on the World Wide Web

Chapter 5: Models of Information Seeking on the World Wide Web

Having examined the intranet as an IT infrastructure for knowledge work and the need for system designers to adopt an information behavioral/ecological approach to intranet design, we now turn our attention away from intranets and towards the broader utilization of the World Wide Web as an information seeking platform. Our focus in this section of the book is on the activities people take when they use the Web as an information source or channel. Specifically in this chapter, we present an overview of the different approaches and models to studying information seeking on the World Wide Web.

Recently there has been several efforts to model information seeking on the Web. These have drawn upon metaphors and methods from fields as diverse as evolutionary biology, informetrics, and organization science. This chapter presents models of information seeking on the Web from three specific areas of research: information foraging; bibliometrics, and user browsing. To round out our description of these models, we summarize findings from recent Web user studies. This leads directly into the next chapter where we present our own in-depth study of organizational Web use.

5.1 Information Foraging

One attempt to analyze information seeking behavior is made via the theories relating to foraging for sustenance. Stephens and Krebs (1986), in their book *Foraging Theory*, point out that foraging models have a number of uses, most notably to analyze behavioral mechanisms. They also concede that foraging models can "serve as a general background against which to organize observations about individual behavior" and that "studies, although not to explicitly aiming to 'test' foraging models, use the general ideas of foraging to organize data and ideas" (p. 184).

Sandstrom (1994) was one of the first to draw attention to the parallels between information seeking and foraging for sustenance. Just as animals evolve different methods of gathering and hunting food or prey to increase their intake of nutrition, humans also adopt different strategies of seeking information to increase their intake of knowledge.

Foraging for information on the Web and foraging for food share common features: both resources tend to be unevenly distributed in the environment, uncertainty and risk characterize resource procurement, and all foragers are limited by time and opportunity costs as they choose to exploit one resource over another. Successful foragers are those who adopt strategies that maximize their harvest rates and their chances of survival. As a model in evolutionary biology, foraging theory requires some proxy currency as a measure of survival fitness. Since information does not deplete no matter how many have been 'feeding' on it, Sandstrom suggests that another characteristic of information, namely its novelty to the information seeker (and to his or her audience), be operationalized as a fitness currency.

According to Sandstrom (p. 416), "because optimal foraging theory integrates deductive models of evolutionary ecology, microeconomics, and evolutionary genetics, it lays the ground work for cost-benefit analyses that can be successfully applied to all human choice-making phenomena". As such, optimal foraging theory can be a relevant approach to studying human searching behavior in that it models how actors calculate costs and benefits within a set of constraints and use certain strategies to enact these calculations. A host of constraints include terrain, travel time, the climate, density of resources, their mobility and their distribution along the terrain. Combining these constraints with an actor's abilities, technologies, skills, understanding of the environment, and availability for teamwork, one can use optimal foraging theory to build a robust individual-oriented behavioral framework that can be applied to how we search for and make choices about the information we use.

Sandstrom presents three broad categories of optimal foraging: "(1) the prey choice and diet breadth of foragers, (2) their time allocation and choice of patch or habitat, and (3) their foraging-group size and settlement patterns in relation to resource distribution" (p. 424). Prey choice assumes that foragers consistently select similar items over time in that they know what they like and therefore seek similar prey consistently given that retrieval and processing costs are acceptable, such as understanding a new environment, or in some cases, a new technology.

Diet breadth is a measure of the range of items selected, which indicates that foragers consistently choose particular items. Time allocation simply seeks to gauge the amount of time that is optimally spent at a patch of information before moving to another patch, or completely foraging the existing patch. For organizational users, the availability of "local" intranet sources of information might constitute little actual discovery foraging. In effect, information foragers may capitalize on information farms of locally produced resources. Patches of information may also be personal, such as bookmarks or previously gathered information resources, making these resources more predominant in an information diet due to their availability.

Group size of optimal foraging looks for measures of individual versus group foraging with the belief that species adapt to work in groups because "aggregation increases the efficiency or effectiveness of individual foragers" (Winterhalder 1981, p. 30). Cooperation among members of a group can result in the monitoring of large areas. For example, group members can exchange information at a central place about the patches of possible information resources. This at least metaphorically echoes the idea that a central location for information exchange can help a group optimize their information diet and even possibly promote their relationships between each other.

Pirolli and Card (1995) build upon Sandstrom's ideas and provide some examples of systems for information foraging in information access environments. They argue that

> "in an information-rich world, the real design problem to be solved is not so much how to collect more information, but rather, how to optimize the user's time, and we have deployed these principles in an attempt to increase relevant information gained per unit time expended. But for task analysis, design exploitation, and evaluation of information systems, a more developed theory is needed." (p. 51)

In response, they choose information foraging theory to account for

> "the adaptiveness of human-system designs in the context of the information ecologies in which tasks are performed. Typically, this involves understanding the variations in activity afforded by some space of human-system design parameters, and understanding how these variations trade-off the value of information gained against the costs of performing the activity ... information foraging theory emphasizes a larger time-scale of behavior, the cost structure of external information- bearing environments, and human adaptation." (p. 52)

In other words, information foraging refers to activities associated with assessing, seeking, and handling information sources, particularly in networked environments. Such search can be adaptive to the extent that it makes optimal use of knowledge about expected information value and expected costs of accessing and extracting the relevant information (Pirolli and Card 1995; Pirolli, Pitkow and Rao 1996).

There are different styles of information foraging. For instance, a wolf hunts for prey, but a spider builds a web and waits for the prey to come to it. Humans seeking information also adopt different strategies, sometimes with close parallels to those of animal foragers. Pirolli and Card (1995) note that the wolf-prey strategy resembles classic information retrieval, while the spider-web strategy is akin to information filtering. Pirolli, Pitkow and Rao (1996) suggest that the optimal selection of Web pages from a collection of related pages to satisfy a user's information needs is a kind of optimal information diet problem. Optimality of the diet or pursuit sequence chosen by users will depend on their ability to categorize rapidly the Web page types, rank category members, assess their popularity on the Web locality, assess the expected amount of return over cost of pursuit, and decide which categories to pursue and which to ignore.

This view of information foraging focuses on tasks involved such as assessing, seeking, and handling information along with strategies akin to animal foragers. Foraging groups are taken into consideration, noting that the overall mean for the foraging group may be lower than an individual, but the group provides more stability for sustenance over time. Pirolli and Card point out that this is seen in information foraging by analysts who cross-reference information to reduce the chance of missing a piece of information. Essentially, the analysts are collaborating with remote foragers, finding, scouring, and exhausting patches of related information for consumption.

Optimal foraging is the goal for any system that aids information foraging. Three assumptions for optimal foraging are presented: 1) decision—identifying problems and making choices; 2) currency—evaluating these problems and noting their use for maximizing, minimizing, and stability of sources; and 3) constraints—limiting and understanding the relationships between the decisions and currency of foraging assumptions. Despite the clarity with which these principles are presented, human behavior is not always perfectly rational; "satisficing" (Simon 1979) can occur where the forager either ignores these activities or their results.

Pirolli and Card elaborate these ideas with three examples: 1) an information patch model using a Scatter/Gather interface to promote browsing information; 2) an information diet model that focuses on ranking an information resource's possible gains, time to acquire and process, and opportunity costs of acquisition; and 3) a dynamic foraging model which accounts for changes in both the information foraging environment and the information forager involving experienced system users and narrowing use of information clusters to forage from. These examples provide valuable guidelines and measurements for further information foraging system development.

Taking these ideas towards information seeking on the Web, Pirolli, et. al. (1996) address how "informavores" optimally forage the World Wide Web for information. Much like Sandstrom's inclusion of patches of information, Pirolli, Pitkow and Rao use the term "Web locality" to specify a collection of related WWW pages. They describe how informavores seek to derive an optimal information diet by focusing on relevant and highly valued information. They argue that when coming upon an information patch or Web site, the user is similar to a predator evaluating prey where the type of prey must be identified and make a decision to pursue the prey. Within this ecology of Web resources, Pirolli, et. al believe it is possible to use the native information in and about a Web resource (an individual Web page or entire Web site) to help make these prey categorization decisions.

In a related work, Cronin and Hert (1995) use information foraging to study how scholars access and use information. They begin by pointing out that a huge variety of information sources is available to modern scholars by electronic means. Recognition of this fact prompts questions as to how they discriminate between sources, and in particular, why they select some and not others. The essentially disorganized nature of the World Wide Web suggests that scholars are likely to adopt what is termed a 'foraging' strategy in order to retrieve information. They will select different areas at different times for different purposes, and search them with varying levels of intensity.

Such an approach is not suited for the existing tools devised to exploit the orderly, structured world of conventional, commercial online databases. Concepts such as recall and precision are no longer necessarily valid. Whereas commercial databases tend to be highly focused, those on the Web are broad, diffuse, fluctuating and even unstable. The search strategy must be characterized by attempts to manage this breadth and diversity. We might expect scholars to seek novelty—new concepts and insights—to stimulate their own research. If this is the case, there are implications for the design of the search tools to be employed. Specifically, the emphasis must shift from matching to foraging. Cronin and Hert tested this idea of foraging for information on the Web, however, the results were disappointing as regards the generation of useful novel associations with search terms. More research needs to be done in such areas as defining 'patches' where foraging takes place, the manner in which it is undertaken, and the mechanisms necessary to make novel items available to scholars. Only then are more relevant search tools likely to appear.

Overall, the foraging perspective represents an approach in analyzing information seeking *behaviors* that has been applied with interesting results in Web-based information environments. While the foraging metaphor includes the concept of value to the user ("hunter") by analyzing dimensions such as nutrition, novelty and diet-breadth, it basically treats information as a sustenance-providing "object" or resource. This view of information as food thus differs somewhat from the conceptualization of information in this volume as the outcome of people actively constructing the meaning and value of information through practices that engage mental and affective processes in particular contexts or situations.

5.2 Bibliometrics

To develop a better understanding of information seeking in practice, the attributes of authorship, publications, and their influences on each other are worth examining. Bibliometrics, a quantitative method for the study of literatures, offers good insights. Originally derived for published information, bibliometrics is particularly applicable to studying how Web documents, Web sites, and Web users are all related through reference and use.

5.2.1 Bibliometrics of Use

Bibliometrics stems from the idea that distribution and use of information has patterns that can be analyzed by counting and analyzing citations, finding relationships between these references based on frequency, and using other statistical measures. Common sources of standard, publication bibliometric data are the Science Citation Index or Social Science Citation Index, where an author's publication influence can be seen by how often the author is referenced.

Bibliometric use is a progressively cyclical process inherent in most communication and specifically in scientific communication. A few basic bibliometric measures track this information use. One of the classic bibliometric analysis techniques begins by counting all types of citations with little or any weight to reference types. A refinement of mass citation counting, direct citation counting is tracking the quantity of citations over a given period of time to test for aspects of an author's, article's or journal's impact. The standard formula for impact is:

number of citations / number of citable articles published

While somewhat blunt, applying and averaging citations along certain scales, such as timeframes and subject fields, begins to become quite useful. It is quite easy to imagine this process for printed documents, however, calculating impact on the WWW can be more complex. Initially, simple comparisons of URLs visited from proxy server logs, search engines, or links could provide this type of metric. Web domain names could be substituted for journals while URLs within the Web domain could be considered as articles. Thus, impact could be dominance of Web usage per user per Web domain or by groups of Web users.

Another basic bibliometric technique is calculating an immediacy index of influence by a publication using this formula:

> number of citations received by article during the year / total number of citable articles published

This is a useful metric to see a broader view of an article's impact, but it is not wholly objective as time frames can be far more variable than a year. This can also be applied to Web data by examining intra-Web domain links and extra-Web domain links between documents. This might also be applied by discovering the different paths a user traverses to arrive at the same URL.

5.2.2 Bibliometric Coupling

The most naturally useful activity of applying bibliometrics is a technique known as bibliographic coupling: measuring the number of references two papers have in common to test for similarity. Kessler (1963) showed that a clustering based on this measure yields meaningful groupings of papers for research and information retrieval by finding "a number of papers bear a meaningful relation to each other when they have one or more references in common" (p. 10). On the Web, this could be measured by noting visits between URLs, where higher relationships would equal more coupling, or at a content level by examining Web pages for similar external links.

Kessler also found a high correlation between groups formed by coupling and groups formed by subject indexing. As bibliometrics has become more automated, many have tried to take these techniques and engineer software to detect patterns and establish relationships between articles (Price and Schiminovich, 1968). The first of these studies by Schiminovich (1971) made the first real steps towards applying bibliometrics to electronic publications, notably physics literature stored on a time-sharing system at MIT, to begin automatically unearthing these types of coupling patterns. With electronically stored publications, metrics like bibliometric coupling could finally be applied on a scale that made them tremendously useful and timely. This is also true for the potential of measuring URL coupling on the Web. Use can be measured via subject categories, such as those seen on the WWW now in sites such as Yahoo!, and relationships found by coupling measures, such as by looking for similarly linked Web pages, or a page that links to a specific Web page—both features supported by most Web search engines. In some fashion, the current trend towards Web meta-search engines takes advantage of coupling to compare search results between the search engines to present a smaller set of resulting resources that should prove to be more accurate.

5.2.3 Co-citation Analysis

Marshakova (1973) and Small (1973) independently developed coupling further by noting that if two references are cited together in a publication then the two references are themselves related. The greater the number of times they are cited together, the greater their co-citation strength. The major refinement between bibliometric coupling and co-citation is that while coupling measures the relationship between source documents, co-citation measures the relations between cited documents. This implies that an author purposefully chose to relate two articles together, not merely an association between two articles as coupling reveals.

For the Web or an organization's intranet, co-citation-like measurements could be made a number of ways such as by using Proxy Server logs to look for Web pages that are used together in one browsing session. In some cases, it is possible that similarities in URL paths of Web documents might indicate that Webmasters grouped like files by directory paths or naming conventions. In some fashion, this is similar to an author citing two documents in his article.

5.2.4 Bibliometric Laws

These three main bibliometric laws: Zipf's Law, Lotka's Law, and Bradford's Law of Scattering are the most widely-known and used bibliometric measures. They are mathematically related to each other, not unlike the very relationships each law seeks to unearth. In fact, both Bradford and Lotka's Laws are actually derived from Zipf's Law. Like physical laws, they seek to describe the working of a system by mathematical means. All of these laws can be applied to World Wide Web content and in discovering patterns of Web usage. Each of these is examined in this section as well as some corollaries and supporting ideas.

5.2.4.1 Zipf's Law

The most powerful, wide-ranging law of bibliometrics is Zipf's Law. In his book *Human Behavior & The Principle of Least Effort*, George K. Zipf defines the essence of what became known as his law, called The Principle of Least Effort, as "the primary principle that governs our entire individual and collective behavior or all sorts, including the behavior of our language and preconceptions" (1949, p. viii). Zipf is saying that the main predictor of human behavior is that we always attempt to minimize our effort. Therefore, Zipf's work applies to almost any field where human production is involved. He notes that his principle shows that a person will

> "expend in solving *both* his immediate problems *and his probable future problems*. That in turn means that the person will strive to minimize the *probable average rate of his work-expenditure* (over time). And in doing so he will be minimizing his *effort*, by our definition of effort. Least effort, therefore, is a variant of least work." (p. 1)

Zipf also applies his principle to other aspects of our efforts of communication; from the distribution of population sizes among towns and cities to the number of newspapers; and to the balance of tools and work.

Originally, Zipf's Law essentially predicts the phenomenon that as we write, we use familiar words with high frequency. In order to minimize effort in remembering or alternating similar word use, we tend to keep using the same words and phrases continually in a document. Specifically, for a distribution applied to word frequency in a text, a word's rank r occurs f times (frequency) where c is the constant for the text analyzed. This gives us the formula $r \; x \; f = c$. For analysis, this can be applied by counting all of the words in a document with the most frequent occurrences representing the subject matter of the document. We could also use relative frequency instead of absolute frequency to determine when a new word is entering a vocabulary.

But what makes Zipf's law so memorable is its use in other fields as well. In fact, the general applicability of Zipfs Law can ironically be used to prove itself. Being so widely known, it is widely used, perhaps so much so in significance that is becomes the bibliometric law used and referred to with the highest frequency by far. Zipf points out

> "that individuals will at all times try to minimize effort, then it follows that the reason for their buying and reading newspapers is that such conduct is an economical method of learning of those events in their environment that may be of positive or negative value for their particular economies... in order to lure these potential buyers into the paper's reader population for the sake of increasing the circulation, the editor must increase the *diversity* of his news items."

This can apply to more than just newspapers, it could be any information source. The World Wide Web is truly diversified and not limited by page size (as Zipf was concerned with for print), but financial resources limit the amount any one organization can publish.

For example, Huberman et. al. (1998) point out in an empirical study of Web use that there are Zipf-like distributions in path lengths (i.e. the number of characters in the Web page's URL) and page visits to sites on the World Wide Web. In other words, the farther down the number of links a user must travel to view a Web page, the smaller the number of visits a Web page received. However, as World Wide Web publishing gets easier, Web search engines become more sophisticated, and more people have access to the Web, will Zipfs distribution still hold?

5.2.4.2 Lotka's Law

Lotka's law looks not at frequencies of information in documents, but the number of documents produced by authors. Lotka found that among authors in a subject field, there are some that are immensely prolific, others marginally productive, and a few who only occasionally, if not singularly compose articles. Lotka (1926) developed the formula $x^n y=c$, with y as the number of authors, x as the number of contributions, and n and c as values that depend on the subject field. This means Lotka's Law is roughly an inverse square law where, for example, every 100 authors contributing one article, 25 will contribute two, 11 will contribute three, and six will contribute four each. We see a general decrease in performance among a body of authors following an inverse square law, represented as $1:n^2$, with n as the number of articles. This ratio shows that some produce much more than the average, which seems true for all kinds of content creation.

However, Lotka does not take impact into account, only production numbers. Furthermore, Voos (1974) found that in Information Science, the ratio was currently $1{:}n^{3.5}$. Thus, we can say that Lotka's Law may not be constant in value, but does follow the inverse square. The challenge will then be to find the values for different subject fields and disciplines as well as for the Web, among Web sites or individual Web page authors. It may also be possible that for the Web, instead of just distributions for authoring, there will also be distributions for Web browsing.

5.2.4.3 *Bradford's Law*

Bradford (1934) revealed a pattern of how literature for a particular subject field is distributed in journals. Bradford called this his Law of Scattering. He developed this by noticing that the publication patterns of papers in a set of journals seemed to be consistent. If, for a certain time frame, a set of journals about a given subject field are analyzed for articles, a core of journals cover a specific field, with a few other groups giving far less coverage . This essentially indicates that publications maintain a regular distribution or "core and scatter" phenomenon where a few core journals are prolific in publishing articles while other journals publish progressively fewer articles about a subject field or topic.

These more prolific, or core journals occupy the core Bradford zone with two following scatter zones of much less influence, as shown by the number of journals required to equate with the core total. A sample distribution (Diodato, 1994):

1) the top 8 journals produce 110 articles;

2) the next 29 journals produce 133 articles;

3) the next 127 journals produce 152 articles

shows that the numbers of the three groups of journals to produce nearly equal number of articles is roughly in proportion to 1:4:16 or $4^0{:}4^1{:}4^2$. This makes the Bradford multiplier, *n*, equal to 4 in $1{:}n{:}n^2$.

Bradford's Law can also be used to measure a rate of obsolescence over time, by distinguishing between the usage levels of items. Essentially, this is a method of clustering. For example, a collection of journal articles in nine journals may account for 429 articles, the next 59 journals may account for 499 articles, while the last 258 journals can account for 404. We roughly get three groupings (ranging from 404 to 499) of articles. Bradford noticed this consistent number of titles it takes to contribute to each third of the total population of articles. Bradford discovered this regularity by calculating the number of titles in each of the three groups: 9 titles, 9 x 5 titles, 9 x 5 x 5 titles. Drott suggests that we can apply this widely, as long as we account for sample sizes, area of (journal) specialization and journal policies (Drott, 1981).

Brookes (1973) notes that Bradford's Law is correct assuming that there are a finite, manageable, and relevant number of journals only. Brookes contends that editorial selection and publishing costs influence much of the structure and content amount of most publications, which itself moderates and distributes information in a subject field. This criticism of Bradford's Law becomes an interesting point to study when we think of the low barriers for publishing on the Web. Will this distribution hold, change or not apply at all? With a deluge of Web-based information, we may find the limits to this law.

More positively, we may discover that there is a "half-life" during which Bradford's Law applies. As time passes, we can observe a fairly regular increased use of a term or citation, followed by a relatively steep and permanent reduction later. We can examine this phenomenon over time, to see that citations originally counted year by year can be expressed as the geometric sequence:

$$R, Ra, Ra^2, Ra^3, Ra^4, \ldots, Ra^{t-1}$$

where R is the presumed number of citations during the first year (some which could not immediately be referenced in publication), but as $a < 1$, the sum of the sequence converges to the finite limit $R / (1-a)$. After a predictable time (for each area of study) usage drops off. This type of measurement has utility when examining information on the World Wide Web as well. As the Web, by nature, expands with information prolifically and often about technical information or general news (which again, changes rapidly) we see how thinking about what constitutes a "Web year" of time might impact Web documents.

Most Web users agree that information use seems to evolve much faster on the Web (or due to the Web). If a Web site or page is useful, its use will be further amplified by links to it, other sources commenting on it, or other Web sites similar to it being created. Sites that are not read much (if the author is aware of the site's readership) seem to naturally never to be updated or eventually lose their place in the attention of the Web. These "ghost sites" rankings in search engines descend; Web indexes no longer point to them; links to their pages are not updated or eventually atrophy off the list; and interest shifts to a more novel coverage of the topic or another topic altogether. One possible means of measuring this may be to compare the date of a user's Web page request to the date of the Web page's last modification (via the HTTP header) to get some measure of impact over time.

5.2.5 Bibliometrics and Web Documents

Currently, only a few studies have examined the bibliometric characteristics of Web resources on a large scale. Mostly individual pages have been collected and analyzed. Woodruff, et. al (1996) used the Inktomi search engine and a number of other tools to make a comprehensive analysis of over 2.6 million Web documents. They examined Web documents for many characteristics such as document sizes had a mean of 4.4 KB and a median of 2.0KB. They also found that 20% of the domains were for .com addresses, 27% for .edu, other domains at 41% (such as .uk or .dk), with the remaining percentages scattered among .org, .mil. and .net. The Web sites with the most links to themselves were found to be www.xerox.com with 28,188 links; www.yahoo.com with 19424; and cool.infi.net (the "Cool Site of the day" Web page host) with 19028 —a large number of the major Web sites contained many thousands of links to their own internal pages.

Other data was aggregated to create a number of ranked lists such as the ten most-used tags and the ten most common HTML errors. Woodruff et. al. also found that documents from different domains had some differences in stylistic attributes such as sentence length. In total, this data begins to support that with this many available characteristics to measure in a document, a "document fingerprint" might be possible to identify types of Web pages. This type of identification could then be used to compare and identify Web browser user's behavior regarding a particular type of Web document. However, Woodruff notes that to do this on the scale of the entire Web would be quite arduous and suggests a longitudinal study (perhaps with sampling) to help track the trends in Web document characteristics.

In another study, Wulfekuhler, et. al. (1997) examine techniques that detect common features in sets of pre-categorized documents, to find similar documents on the World Wide Web. They found that extracting word clusters from the raw document features proved successful in discovering word groups that can be used to find similar Web documents.

When comparing these results to pattern recognition via training samples from known categories to form a decision rule for unknown patterns, they found not knowing the number and labels of categories of Web documents made accuracy difficult. They discovered that clustering techniques are unsupervised, requiring no external knowledge of categories and only group similar patterns into clusters whose members are more similar to each other (according to some distance measure) than to members of other clusters. They also point out that pattern recognition requires a greater number of documents. For their "4 class problem and 5190 features, this means we would need one to two hundred thousand training documents. Clearly this is not possible for this domain" (p. 5). They note that additional techniques can help to reduce the number of training samples, but seem content to work with word clustering for now.

Many concepts bibliometrics formally captured can be and are used to deduce how to manage and measure Web resources. By measuring resource access and to test the utility of a document (assuming that a visit or return visit implies the document was useful), the most-used documents can be enhanced or used as a starting point for other topic selections. Even Web page caching can be (and is) helped with bibliometric-oriented concepts: keeping the most frequently accessed Web pages available in the cache for the quickest access is good optimization of Web server resources and formerly for managing access to collections of print publications.

However, this in turn might cause cached files to be requested more often simply because the reliability of being received by a Web browser is higher. Essentially, this is Price's (1976) "cumulative advantage model" where success breeds success. However, it also implies that an obsolescence factor is at work, in that information that is not used will atrophy on the Web.

The operational methods of bibliometrics can be useful to produce quantitative data and subsequent analysis to understand and improve information systems use. In many ways bibliometric techniques are similar to what is currently known as knowledge discovery in databases or data mining techniques, but with an emphasis on the content of the data. However, many of the techniques employed by bibliometrics concern the content of a document as well, which is currently called text-based data mining. Much of this type analysis could be undertaken by retrieving all of the pages noted in a Web usage log and analyzing the Web pages' content.

5.2.6 Bibliometrics and the Web - Webometrics

In 1996, Larson made an exploratory study applying bibliometric measures to a set of World Wide Web documents in one subject field. He used a combination of Web-based tools: a Web crawler and a Web search engine to measure the characteristics and co-citation relationships of over 30 gigabytes of Web documents. The goal was to determine highly-cited Web documents and their characteristics from a snapshot of the Web from two different time periods in 1995. Data collection was chosen from a set of Web searches, then narrowed to focus only on sites that linked to (cited) two specific subject field pages. Pages were then narrowed to relevant pages within the subject field, then sorted to eliminate duplicate URLs and URLs that appeared in less than three other of this group of Web pages. This left a total of 332 potential core Web pages, then retrieved and manually examined, resulting in further editing to 125 Web documents. This was reduced to a "best" set of Web pages, finally narrowing the set to 34 Web pages.

A raw co-citation measure was captured in a frequency table using a Web robot, next it was converted into a correlation matrix to transform the raw co-citation values into proximity measures between Web sites. Sites with high correlations were considered similar in content. After multidimensional scaling, a graphical view of the map of the Web pages was developed to show "the major 'topical' clusters of WWW sites" (p. 76). These mappings closely matched the expectations of the clusters seen during the manual examination process earlier.

Almind and Ingwersen (1997) coin a new term for their bibliometric analysis of the Web— "webometrics", adapted from the field of informetrics. They contend, as many others have, that the World Wide Web is a citation network and apply informetric measures to Web pages. They suggest that many HTML tags or other Web page characteristics are similar to citation information commonly found in ISI data files. While generally agreeable, domain names, URL paths (see Spertus, 1997) and more recent Web page attributes such as META tags might provide even more information about Web resources than their suggestions. One noticeable difference is their use of "most cited (Lycos 250)" as an important characteristic. With the expansion of Web pages, and popularity of Web portal and search engine pages, and the constant change of most popular pages (which may be cause or effect of their popularity), this characteristic is doubtfully useful. However, Almind and Ingwersen are aware that their initial idea of webometrics is not perfect. They note that difficulties with access (actual retrieval of the Web documents); difference in data formats (most Web page markup standards are wholly subjective); and the uncertainty of a Web page's host (usually derived from the domain name in the Web page URL, but not always consistently used) all contribute to inaccurate webometrics.

In their study itself, Almind and Ingwersen collected URLs for Web pages using standard search engines, looking only for Web pages with the ".dk" suffix in their URL. They then analyzed this data to develop a ranking of Denmark's position on the Web (similar to an impact factor); how Web pages are distributed over large centers of learning (much like Lotka's law for determining prolific publishers); an overall map of the subject fields represented; and a picture of Web page characteristics. Their more interesting findings were that the Danish Web position did not match its position in population or by standing of Denmark's research and development facilities. They also noted that shifts in the organization of WWW resources over time as Web sites add and alter their content made the analysis of the large centers of learning in Denmark problematic. As for the Web pages themselves, they discovered that for each "home page" there are about nine other pages and the average size of a Web page was 5,779.5 bytes (roughly 6K). One of the more innovative metric they used was labeled Link Density:

> "which measures the size per link ratio ... an interesting new measure as it brings together and normalizes the two measures of size and number of links. The smaller the number of bytes the lower the link density for equal number of links." (p. 420)

The collection of data resulting from their webometrics was not all their study yielded. Almind and Ingwersen also note that current Web data collection tools are not sufficient for two reasons: 1) the tools are not automatic enough (much manual work is still required that makes working with the scale of the Web impractical); and 2) it is impossible to find every Web page (dynamically-generated Web pages, sites that do not choose to be indexed, private Web sites, commercial Web sites with membership access only, and different character sets for text information).

In 1998, Ingwersen undertook a follow-up study with the aim to calculate Web impact factors ("Web-IF"). Web-IF:

> "takes the logical sum of the number of external- and self-linked web pages pointing to a given country or web site divided by the number of pages found in that country or web site—at a given point in time." (p. 237)

He examined a set of seven entire national Web domains, four other large sector Web domains, and some specific institutional Web sites as a series of snapshots of the Web. Ingwersen contends that Web pages exhibit the same referral behavior as other social communication phenomena and this information can be used to determine the importance or attractiveness of a given Web page or entire Web site. He found that by using Web snapshots, Web impact factors are "calculable with high confidence" (p. 236) in national and sector Web domain studies, but that the institutional studies were problematic. One additional finding was that national Web pages contained self-references about half the time, increasing the overall rating necessary to consider a Web page's impact as high. As Web pages are linked intra-site or intra-domain, the ratio for Web-IF will rise. This is similar to the lengths that Web page authors go in adding numerous search terms to their Web pages which in some cases results in more hits on Web search pages.

In all, more important than the statistics generated by this study are its conclusions about using the Web for similar studies. From a technical standpoint, Ingwersen discovered that something as simple as altering the order of Boolean arguments using the Alta Vista search engine may have had some influence on the results of the study. This strengthens his point in his 1997 paper about the immaturity of current research tools for the Web. He also concluded that Web sites that block Web crawlers or robots from their sites actually can increase impact factors as they are not counted, yet links to them are. Once again, language is considered a problem when analyzing impact factors for non-roman alphabet countries' Web pages. Finally, Ingwersen concludes by noting three spin-off effects: 1) webometric studies may provide novel insights into Web retrieval processes; 2) the analysis methods in this study can measure accuracy of Web search engine performance and Web site structure and linking standards; and 3) Web impact factors will introduce concerns about the validity of Web-based studies.

Overall, these studies indicate that the Web and Web documents have characteristics similar to standard publications. Available Web-based tools make surveying, collecting and analyzing Web documents for this and other bibliometric measures a major avenue for further study.

5.2.7 Bibliometric Measures of Group Web Use

In addition to studying Web content from a bibliometric perspective, actual traces of Web use can be studied. It is common to learn about Web use by examining Web server log files using bibliometric techniques as when Downie (1996) analyzed a single Web server's logs to perform the following analyses:

- User-based analyses to discover more about user demographics and unveil preferences based on:
  - who (organization)
  - where (location)
  - what (client browser).

- Request analyses for content.

- Byte-based analyses to measure raw throughput along from certain timeframes. (bytes served per day, etc.).

The power of these different analyses is that they can be merged to develop a detailed scenario of a user's visit(s) to the Web site and their preferences, problems and actions. Many commercial Web site log analysis packages perform a combination of these analyses, often with the use of special Web server applications or by browser cookies. Only rarely are user clustering or any somewhat sophisticated linking statistics generated, except in some electronic commerce or user profiling applications.

When using bibliometric analysis techniques, Downie discovered via a rank-frequency table of Web pages accessed on his server that requests conformed to a Zipf-like distribution. Other results confirmed that poor Web server configuration and lack of access or use to complete log files could cast doubts on any more accurate results. It is also worth noting that Downie attends to ethical observation issues that many Webmasters and information system professionals do not normally consider. However, by only analyzing a single Web server's access logs, an incomplete model of how the Web is really used is formed. We only have a view of how users that visit a particular Web site access and use the pages.

5.3 User Browsing

The information foraging and bibliometric models of information seeking are promising approaches in their ability to reveal global, historic patterns of use, suggest alternative metrics of information value, and provide implications for system design. However, models are also needed that focus on the information behaviors of individuals as they traverse the Web, taking into account the content in which this information seeking is situated, such as addressing the situation as to why the information was needed and how the information was used.

We examine now three main models of information seeking which focus on the behaviour of information seeking: Marchionini's electronic browsing model, Ellis' model of information seeking behaviors, and Aguilar's modes of organizational scanning. A new behavioral model of information seeking on the Web is then proposed which is based on various aspects of these former models.

5.3.1 Marchionini's Electronic Browsing Model

The influence of new technologies, notably the World Wide Web with its search engines and navigational links, is changing what scholars mean when referring to information seeking. Marchionini (1995) defines information seeking as "a process in which humans purposefully engage in order to change their state of knowledge" (p. 5). Even in the nascent days of the World Wide Web, Marchionini (1995) begins to distinguish information seeking as a superset of activities including information retrieval and browsing. He contends that "the term *information seeking* is preferred to *information retrieval* because it is more human oriented and open ended" (Marchionini 1995, p. 5-6) He points out that information retrieval assumes the information sought has been known at some point, while seeking information can cover this activity and beyond. In most cases, learning about a new topic is involved, meaning that the information wasn't known, it may not be discovered in one measurable activity, and may eventually end up not satisfying the initial answer to the question. Browsing is the other component of Marchionini's idea information seeking, an accompaniment to information retrieval. With the new graphical browsing applications, most notably Web browsers, information seeking can be more fluid and less structured than traditional information retrieval processes. This openness to exploration also fits underneath the information seeking umbrella.

Information seeking, with emphasis on seeking, implies that the goal might change as more information is learned; the question can be further refined; the initial question may be realized as too broad; or the information discovered while seeking the answer changes the question altogether. With the advent of the relatively easy to use Web browser and proliferation of information on the Web, users can move more rapidly through larger amounts of information. These two activities, information retrieval and browsing, combine to cover the broad spectrum of information seeking: information retrieval is more suited to highly organized information like databases and strongly-typed text while browsing is more conducive to non-standardized text and other multimedia. Information retrieval requires more planned analytical strategies, with preparation of queries and understanding the search results. Browsing relies more on intuitive strategies based on past browsing experiences, with unplanned, often serendipitous recognition of information and paths to follow. The World Wide Web provides opportunities for both information retrieval and browsing. With the proliferation of search engines and graphical browsers, the entire range of information seeking activities are possible on the Web. This availability provides new opportunities to study all aspects of information seeking, as seen in the different methods in this chapter.

Marchionini (1995) reviewed the research on browsing and observes that "there seems to be agreement on three general types of browsing that may be differentiated by the object of search (the information needed) and by the systematicity of tactics used" (p. 106). Directed browsing occurs when browsing is systematic, focused, and directed by a specific object or target. Examples include scanning a list for a known item, and verifying information such as dates or other attributes. Semidirected browsing occurs when browsing is predictive or generally purposeful: the target is less definite and browsing is less systematic. An example is entering a single, general term into a database and casually examining the retrieved records. Finally, undirected browsing occurs when there is no real goal and very little focus. Examples include flipping through a magazine and "channel-surfing."

Marchionini (1995) proposes another often-cited model of the information-seeking process, tuned perhaps to electronic environments. In his model, the information seeking process is composed of eight sub-processes which develop in parallel: (1) recognize and accept an information problem, (2) define and understand the problem, (3) choose a search system, (4) formulate a query, (5) execute search, (6) examine results, (7) extract information, and (8) reflect/iterate/stop. (Marchionini 1995, p. 49-60).

5.3.2 Ellis' Model of Information Seeking

Ellis (1989), Ellis et al (1993), and Ellis and Haugan (1997) propose and elaborate a general model of information seeking behaviors based on studies of the information seeking patterns of social scientists, research physicists and chemists, and engineers and research scientists in an industrial firm. One version of the model describes six categories of information seeking activities as generic: starting, chaining, browsing, differentiating, monitoring, and extracting.

"Starting" comprises those activities that form the initial search for information—identifying sources of interest that could serve as starting points of the search. Identified sources often include familiar sources that have been used before as well as less familiar sources that are expected to provide relevant information. The likelihood of a source being selected depends on the perceived accessibility of the source, as well as the perceived quality of the information from that source. Perceived accessibility, which is the amount of effort and time needed to make contact with and use a source, has been found to be a strong predictor of source use for many groups of information users (such as engineers and scientists (Allen 1977)). However, in situations when ambiguity is high and when information reliability is especially important, less accessible sources of perceived high quality may be consulted as well (see for example the environment scanning behavior of chief executives in Choo (1998)). While searching the initial sources, these sources are likely to point to, suggest, or recommend additional sources or references.

Following up on these new leads from an initial source is the activity of "chaining". Chaining can be backward or forward. Backward chaining takes place when pointers or references from an initial source are followed, and is a well established routine of information seeking among scientists and researchers. In the reverse direction, forward chaining identifies and follows up on other sources that refer to an initial source or document. Although it can be an effective way of broadening a search, forward chaining is much less commonly used, probably because people are unaware of it or because the required bibliographical tools are unavailable.

Having located sources and documents, "browsing" is the activity of semi-directed search in areas of potential search. The individual often simplifies browsing by looking through tables of contents, lists of titles, subject headings, names of organizations or persons, abstracts and summaries, and so on. Browsing takes place in many situations in which related information has been grouped together according to subject affinity, as when the user views displays at a conference or exhibition, or scans periodicals or books along the shelves of a bookshop or library. Chang and Rice (1993) define browsing as "the process of exposing oneself to a resource space by scanning its content (objects or representations) and/or structure, possibly resulting in awareness of unexpected or new content or paths in that resource space." (p. 258) They regard browsing as a "rich and fundamental human information behavior" that could lead to outcomes such as serendipitous findings, modification of information needs, learning, enjoyment, and so on.

During "differentiating", the individual filters and selects from among the sources scanned by noticing differences between the nature and quality of the information offered. For example, social scientists were found to prioritize sources and types of sources according to three main criteria: by substantive topic; by approach or perspective; and by level, quality, or type of treatment (Ellis 1989). The differentiation process is likely to depend on the individual's prior or initial experiences with the sources, word-of-mouth recommendations from personal contacts, or reviews in published sources. Taylor (1986) points out that for information to be relevant and consequential, it should address not only the subject matter of the problem but also the particular circumstances that affect the resolution of that problem. He identifies six categories of criteria by which individuals select and differentiate between sources: ease of use, noise reduction, quality, adaptability, time savings, and cost savings.

"Monitoring" is the activity of keeping abreast of developments in an area by regularly following particular sources. The individual monitors by concentrating on a small number of what are perceived to be core sources. Core sources vary between professional groups, but usually include both key personal contacts and publications. For example, social scientists and physicists were found to track developments through core journals, online search updates, newspapers, conferences, magazines, books, catalogues, and so on (Ellis et al 1993).

"Extracting" is the activity of systematically working through a particular source or sources in order to identify material of interest. As a form of retrospective searching, extracting may be achieved by directly consulting the source, or by indirectly looking through bibliographies, indexes, or online databases. Retrospective searching tends to be labor intensive, and is more likely when there is a need for comprehensive or historical information on a topic.

Note that although Ellis's extracting activity bears the same name as Marchionini's (1995) sub-process of "extract information", the two processes are different. Marchionini (1995) describes extracting thus:

> "There is an inextricable relationship between judging information to be relevant and extracting it for all or part of the problem's solution. ... To extract information, an information seeker applies skills such as reading, scanning, listening, classifying, copying, and storing information. ... As information is extracted, it is manipulated and integrated into the information seeker's knowledge of the domain." (pp. 57-58)

In Ellis' model, "browsing" and "differentiating" are activities separate from "extracting," which is "systematically working through a particular source or sources to identify material of interest" (Ellis 1989, p. 242). On the Web, we expect extracting (in Ellis' sense) to mean systematically working through a selected web site or set of web pages (typically using search engines) in order to search and retrieve material of interest.

Although the Ellis model is based on studies of academics and researchers, the categories of information seeking behaviors may be applicable to other groups of users as well. For example, Sutton's (1994) analysis of the information seeking behavior of attorneys noted that the three stages of legal research he identified (base-level modeling, context sensitive exploration, and disambiguating the space) could be mapped into Ellis's categories of starting, chaining, and differentiating. The identification of categories of information seeking behavior also suggests that information retrieval systems could increase their usefulness by including features that directly support these activities. Ellis thought that hypertext-based systems would have the capabilities to implement these functions (Ellis 1989). If we visualize the World Wide Web as a hyperlinked information system distributed over numerous networks, most of the information seeking behavior categories in Ellis' model are already being supported by capabilities available in common Web browser software. Thus, an individual could begin surfing the Web from one of a few favourite starting pages or sites (starting); follow hypertextual links to related information resources—in both backward and forward linking directions (chaining); scan the Web pages of the sources selected (browsing); bookmark useful sources for future reference and visits (differentiating); subscribe to e-mail based services that alert the user of new information or developments (monitoring); and search a particular source or site for all information on that site on a particular topic (extracting).

5.3.3 Aguilar's Model of Scanning

Research in organization science suggests that it might be helpful to distinguish between four modes of organizational scanning: undirected viewing, conditioned viewing, informal search, and formal search (Aguilar 1967, 1988; Weick and Daft 1983; Daft and Weick 1984).

In undirected viewing, the individual is exposed to information with no specific informational need in mind. The overall purpose is to scan broadly in order to detect signals of change early. Many and varied sources of information are used, and large amounts of information are screened. The granularity of information is coarse, but large chunks of information are quickly dropped from attention. The goal of broad scanning implies the use of a large number of different sources and different types of sources. These sources should supply up-to-date news and provide a variety of points of views. Information on the Web appears to match these requirements well. The Web is a laissez faire information marketplace offering a huge diversity of sources presenting information through a wide range of perspectives. Information often becomes available on the Web more quickly than through print channels. The immediacy, variety and eclecticism of the Web makes it a useful medium for detecting early, weak signals about trends and phenomena that could become significant over time. As a result of undirected viewing, general areas or topics may be identified as being potentially relevant to the organization's goals or tasks, and the individual becomes sensitive to these areas.

In conditioned viewing, the individual directs viewing to information about selected topics or to certain types of information. The overall purpose is to evaluate the significance of the information encountered in order to assess the general nature of the impact on the organization. The individual has isolated a number of areas of potential concern from undirected viewing, and is now sensitized to assess the significance of developments in those areas. The individual wishes to do this assessment in a cost-effective manner, without having to dedicate substantial time and effort in a formal search. The Web can provide a number of ways of obtaining information to make initial sense of emergent phenomena. For example, market research companies, financial institutions, industry associations, and government organizations make available on Web pages their reports, bulletins, and newsletters that analyze ongoing developments in their areas of watch. Some academics, authors, consultants, industry observers, and knowledgeable experts use the Web to share their insights and predictions, and to stimulate further discussion. If the impact is assessed to be sufficiently significant, the scanning mode changes from scanning to searching.

During informal search, the individual actively looks for information to deepen the knowledge and understanding of a specific issue. It is informal in that it involves a relatively limited and unstructured effort. The overall purpose is to gather information to elaborate an issue so as to determine the need for action by the organization. The individual has determined the potential importance of specific developments, and embarks on a search that would build up knowledge about those developments, and deepen understanding of their implications and consequences. In conducting an informal search, the Web can address the requirement for information that is directed at specific issues, but that still does not cost a great deal of time or money to acquire. On the Web, search engines can be used to locate information on Web pages, newsgroups and mailing list discussions. Librarians and specialists have also compiled Web-based directories and lists of focused Web resources. If a need for a decision or response is perceived, the individual dedicates more time and resources to the search.

During formal search, the individual makes a deliberate or planned effort to obtain specific information or information about a specific issue. Search is formal because it is structured according to some pre-established procedure or methodology. The granularity of information is fine, as search is relatively focused to find detailed information. The overall purpose is to systematically retrieve information relevant to an issue in order to provide a basis for developing a decision or course of action. Formal searches could be a part of for example, competitor intelligence gathering, patents searching, market demographics analysis, and issues management. Formal searches prefer information from sources that are perceived to be knowledgeable, or from information systems and services that make efforts to ensure data quality and accuracy.

The individuals in an organization are simultaneously engaged in all four modes of scanning. They view the environment broadly in order to see the big picture as well as to identify areas that require closer attention. At the same time, they are searching for information on particular issues in order to assess their significance and to develop appropriate responses. Etzioni (1967, 1986) compares this "mixed scanning" to a satellite scanning the earth by using both a wide-angle and a zoom lens: "Mixed scanning ... is akin to scanning by satellites with two lenses: wide and zoom. Instead of taking a close look at all formations, a prohibitive task, or only at the spots of previous trouble, the wide lenses provide clues as to places to zoom in, looking for details" (Etzioni 1986, p. 8). Effective environmental scanning requires both general viewing that sweeps the horizon broadly and purposeful searching that probes issues in sufficient detail to provide the kinds of information needed for decision making.

5.3.4 A Behavioral Model of Web Information Seeking

Aguilar's modes of scanning and Ellis's seeking behaviors may be combined and extended in a new behavioral model of information seeking on the Web. The figure below identifies four main modes of information seeking on the Web: undirected viewing, conditioned viewing, informal search, and formal search. For each mode, the figure indicates which information seeking activities or moves are likely to dominate, as suggested by theory.

	Starting	Chaining	Browsing	Differentiating	Monitoring	Extracting
Undirected Viewing	✓	✓				
Conditioned Viewing			✓	✓	✓	
Informal Search				✓	✓	✓
Formal Search					✓	✓

Figure 5.1 Behavioral Model of Information Seeking on the Web

In the undirected viewing mode, while there are broad areas of interest, there is no particular information need that may be articulated explicitly or formally. Instead, the purpose of viewing is precisely to notice significant developments or issues that then generate new information needs. As noted earlier, typical tactics here would involve viewing a diversity of sources, taking advantage of what's easily accessible, and including sources which may not seem at first to be directly related to the work of the organization.

In terms of information seeking moves on the Web, we may anticipate starting and chaining to dominate. Starting occurs when viewers begin their web use on pre-selected default home pages, or when they visit a favorite page or site to begin their viewing (such as news, newspaper, or magazine sites). Chaining occurs when viewers notice items of interest (often by chance), and then follow hypertext links to more information on those items. Forward chaining of the sort just described is the most typical during undirected viewing. Backward chaining is also possible, since search engines can be used to locate other Web pages that point to the site that the user is currently at.

In the conditioned viewing mode, there are specific topic areas that define the scope and substance of the viewer's information needs. The viewer is sensitive to information about these topics, and is able to assess, in a general way, the significance of the information encountered. To increase knowledge on these topics, typical tactics would involve browsing in sources that the viewer knows to contain potentially useful information.

In terms of information seeking moves on the Web, we may anticipate browsing, differentiating, and monitoring to be common. Differentiating occurs as viewers select Web sites or pages that they expect to provide relevant information. Sites may be differentiated based on prior personal visits, or recommendations by others (such as word-of-mouth or published reviews). Differentiated sites are often bookmarked. When visiting differentiated sites, viewers browse the content by looking through tables of contents, site maps, or list of items and categories. Viewers may also monitor highly differentiated sites by returning regularly to browse, or by keeping abreast of new content (through, for example subscribing to newsletters that report new material on the site).

During informal search, the individual has amassed enough knowledge and awareness about a topic to formulate a query to learn more about a specific issue or development. An informal search query is possible because the individual is able to establish some parameters and boundaries to constrain the search. At the same time, the search is limited as the individual does not wish to expend substantial amounts of time and effort. The purpose is to learn more about the issue in order to determine the need for action or response.

In terms of moves on the Web, we may anticipate differentiating, extracting, and monitoring to be typical. Again, informal search is likely to be attempted at a small number of Web sites that have been differentiated by the individual, based on the individual's knowledge about these sites' information relevance, quality, affiliation, dependability, and so on. Extracting is relatively "informal" in the sense that searching would be localized to looking for information within the selected site(s). Extracting is also likely to make use of the basic, 'simple' search features or commands of the local search engine, in order to get at the most important or most recent information, without attempting to be comprehensive. Monitoring becomes more proactive if the individual sets up push channels or software agents that automatically find and deliver information based on selection of keywords or topics.

During formal search, the individual is prepared to invest substantial time and effort in order to gather information that will enable action to be taken. The search may be formal because it follows some pre-established routine or method. The search is also formal because it is now possible, (with the knowledge from informal search and conditioned viewing,) to elaborate the query in detail—specifying the target of inquiry or retrieval according to desired attributes (authors, institutions, dates, document types, and so on). Information gained from formal search is typically used 'formally' as well, for policy making, strategic planning, and other forms of decision making.

In terms of moves on the Web, we may anticipate primarily extracting operations, with some complementary monitoring activity. Formal search makes use of search engines that cover the Web relatively comprehensively, and that provide a powerful set of search features that can focus retrieval. Because the individual wishes not to miss any important information, there is a willingness to spend more time in the search, to learn and use complex search features, and to evaluate the sources that are found in terms of quality or accuracy. Formal search may be two-staged: multi-site searching that identify significant sources is then followed by within-site searching. Within-site searching may involve fairly intensive foraging. Extracting may be supported by monitoring activity, again through services such as Web site alerts, push channels, and software agents, in order to keep up with late-breaking information.

5.4 Web Use Studies

Having presented various theoretical interpretations of how people use the Web to find information, we turn now to recent empirical work in this area. Despite the Web's growing popularity, until recently there were few direct, rigorous studies of Web browsing behavior. One reason for this is the difficulty in obtaining an accurate and complete set of data that describes Web browsing sessions. In order to collect representative data on Web information seeking, Web use logs must be collected on the Web browsing client system. Though Web or proxy server logs provide excellent volume on Web usage, they miss Web access from the browser's local cache which provides most of the Web pages requested via the Back and Forward buttons in Web browsers. As well, other browser features are not recorded in proxy server logs such as bookmarking or printing a Web page.

Catledge and Pitkow (1995) were the first to publish a major study of Web browsing behavior by modifying the source code for a version of XMosaic, the dominant X Windows browser at the time. They configured the browser to generate a client-side log file that showed user navigation strategies and interface selections. They deployed this modified browser to the Computer Science department students who ran Mosaic from X Terminals in the various departmental computing labs at Georgia Tech. Their results were measured using a task-oriented method to determine session boundaries artificially by analyzing the time between each event for all events with a mean time of 9.3 minutes between each user interface event.

> "In order to determine session boundaries, all events that occurred over 25.5 minutes apart were delineated as a new session. This means that most statistically significant events occurred within 1-1/2 standard deviations (25.5 minutes) from the mean. Thus, a new log file was derived that indicated sessions for each user. Interestingly, a consistent third quartile was observed across all users, though we note no clear explanation for this effect." (p.3-4)

Catledge and Pitkow's method is currently the most-commonly used method to begin to determine session boundaries. In most cases, the 25 minute boundary has become standard in estimating user browsing sessions.

Additionally, their study revealed a few unexpected results. Web pages that users bookmarked did not match the most-popular sites visited as a whole from the group. Interestingly, only 2% of Web pages were either saved locally or printed. Of course, these results could be influenced by the users' environment, such as the capabilities of bookmarking in XMosaic or the availability of printers. As for types of Web users in their study, Catledge and Pitkow hypothesized that users categorized as "browsers" spend less time on a Web page than "searchers".

Tauscher and Greenberg (1997a, 1997b) look at another view of individual Web use, by studying the history mechanisms that Web browsers use to manage the recently-requested Web pages browsed in a session of Web information seeking. They also used a modified XMosaic browser to collect Web browsing data for over six weeks from 23 participants. They recorded and examined the rate that Web pages were visited; how users visited old and new Web pages; the distance (in terms of URLs) between repeated Web page visits; the frequency of Web page visits, the extent of browsing in one cluster of Web pages; and repeated sequences of "path-following behavior" (p. 400, 1997a).

Most significantly, they found that 58% of the pages visited during a Web browsing session are re-visits. This results less from any kind of Zipf-like behavior of page visits, but more likely the navigational structure of most Web sites and user preference to use the Web browser's functionality to help navigate rather than the links on a Web page. Furthermore, Tauscher and Greenberg reveal that overall, users also only access a few pages frequently (60% once, and 19% twice) and browse in very small clusters of pages. They contend that Web browsing activity is a "*recurring system*... where users predominantly repeat activities they had invoked before, while still selecting new actions from the many that are possible" (p 400, 1997a from Greenberg, 1993). Through post-study interviews they found that people stated that they revisited Web pages because

> "the information contained by them changes; they wish to explore the page further; the page has a special purpose (e.g. search engine, home page); they are authoring a page; or the page is on a path to another revisited page." (p. 400, 1997a)

Tauscher and Greenberg identified seven Web browsing patterns: first-time visits to a cluster of pages; revisits to pages; page authoring (where the subject used Reload to view the newly modified page); use of web-based applications; hub-and-spoke visits (navigating to each new page from around a central page); a guided tour where links guide navigation through the Web pages; and a depth-first search where link paths are followed without returning to the first page in some cases.

Like Catledge and Pitkow, they agree that the "Back" button is heavily used and that it is a good predictor of what Web pages are revisited. This is important in light of their finding that there are no strong repeatable linear patterns of browsing among Web pages. However, by comparing the different browsing history mechanisms, Tauscher and Greenberg discovered "the stack-based prediction method prevalent in commercial browsers is inferior to the simpler approach of showing the last few recently visited URLs with duplicates removed" (p. 97, 1997b). They assert that an improved history mechanism helps with Web navigation, decrease searching for previously-viewed pages, and reduce "cognitive and physical burdens, as pages can be returned to with little effort, and users can see where they have been" (p. 399, 1997a). We can see how even the smallest improvement in a Web browser could substantially change how Web user seek information.

Crovella and Bestavros (1996) also analyze Web usage by looking at the network traffic generated by Web browser users. They collected over half a million Web page requests using an instrumented NSCA Mosaic client, again similar to Catledge and Pitkow's 1995 study. Their analysis was primarily on the busiest hours of use to provide a basis of comparison to past studies of network traffic. They found that Web transfer times were noticeably heavy-tailed in that smaller Web documents were retrieved much more quickly than larger Web documents, but not consistent by size as a power law would indicate. This might indicate that client caches impact performance more than expected, or simply that Web users select more shorter Web documents. Furthermore, this might also indicate a Zipfian tendency to select files that require the least effort (wait time) to retrieve or read. Moreover, they contend "that silent times also may be heavily-tailed, primarily due to the influence of user 'think time'" (p. 9), indicating that any technical changes in Web architecture should not impact this self-similarity as its cause is mostly by Web users.

Overall, Crovella and Bestavros conclude that this network traffic does exhibit self-similar behavior consistent with other traffic models based on Web document sizes; the effects of Web page caching; user preferences in file transfer; the effect of user "think time"; and the overlap of many requests by the local area network serving the Web documents. They found that Web traffic exhibited self-similar characteristics over four orders of magnitude, from small groups of pages to very large collections. This implies that the same activities that cause this self-similarity occur regularly and therefore that Web information seeking has continuous similarities of use among different users and with different Web technologies.

Pitkow (1997) provides a comprehensive overview of many studies of Web characterizations. He samples from the body of research on studying Web server logs, Proxy Server logs, client trace logs, and results tabulated from Web search engines. He notes some of the overall findings, most notably from a Bibliometric standpoint that file requests follow a Zipfian distribution and that for site popularity, "roughly 25% of the servers account for over 85% of the traffic" (p. 6). As for specific Information Seeking activities, the average reading time per Web page averages about 30 seconds, with a mean of 7 seconds, and a standard deviation of 100 seconds.

More recently, Huberman et. al. (1998) note regularities in Web user surfing patterns they call the "law of surfing, ... that determines the probability distribution of the depth—that is, the number of page a user visits within a Web site" (p. 95). Their model starts with a model of probability for the number of links a user might follow on a Web site. Next they calculate a value for the current page and relate this value to the next page accessed that leads to examining the cost of continuing surfing. When the cost of moving to the next Web page is more than its expected value, the user stops Web surfing. They analyzed data collected from a sample of AOL (America Online) users for each of five days, a huge amount of data. One day alone (December 5, 1997) yielded 23,692 AOL users who surfed 3,247,054 total Web pages from 1,090,168 unique Web pages. This amount of data is staggering compared to previous studies of Web use.

To contrast this user-centric data, Huberman, et. al. also examined Web server logs of the Xerox external Web site to obtain a constrained set of Web page requests. They also used "cookies" to help track the paths of individual users as they surfed through the Web site. Overall, they found a "strong fit" to their law of surfing model which was consistent through each day of the study. By applying this model along with a spreading activation algorithm, they can predict the number of requests for each Web page in a Web site. As they point out, this has implications for e-commerce applications and Web site organization, not to mention a more robust understanding of overall information seeking activities concerning the Web.

Like others, they also found a Zipf-like distribution of Web page hits for total Web page use, which echoes other studies in showing that "surfing patterns on the Web display strong statistical regularities that can be described by a universal law. In addition, the success of the model points to the existence of utility maximizing behavior underlying surfing" (p. 97). These findings do not signal the end of new findings about Web information seeking, but do establish a firm foundation to build upon in further research.

5.5 Conclusion

This chapter has explored different avenues of research that model or attempt to understand information seeking on the Web. The first was information foraging which compares the seeking and acquisition of information to evolutionary biological activity, namely the hunting and gathering behavior of animals in their quest for food and sustenance. The second was bibliometrics which views the Web as a huge citation network and approaches the phenomenon of information seeking from a mathematical perspective. The third was to investigate various user browsing models; two of which were combined and extended as a new behavioral model of information seeking on the Web.

The purpose of illustrating these various perspectives was to highlight the complexity and richness of Web information seeking. As academics attempt to understand and explicate how humans find information on the Web, new approaches and viewpoints are likely to be developed. Our overview of recent Web use studies illustrates the fervor of activity taking place in this area of study. This sets the stage for the next chapter where we present our empirical work towards understanding and describing Web information seeking behavior.

Chapter 6: Understanding Organizational Web Use

This chapter presents findings from a recent investigation by the authors of how knowledge workers in organizations utilize the Web to seek external information as part of their daily work (Choo, Detlor, & Turnbull, 2000). Though other studies of Web use presented in the last chapter cover a broad range of Web users, most Web usage studies tend to concentrate on students and home users (Kehoe, Pitkow & Rogers, 1998). In contrast, the study presented here focuses exclusively on corporate Web users who utilize the Web as an integral part of their daily work. All participants in our study used the Web to carry out various work-related activities and were connected to the Internet through continuous leased-line access and relatively high-powered machines. The purpose of our research was to focus on these "work-oriented" Web users in the hope that we would be able to understand and predict trends and patterns in organizational Web use.

6.1 Study Introduction

The study began by recruiting participation from corporations with guarantees of confidentiality and promising to deliver an anonymized report of overall Web usage to compare and contrast individual and inter-organizational Web use. In some cases, individual analysis of participant Web use was also delivered which included recommendations of new Web sites to visit and tips on how to utilize the Web browser more effectively.

Since participants were required who were adept and comfortable with using information technology in their daily work practice, volunteers were recruited through solicitations at various information technology-related workshops and conferences; calls for participation via technology-focused listservs; and direct e-mail contact with colleagues and associates at large technology-oriented companies. In total, 52 participants from nine different companies participated in various stages of the project. Specifically, the nine participating companies comprised one large international bank, two large utility companies, one large computer hardware and systems solution provider, one large magazine publisher; one medium-sized University research library, one medium-sized marketing agency, and two small software consulting firms.

The participants were predominantly a mix of information technology specialists and managers from various departments: 23 held IT technologist/analyst job titles; 15 were managers; 12 held research/marketing/consultant positions; and 2 were administrative support staff. Only a small percentage of participants were novices to the World Wide Web; most routinely used the Web as part of their daily work.

Once permission was obtained to study an organization, an initial briefing for all participants was conducted at each organizational work site. At these briefings, participants were told of the purpose and confidential nature of the study, as well as what their personal involvement would entail. At each briefing, participants were given the opportunity to ask any questions they might have.

At the conclusion of each session, a questionnaire was distributed for participants to complete. During this time, individual appointments were scheduled to install custom-built Web tracking software on each participant's machine. During the installation, participants were given a walk-through of how the software works and shown how to view the log files that recorded their personal Web usage activity. Note that each participant was shown how to disable this monitoring, if the participant so chose. After a ten business day monitoring period, a follow-up interview was conducted with each participant to discuss significant episodes of Web activity identified in the individual tracking logs.

The triangulation of a diverse set of data collection and analysis methods, namely the questionnaires, Web tracking software, and one-on-one interviews, allowed us to obtain a rich understanding of organizational Web use. The following sections describe the application of these methods and their results.

6.2 Questionnaires

The questionnaire instrument was adapted from one devised by Auster & Choo (1993) in a study on the environmental scanning behavior of Chief Executive Officers in two Canadian industries. Eleven information sources were selected from Auster & Choo's original list of sixteen sources; these were based on the sources used in past research on how people acquire information about the external business environment (Aguilar, 1967; Keegan, 1974; Culnan, 1983; Preble et. al., 1988; Daft et. al., 1988). These 11 information sources plus the World Wide Web were grouped into a classification scheme of information sources as proposed by Auster & Choo (1993). Table 6.1 outlines the various categories and information sources used in the questionnaire instrument. External sources were ones concentrated outside a company's organizational structure, while internal sources were ones available within an organization only. People sources were ones which communicated information personally, while non-people sources were ones which communicated information to broad audiences or through formalized, group communication activities.

Information Source Categories	Information Source
External People Sources	Customers
	Business Associates
	Competitors
External Non-People Sources	World Wide Web
	Radio/TV/Newspapers
	External Reports/Studies
Internal People Sources	Managers/Supervisors
	Colleagues in same dept
	Colleagues in other dept
Internal Non-People Sources	Internal Reports/Studies
	Internal Memos
	Internal Library/Info Center

Table 6.1 Information Sources Used

The questionnaire instrument was composed of two broad sections. The first dealt with the perception and use of information sources by participants. The idea was to capture and measure participant perception of the World Wide Web compared to other information sources used in typical work activity. In this section, participants were asked to rate their frequency of usage of each of the twelve sources, and to give their perceptions of each source in terms of its quality and accessibility.

The first question of the questionnaire asked users the following question:

> 1) How *frequently* do you use each of the following information sources to identify trends and events outside your organization?

Participants responded by rating each information source on an incremental scale with six categories: 1: never; 2: < once a year; 3: few times a year; 4: >= once a month; 5: >= once a week; 6: >= once a day.

The next two questions of the questionnaire asked users to describe the quality of each source:

> 2) How *relevant* is the information from each source in identifying trends and events outside of your organization?
>
> 3) How *reliable* is the information from each source in identifying trends and events outside of your organization?

Here, relevant information was defined as information that was needed and useful with respect to the goals and activities of the organization, and measured on an ascending Likert scale of 1 to 5 (1 being "very irrelevant" and 5 being "very relevant"). Reliable information was defined as being authoritative and dependable—information that was personally trusted. It was also measured on an increasing Likert scale of 1 to 5 (1 being "very unreliable" and 5 being "very reliable"). The response scores from these two sources were summed into an index of the perceived source quality of each source.

The following two questions asked users to describe the accessibility of each source:

> 4) How much of your *time and effort* is needed to approach, contact, or locate each information source?
>
> 5) After contacting or locating the source, how *easy* is it to get the desired information from that source?

For each of the 12 information sources, participants indicated their responses to these questions on ascending scales. The fourth question used a Likert scale of 1 to 5 (1 being a "very great deal" and 5 being "very little). The fifth question used a Likert scale of 1 to 5 (1 being "very hard" and 5 being "very easy"). The response scores from these two questions were summed into an index of the perceived accessibility of each source.

The second section of the questionnaire gathered participant background information to generate user profiles of the participant base. Ten questions were asked in this section. These polled the job titles and functional departments in which the users worked, the familiarity of the participants with computers and World Wide Web technology, and the number of hours worked and spent seeking information on the Web by each respondent.

Again, this questionnaire was administered at the participants' workplaces during the first visit to each site. Further, through informal conversations during the visits, we were able to develop a general impression of the style and scope of each participant's Web use.

In terms of findings, the questionnaire provided insights into the frequency and accessibility of the World Wide Web in relation to other information sources typically used by organizational participants in their day-to-day activities. Figure 6.1 shows the mean frequency with which the participants used each source. A high numerical score indicates a frequently used source.

The *World Wide Web* was the second-most frequently used source (mean=5.29, sd=0.75), closely behind the most frequently used source of *Radio/TV/Newspapers* (mean=5.35, sd=0.84). From these two highly-rated sources, our findings indicated that participants heavily frequent external non-people sources to seek information. As found with other scanning studies, people sources ranked favorably well. Similar to Auster and Choo's (1993) findings, our study showed a preference of internal-people sources, such as *Colleagues in the Same Department* and *Managers*, over external-people sources such as *Customers* and *Competitors*.

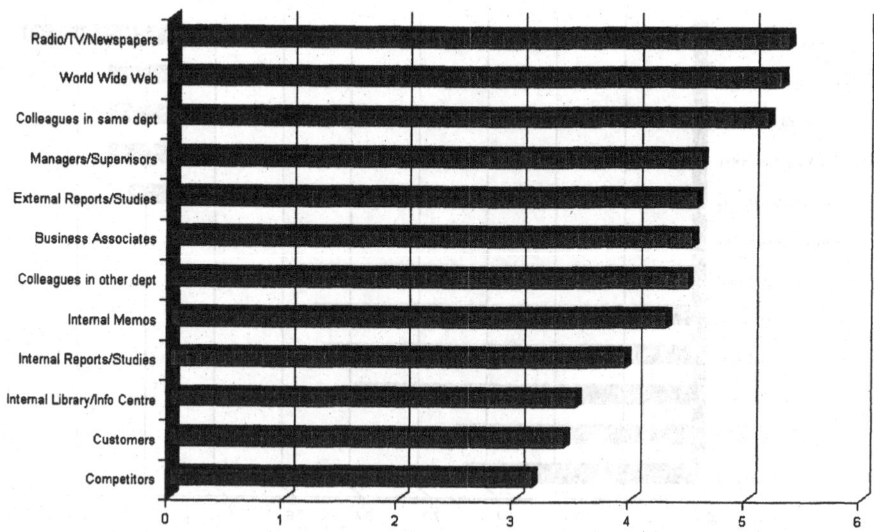

1: never; 2: < once a year; 3: few times a year; 4: >= once a month; 5: >= once a week; 6: >= once a day

Figure 6.1 Frequency of Information Source Usage

Figure 6.2 shows how participants perceived the quality of each information source. The higher the numerical score, the higher the perceived quality of the source.

The *World Wide Web* (mean=8.12; sd=1.25) tied with *External Reports/Studies* (mean=8.12; sd=1.25) and *Business Associates* (mean=8.12; sd=1.29) as the second-most highly-rated source in terms of relevance and reliability. The most highly-rated source in terms of quality was *Colleagues in the Same Department* (mean=8.37; sd=1.39). All of the second-rated sources are in the external source category, contradicting a trend found in the Auster & Choo (1993) study for a preference for internal sources in terms of quality information. Interestingly, two of the other external sources of *Customers* and *Competitors* had the lowest mean quality scores implying that information from these sources is viewed as less relevant and reliable.

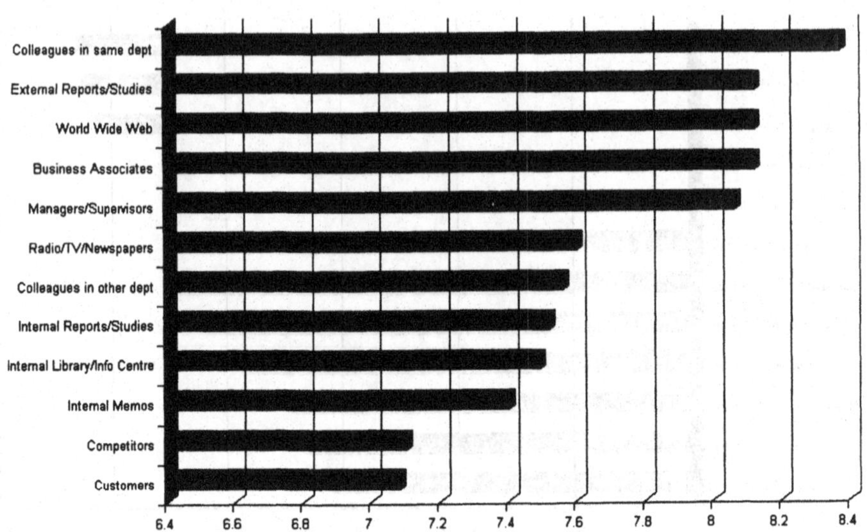

Figure 6.2 Perceived Source Quality

The frequency of using each information source was correlated with the calculated perceived source quality index and is shown in Table 6.2 below. There is no significant relationship between World Wide Web use and source quality. However, the table shows that source use was significantly correlated with source quality (p<.05) for *Customers, Competitors, External Reports/Studies, Colleagues in the Same Department, Internal Report/Studies, Internal Memos* and the *Internal Library/Information Center*. The correlation coefficients range between 0.3 and 0.4, the two highest occurring for *Internal Reports/Studies* and the *Internal Library/Information Center*.

Information Source	Pearson's r
Customers	0.33645[b]
Business Associates	0.0791
Competitors	0.32438[b]
World Wide Web	0.1105
Radio/TV/Newspapers	0.2332[a]
External Reports/Studies	0.34355[b]
Managers/Supervisors	0.25891[a]
Colleagues in same dept	0.29746[b]
Colleagues in other dept	0.2517[a]
Internal Reports/Studies	0.40172[c]
Internal Memos	0.2964[b]
Internal Library/Info Center	0.43722[c]

[a]p<=.10; [b]p<=.05; [c]p<=.01

Table 6.2 Correlation between Frequency of Source Use and Perceived Source Quality

Figure 6.3 shows how participants perceived the accessibility of each information source. The higher the numerical score, the higher the perceived accessibility of the source.

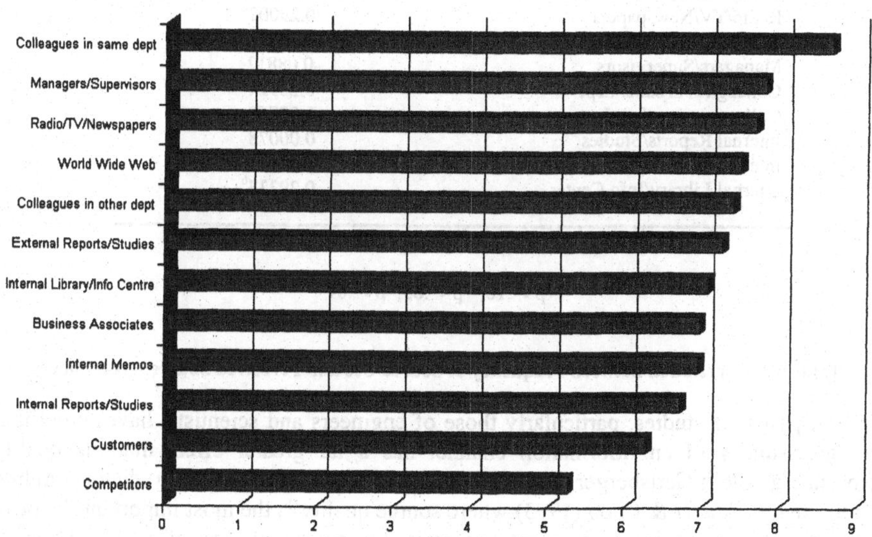

Figure 6.3 Perceived Source Accessibility

The *World Wide Web* was the fourth highly-rated source in terms of accessibility (mean=7.46; sd=2.02). The most highly-rated source was *Colleagues in the Same Department* (mean=8.65, sd=1.34), followed by *Managers/Supervisors* (mean=7.77, sd=1.28) and *Radio/TV/Newspapers* (mean=7.65, sd=1.71). These results indicate a mixed preference of external non-people and internal people sources in terms of accessibility. The least accessible sources were external people sources such as *Customers* and *Competitors*, which supports a similar finding as described in the Auster & Choo (1993) study.

The frequency of using each information source was correlated with the calculated perceived source accessibility index and is shown in Table 6.3. There is no significant relationship between World Wide Web use and source accessibility. The table shows that source use was significantly correlated with source accessibility ($p<.05$) for *Business Associates*, *Radio/TV/Newspapers*, *External Reports/Studies* and the *Internal Library/Information Center*. The correlation coefficients range between 0.3 and 0.4; the two highest were for *Business Associates* and *External Reports/Studies*.

Information Source	Pearson's r
Customers	0.08626
Business Associates	0.31116[b]
Competitors	0.24334[a]
World Wide Web	0.23356[a]
Radio/TV/Newspapers	0.29007[b]
External Reports/Studies	0.36006[c]
Managers/Supervisors	-0.08812
Colleagues in same dept	0.23924[a]
Colleagues in other dept	0.02769
Internal Reports/Studies	0.00078
Internal Memos	-0.10611
Internal Library/Info Center	0.29237[b]

[a]p<=.10; [b]p<=.05; [c]p<=.01

Table 6.3 Correlation between Frequency of Source Use and Perceived Source Accessibility

Several past user studies, particularly those of engineers and scientists, have found that the accessibility of an information channel has a far greater effect than its quality (Rosenberg, 1967; Gertsberger & Allen, 1968; and Allen, 1977). A contradictory finding is reported by Auster & Choo (1993) where source quality is the most important factor in explaining source use in environmental scanning by senior managers of organizations. In terms of our study focusing on Web use, which has representatives from both population groups– namely information technologists and corporate managers, we find no evidence of a significant relationship between source quality or source accessibility with the frequency of World Wide Web use.

We offer two plausible explanations for this finding. The first is that participants use the Web frequently, not because of its perceived quality or accessibility, but because it is presumed by users to be a source which *actually does* contain the information desired. The second is that users have *no choice* but to use the World Wide Web to seek information. That is, they need information which they assume is not reasonably obtainable from any other available information source. These explanations hint at the increasing reliance on Web use in the workplace.

In terms of the profile of the participant base, the users were found to be avid Web users with a high degree of comfort with computer technology. On average, Web usage accounted for 18% of the participant's work day. That is, for an average work day of 9.06 hours, participants used the Web for an average of 1.48 hours. Further, participants rated themselves between the "intermediate" and "intermediate/expert" levels in terms of both their computer background and Web expertise.

6.3 WebTracker

The second tool used in this study, WebTracker, was a tool for gathering Web browsing metrics developed for the Faculty of Information Studies at the University of Toronto. WebTracker was designed because of the inaccuracy of using Proxy or Firewall servers (Pitkow, 1997) to study micro moves when using the Web and the lack of current, publicly-available browser code for the Windows environment to instrument a browser. Previous studies used XMosaic (Catledge & Pitkow, 1995 and Cuhna, Bestavros, & Corvella, 1995) on UNIX systems, but as our study focused on corporate users who predominantly worked on Microsoft Windows platforms, we required a different tool. Despite the presence of newer, Windows-specific Web browser source code from the Mozilla project (Eich et. al, 1998) we felt installing a new, instrumented browser would not allow us to observe the actual behavior of users. With our software, users could simply work on the Web as they did before, with their usual technical configurations and browser preferences including bookmarks and toolbar choices.

WebTracker runs on Windows 3.1, Windows 95, Windows NT 3.5x and 4, and Windows 98 environments. It is a 32-bit application with standard Windows controls and behaviors. Moreover, WebTracker runs like any typical Windows application, using normal install procedures, standard systems processes, and can therefore be uninstalled easily as well. Primarily, WebTracker watches the Web browser and collects menu choices, button bar selections, and keystroke actions. These actions are associated with the open Web page (URL), tagged with a date-time stamp and recorded in a daily log file. This tracking method enables log analysis that can essentially reconstruct move-by-move how participants looked for information. Figure 6.4 displays the log file format:

User ID	Browser Action	Date-Time Stamp	URL	Web Page Title

Figure 6.4 WebTracker Log File Format

The UserID field is taken from the entry in WebTracker via the User Identification dialog while Browser Action is taken from a code file installed in the WebTracker directory that is specific to the browser version on the participant's machine. The Date-Time Stamp is taken from the system clock and the URL is the actual protocol and address of the page loaded into the Web browser. Finally, the Web Page Title is taken from the HTML <TITLE> tag in each Web page displayed by the browser in its Title Bar.

WebTracker was designed to collect the most relevant browser actions, mainly interaction using buttons, menus, and the keys that control the Web browser functionality. Mouse clicks are only recorded when a link is selected on the current Web page. Tables 6.4, 6.5, and 6.6 show all of the different actions logged. Note that scroll bar use and certain menu functions were specifically not implemented but could be added for future studies. Browser actions are recorded in an ASCII text, tab-delimited log file named with the system date using a ".TXT" extension (e.g. 110198.TXT). For each day of use, WebTracker creates a separate log file. These files can be viewed with any text editor application.

Object	Action	User Activity
Button	Back	The Back button on the Navigation Toolbar
Button	Forward	The Forward button on the Navigation Toolbar
Button	Reload	The Reload button used to reload the Web page
Button	Home	The Home button on the Navigation Toolbar
Button	Search	The Search button on the Navigation Toolbar
Button	Guide	The Netscape button on the Navigation Toolbar
Button	Print	The Print button on the Navigation Toolbar
Button	Security	The Security button on the Navigation Toolbar
Button	Stop	The Stop button on the Navigation Toolbar

Table 6.4 Button Browser Actions Recorded by WebTracker

Object	Action	User Activity
Key	Edit bookmark	Ctrl + B to open the Bookmark file
Key	Copy	Ctrl + C to copy selected text onto the Windows Clipboard
Key	Add bookmark	Ctrl + D to add the current Web page to the bookmark file
Key	History	Ctrl + H to open the browser's History window
Key	New window	Ctrl + N to open another browser window
Key	Open page	Ctrl + O to enter a URL to open
Key	Print	Ctrl + P to print the URL
Key	Reload	Ctrl + R to reload the Web page
Key	Save as	Ctrl + S to save the Web page locally
Key	Page source	Ctrl + U to view the HTML of the Web page
Key	Back	Alt + ← (left arrow key)
Key	Forward	Alt + → (right arrow key)
Key	Stop	The Esc key to stop the Web page from loading
Key	Page up	The PageUp key to move through the Web page
Key	Page down	The PageDown key to move through the Web page

Table 6.5 Key Browser Actions Recorded by WebTracker

Object	Action	User Activity
Menu	File new	File - New to open another Browser window
Menu	File open	File - Open Page.. to enter a URL to access/open a local file
Menu	Save as	File - Save As.... To save the Web page locally
Menu	Send page	File - Send Page... to send a page
Menu	Open page	File - Open Page to open the page in the browser's Editor
Menu	Print preview	File - Print Preview
Menu	Print	File - Print...
Menu	Edit copy	Edit - Copy to copy selected text onto the Clipboard
Menu	Select all	Edit - Select All
Menu	Find in page	Edit - Find in Page...
Menu	Search internet	Edit - Search Internet...
Menu	Search directory	Edit - Search Directory...
Menu	Reload	View - Reload
Menu	Refresh	View - Refresh
Menu	Page source	View - Page Source
Menu	Back	Go - Back
Menu	Forward	Go - Forward
Menu	Go home	Go - Home to return to the user-specified Home page
Menu	Add bookmarks	Communicator - Bookmarks - Add Bookmark
Menu	Edit bookmarks	Communicator - Bookmarks - Edit Bookmarks
Menu	History	Communicator - Tools - History

Table 6.6 Menu Browser Actions Recorded by WebTracker

During the initial stages of the study, we physically visited the users' individual work environments and installed WebTracker to run at system startup as a minimized application. By developing WebTracker as a standalone, typical Windows application, participants could "see" it running and have WebTracker available for suspending or viewing their usage logs. After verifying that WebTracker was functional, we again explained how WebTracker worked by showing the few user functions available. These included the option of turning WebTracker logging off by selecting the "Web Tracker is

INACTIVE" radio button. As shown in Figure 6.5, the current WebTracker log file can be viewed by selecting Today's Data from the View menu.

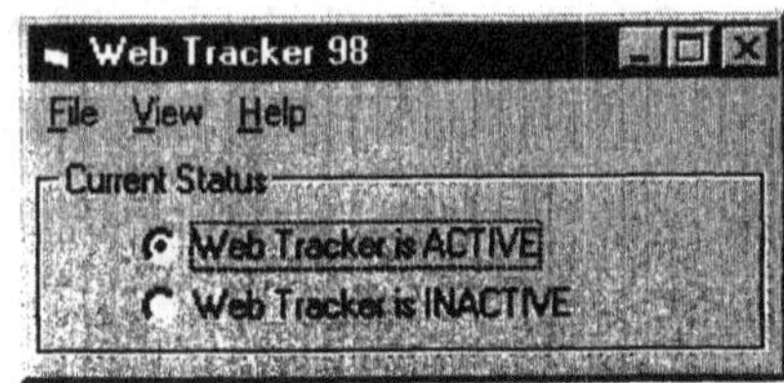

Figure 6.5 WebTracker Main Window

Next, we showed each participant how to enter a User Identification string that is appended to each entry in the WebTracker log file (see Fig. 6.6). This is the only actual interaction with WebTracker that is required by the participant. Once configured to load at system startup as minimized, WebTracker ran without any additional intervention for the duration of the study.

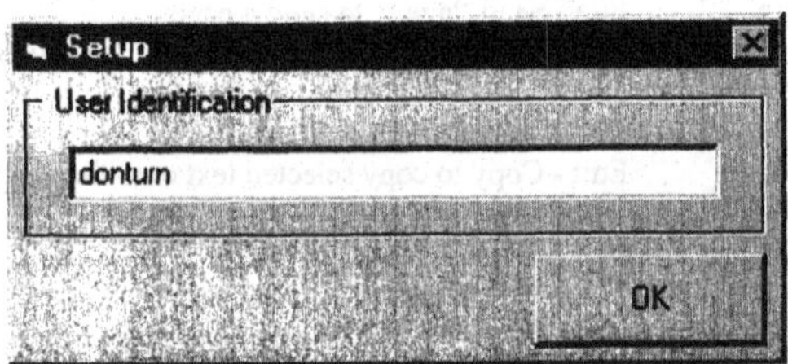

Figure 6.6 WebTracker Setup Window

As shown in Figure 6.7 below, the Expanded window mode also allows the user to make logging either active or inactive and adjust the interval at which the Web browser is polled for data. This interval can be adjusted from 1 to 5 seconds to accommodate various system speeds, eliminate double log entries, and prevent interference with other client applications. Figure 6.7 also displays a Message History box which shows codes that correspond to the user action in the Web browser. In this example, a URL http://witanweb.iit.nrc.ca/www/AuthorFAQ is being selected by the user from a link on the current Web page and noted in the Last Event display box as the "LINK_TO" activity.

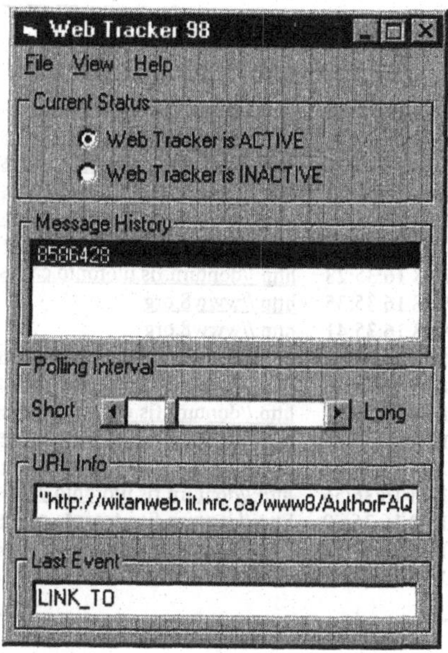

Figure 6.7 WebTracker Expanded Window

Once WebTracker had been demonstrated, participants were encouraged to use their Web browsers as they normally would. From that point on, their Web use was collected into log files.

Table 6.7 shows a short, but typical set of log entries that WebTracker might record when using a Web browser. In the example, the Web browser was started at 4:29 p.m. on November 1, 1998. The "Test Site Home" Web page was accessed, as it was the default browser Home Page. From there, a link from that page was followed to the "Test Site Page 1" Web page, and then the Back button was clicked on the Navigation toolbar to return to the previous page. Next, this page was bookmarked. While on the "Test Site Home" page, the Ctrl-O keystroke was used to open the Open Page dialog box where the URL "www8.org" was entered. The "WWW8" page was loaded, then the Back button was selected while on that page, returning to the previous page "Test Site Home". Next, this page was subsequently saved as a file on the local hard drive by using the File - Save As… menu command. Next, the "Test Site Print Me" link was selected, opening that page in the browser. The page was printed using the File - Print… menu command and then the Back toolbar button was selected to return to the "Test Site Home" page. The Reload toolbar button was selected, the page was reloaded into the browser window, and finally the browser was closed at 4:41 p.m.

User ID	Browser Action	Date and Time	URL Visited	Web Page Title
DT	STARTUP	11/1/98 16:29:44		
DT	LINK_TO	11/1/98 16:34:59	http://donturn.fis.utoronto.ca/test/index.html	Test Site Home
DT	LINK_TO	11/1/98 16:35:08	http://donturn.fis.utoronto.ca/test/test1.html	Test Site Page 1
DT	Button back	11/1/98 16:35:09	http://donturn.fis.utoronto.ca/test/test1.html	Test Site Page 1
DT	LINK_TO	11/1/98 16:35:17	http://donturn.fis.utoronto.ca/test/index.html	Test Site Home
DT	Key add bookmark	11/1/98 16:35:17	http://donturn.fis.utoronto.ca/test/index.html	Test Site Home
DT	Key open page	11/1/98 16:35:28	http://donturn.fis.utoronto.ca/test/index.html	Test Site Home
DT	LINK_TO	11/1/98 16:35:35	http://www8.org	WWW8
DT	Key back	11/1/98 16:35:41	http://www8.org	WWW8
DT	LINK_TO	11/1/98 16:35:44	http://donturn.fis.utoronto.ca/test/index.html	Test Site Home
DT	Menu save as	11/1/98 16:35:46	http://donturn.fis.utoronto.ca/test/index.html	Test Site Home
DT	LINK_TO	11/1/98 16:36:11	http://donturn.fis.utoronto.ca/test/printme.html	Test Site Print
DT	Menu print	11/1/98 16:36:15	http://donturn.fis.utoronto.ca/test/printme.html	Test Site Print
DT	Button back	11/1/98 16:36:46	http://donturn.fis.utoronto.ca/test/printme.html	Test Site Print
DT	LINK_TO	11/1/98 16:36:56	http://donturn.fis.utoronto.ca/test/index.html	Test Site Home
DT	Button reload	11/1/98 16:36:59	http://donturn.fis.utoronto.ca/test/index.html	Test Site Home
DT	LINK_TO	11/1/98 16:37:14	http://donturn.fis.utoronto.ca/test/index.html	Test Site Home
DT	SHUTDOWN	11/1/98 16:41:11		

Table 6.7 WebTracker Log View

After the ten business day tracking period, we visited each user site and uninstalled WebTracker, while collecting individual log files for analysis.

The tracking logs from participants were collected and analysed. Part of this process involved the delineation of Web use sessions utilizing a 30-minute gap heuristic developed by Catledge and Pitkow (1994). A session refers to constant Web use without gaps in time over a 30 minute period. The intent of this timeframe boundary is to provide a comparative measure of how many times participants use the Web to seek information. Gaps of over 30 minutes between Web use are assumed to indicate that participants were otherwise occupied, away from their desks, or utilizing their computers for other purposes.To facilitate the process of identifying such gaps, log files were reviewed manually to find obvious session boundaries and remove invalid ones, such as when a Web page access was attempted and Internet access was temporarily not available.

Table 6.8 below displays the overall statistics of Web use behavior exhibited by the participants. Note that the average number of sessions per day was fairly low—slightly over two sessions per day. The session per day measure might indicate how often a participant went to the Web to answer a question, or complete a work-related activity using Web resources.

While some sessions were lengthy, some lasting up to 3 hours in duration, most were no more than 40 minutes long. The total number of Web pages visited by each participant was high; this can be primarily attributed to participants using search engines to branch out to many different possible sites and also suggests how wide participant information needs can vary.

The fewer number of unique sites or domains visited points to the frequent use of familiar, useful Web sites by participants. As Web portals increase in popularity, this total may decrease due to a portal's relative homogeneity of linked Web pages, such as news pages from one particular wire service.

The A.M. percentage column is simply an attempt to discover if participants used the Web more in the mornings (i.e. to read morning news) or in the afternoons. No wide difference in time of use was noted, with a slight preference for A.M. use.

	# of Hours	# of Days	# of Hours per Day	# of Sessions	# of Sessions per Day	# of URLs	# of Unique Domains	AM %
Total	605.87	319	61.92	676	73.8	17634	1616.76	—
Average	16.83	8.86	1.72	18.78	2.05	489.83	44.91	54.24%

Table 6.8 Total Time of Web Use

Table 6.9 lists some examples of typical Web usage activity exhibited by the participants. Participant number 8 represents an average user in terms of the frequency and diversity of Web sites visited over the data collection time. Participant number 16 represents a morning Web newspaper reader— his results show a significant amount of total Web use during the morning hours with a slightly lower than average total number of unique domains. A very small number of Web sites are visited per day, indicating that a few domains (in this case, newspaper Web sites) are heavily accessed, with only occasional forays into the rest of the Web. Participant number 19 represents an active Web user. In reality, for this participant, locating and tracking down information is a primary part of her work responsibilities. As a result, her findings indicate a large number of URLs and unique domains visited, above average number of hours used, and multiple Web sessions.

Participant Number	# of Hours	# of Days	# of Hours per Day	# of Sessions	# of Sessions per Day	# of URLs	# of Unique Domains	AM %
#8	19.31	9	2.15	10	1.11	454	50	31.72%
#16	7.28	9	0.81	8	0.89	83	9	87.95%
#19	65.81	17	3.87	57	3.35	2313	136	54.69%

Table 6.9 Participant Examples of Web Use

In terms of search engine use, participants showed a strong preference to utilize a common set of popular search engines with a select few being used more frequently to find information on the Web. Table 6.10 below displays the frequency with which various search engines were used by participants during the tracking period. The Total

Visits column includes re-visits to a Web page for a particular query when a participant entered a query term, followed a link, then revisited the query page to follow another link. The column also incorporates visits to the Microsoft and Netscape home pages, as these pages were used as default startup pages for some participants, and used, to look for information off the Web.

Search Engine	Total Visits	Total Visits %
1) Lycos	9	0.46%
2) Looksmart	16	0.81%
3) MSN	30	1.52%
4) Hotbot	36	1.82%
5) Excite	64	3.24%
6) Metacrawler	78	3.95%
7) Dogpile	98	4.96%
8) Infoseek	199	10.08%
9) AltaVista	256	12.97%
10) Yahoo	316	16.01%
11) Netscape	408	20.67%
12) Microsoft	464	23.51%

Table 6.10 Search Engine Visits

It is interesting to note that during the data collection period, the Netscape home page did provide a search function, enabling searching directly from a participant's default home page. The Microsoft site however, provided a Search function via another Web page, and in some cases, participants used this search page to search the entire Web while in reality they were searching the Microsoft Web site only.

Figure 6.8 below shows a distribution of search engine use sorted by frequency. Overall, there are three rough clusters of search engines used by the participants, clusters A, B and C. Similar to a Bradford-like clustering as overviewed in Chapter 5, there are more infrequently used search engines (Cluster A), less than half that moderately used search engines in cluster B, and very frequently used (in addition to being the default homepage for less than half of the participants) cluster C.

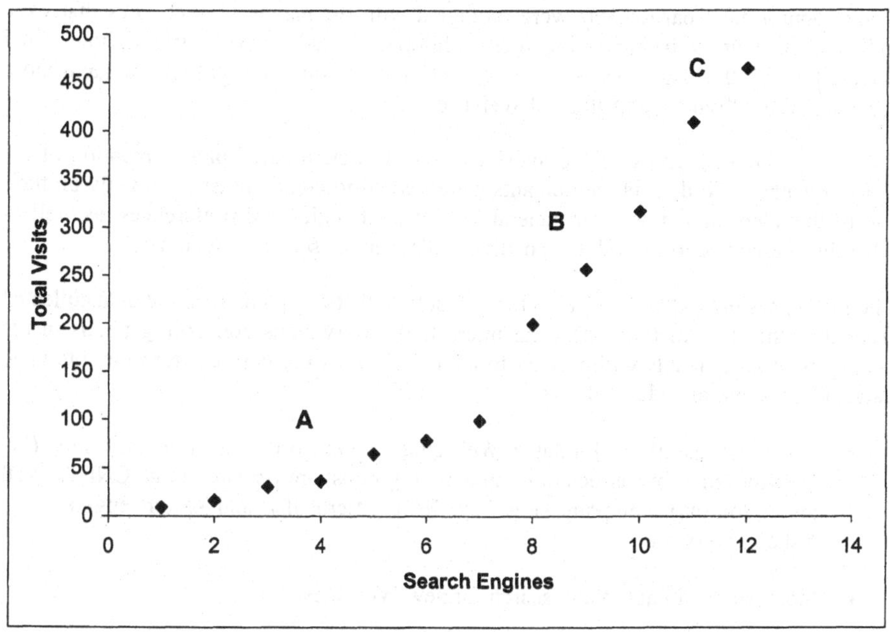

Figure 6.8 Search Engine Use Distribution

6.4 Interviews

After the two week monitoring period, participant logs were collected by the researchers. The logs were analyzed to determine significant episodes of activity which were i) recurring events and ii) events that took a relatively substantial amount of time in relation to other Web activities in the tracking logs. After this analysis, one-on-one interviews were conducted with 33 of the 52 participants to obtain a better understanding of the significant episodes identified in the logs.

The interviews served two broad purposes. The first was to understand better the context behind individual Web usage activity recorded in the tracking logs. The interview format was based on the principles of the Critical Incident Technique (Flanagan 1954), in which the 'incident' to be studied should be recent, sufficiently complete, and its effects or consequences sufficiently clear. In the interviews, participants described two 'critical incidents' of Web information seeking and use in reply to the following question:

> "Please try to recall a recent instance in which you found important information on the Web, information that led to some significant action or decision. Would you please describe that incident for me in enough detail so that I can visualize the situation?"

Where appropriate, participants were prompted with the names of Web sites that were indicated in their WebTracker log files. Additional questions were asked about noted regularities in the log files as well as isolated, unique log entries to gain more understanding of typical and atypical Web use.

The second broad purpose of the interviews was to obtain participant perception of the Web in general. To do this, participants were invited to comment more broadly on their use of the Web, including their general Web use strategies and preferences, as well as what they perceived to be both the positive and negative aspects of Web use.

The interviews proved to be a rich interview source that complemented the data collected from the other two methods. Several interesting observations concerning trends in the behaviors of participants with respect to their Web use were derived from the interview data and are summarized as follows:

- The most useful work-related Web sites in rank order are directory sites (i.e. resource sites by associations and user groups), news sites (e.g. CNET, Wall Street Journal), company sites (e.g. IBM, Microsoft), and search engines (e.g. Yahoo, AltaVista).

- Most people do not avidly search for new Web sites.

- The top three methods of identifying new Web sites of interest in rank order are search engines, magazines & newsletters, and other people/colleagues.

- Twice as many people spend most of their Web time visiting old sites as opposed to those who tend to visit new sites of interest.

- The decision criteria to bookmark a Web site is largely based on a site's ability to provide relevant and up-to-date information.

- The top four types of information sought on the Web in rank order are: 1) competitive information on other companies; 2) technical information; 3) research information; and 4) product information.

- The top three things liked best about the Web in rank order are: 1) convenient & quick access to information; 2) abundance of information; and 3) unfiltered/personal control over information.

- The top three things liked least about the Web in rank order are: 1) poor search tools & services; 2) slow response/download speed; and 3) poor site designs.

6.5 The Behavioral Model of Information Seeking

Recall the Behavioral Model of Information Seeking on the Web presented back in Chapter 5 (section 5.3.4) which related Aguilar's four main modes of information seeking on the Web with dominate information seeking activities/moves proposed by Ellis. That model was utilized to structure significant episodes of activity identified in the interview transcripts and Web traffic logs. Figure 6.9 below illustrates the distribution of episodes over four modes of viewing and searching and six classes of possible Web moves.

Information Seeking on the Web

<table>
<tr><th></th><th>Starting</th><th>Chaining</th><th>Browsing</th><th>Differentiating</th><th>Monitoring</th><th>Extracting</th></tr>
<tr><td>Undirected Viewing</td><td colspan="2">12 Episodes</td><td></td><td></td><td></td><td></td></tr>
<tr><td>Conditioned Viewing</td><td></td><td></td><td colspan="2">18 Episodes</td><td></td><td></td></tr>
<tr><td>Informal Search</td><td></td><td></td><td></td><td colspan="3">23 Episodes</td></tr>
<tr><td>Formal Search</td><td></td><td></td><td></td><td></td><td></td><td>8 Episodes</td></tr>
</table>

Figure 6.9 Episodes of Information Seeking on the Web

Generating the distribution of episodes required exhaustive analysis of the interview and tracking data. First, Web modes of viewing and searching had to be identified. Second, these had to be analysed in terms of participant Web moves. Such analysis essentially required two passes through the data.

The first pass involved identifying significant episodes and categorizing these into Web modes of information seeking. Recall that during the interviews, participants were asked to describe "critical incidents" or significant episodes of finding and using information on the Web. By reading the transcripts, each episode was analyzed according to its information need, amount of effort, number of web sources consulted, and information use. Based on this analysis, an episode was categorized according to one of Aguilar's (1967) four modes of scanning (undirected/conditioned viewing; informal/formal searching). WebTracker logs were also examined to identify additional significant episodes. Two criteria were used to select episodes: the episode consumed a substantial amount of time and effort; or the episode was a frequently or regularly repeated activity.

In total, 61 significant episodes were identified. Of these, 12 were categorized as undirected viewing. The most common example of undirected viewing consisted of visits to general news websites such as those of NewsEdge, news.com, and newspapers. In the words of one participant, the goal was to "keep up with what's happening in the world." General news sites acted as gateways to information covering many different subject areas, and provided an efficient way of surveying current developments without a specific information need in mind. Other channels of undirected viewing included portal sites such as CANOE, and large magazine sites such as ZDnet.

Eighteen episodes were categorized as conditioned viewing. The most common examples were regular return visits to bookmarked sites, and starting from a particular page that contained links to sites of interest. Thus, a number of participants regularly visited the websites of Microsoft, Novell, and Sun Microsystems in order to monitor new content in selected sections. One participant regularly visited the Novell site for information on upcoming training courses, seminars, and software updates. Another returned to Sun's Java home page periodically to follow developments in the Electronic Commerce Framework and E-commerce tools. A third person habitually scanned the Canada Newswire Site to view press releases from the Federal and Provincial governments. Yet another customized his start-page at MSN with his own topic headings and keywords.

Twenty three episodes were categorized as informal search, and these constituted the largest group. The most common examples of informal search were when participants made use of specific query terms such as names of companies, products or technologies to perform simple searches on easily accessible search engines. There were several examples of selecting search engines that were local to a specific site (e.g. a search engine maintained by a company that only indexed its own web pages). Thus, two participants used the local search engine on the website of Forrester Research (a market research firm) to retrieve information about specific companies; another participant used the search engine at the Environmental Protection Agency to retrieve information on ventilation-heating systems for school buildings. Several of the informal searches used well-known search services from Yahoo and AltaVista.

Eight episodes were categorized as formal search. Here, participants were intending to use the information formally (e.g. to write policy or planning documents, to provide definitions). Three formal searches utilized several search engines, including meta search services. Two searches attempted to be exhaustively comprehensive: one used four meta search engines to locate a good example of an action plan that could be formally presented to a manager; the other used the DejaNews search engine to retrieve two author profiles and scan all their postings. Another search was carried out over four days, retrieving high quality resources on Women Advocacy to be included on an institutional site for International Women and Human Rights.

The second pass of data analysis involved examining the episodes in each mode in terms of Ellis' (1989) Web moves (starting, chaining, browsing, differentiating, monitoring, or extracting). That is, for each significant information seeking episode categorized, the corresponding section of the WebTracker logs were analyzed to determine the browser-based actions that best characterized that episode. Data about the sequence of site visits, repetitions of these sequences, movements backwards and forwards between pages, the use of bookmarking, the selection of sites from stored bookmarks, the use of search engines, printing, and other actions and events captured by the Web Tracker were examined to trace the selection and development of information seeking moves over the duration of each episode.

The most common examples of starting moves took the form of participants starting their Web sessions from (1) jumpsites that contained links of interest; (2) portal sites; and (3) Intranet entry pages of their organizations. Chaining moves occurred when participants followed links from the starting page or some other page. Chaining could be in either direction (backward/forward). Browsing moves occurred when participants looked through top-level pages, examined lists of headings, or viewed sitemaps. Differentiating moves were when participants bookmarked a page, printed it, or copied its contents. Another indication of differentiating was when a person went direcly to a specific site of known content (e.g. the Microsoft site) by entering its URL. Monitoring moves were when participants revisited favorite sites (that have for example been bookmarked or entered into a customized list/page). Although this was uncommon, another indication would be when participants signed up for email or alert services that informed them of new content on the monitored pages. Extracting moves were characterized by participants systematically working through a website to extract information of interest. A common method of extracting was to use local search engines that indexed material at their parent sites.

In the undirected viewing episodes, data collected by the WebTracker application indicated that the most frequently occurring moves were starting and chaining. Thus, participants began at favorite starting pages (news or portal sites) and followed links that they found interesting on those pages. This was usually characterized by a certain amount of movement back and forth using the starting page as anchor.

In the conditioned viewing episodes, the most frequently occurring moves were differentiating, browsing, and monitoring. Thus, participants selected a bookmarked page/site, or entered the URL of a site they remembered (differentiating). Another example of differentiating was when participants printed useful pages for their own files or to show to others. These sites/pages were then examined to locate new content of interest (browsing). The most important characteristic of conditioned viewing was that participants regularly or frequently returned to their selected or differentiated sites/pages to check for new information (monitoring).

In the informal search episodes, the most frequently occurring moves were differentiating and localized extracting. Thus, participants went directly to selected sites where they expected that the searching they intend to do would likely yield results, e.g. going to a market research firm's site to search for company data, or to a software vendor site to search for software patches (differentiating). Searching at these sites would make use of the local search engines that were dedicated to retrieving information from those sites (localized extracting). Some participants frequently returned to specific sites to perform their informal searches (monitoring).

In the formal search episodes, the most frequently occurring move was a relatively intensive and thorough form of extracting, compared with the localized extracting that characterized informal searching. Thus, participants systematically worked through a number of search engines or meta search engines so as to find (all) important information about a topic or item. Formal searches often involved the use of search engines known for their comprehensive coverage, currency, or the inclusion of historical data. The Behavioral Model of information seeking presented in Chapter 5 suggested that monitoring would be part of formal searching. However, for this group of participants, there were no explicit instances of monitoring to support extracting.

Overall, the distribution of information seeking episodes shown in Figure 6.9 suggests that people who use the Web as part of their work engage in four complementary modes of information seeking as proposed by the Behavioral Model. Each mode is set apart by its information needs, information seeking scope and effort, and the purpose of information use. Moreover, each mode of information seeking is characterized by information seeking moves that are revealed through recurrent sequences of participants' use of browser functions and features. Undirected viewing is mainly characterized by starting and chaining; conditioned viewing by differentiating, browsing, and monitoring; informal search by differentiating, and localized extracting; and formal search by systematic, thorough extracting.

The study also introduces an experimental method by which to operationalize and measure the six patterns of information seeking behaviors identified by Ellis (1989, 1993, 1997) as browser-based actions and events. Recurrent patterns of these actions would indicate that a user is engaging in a particular mode of viewing or searching on the Web. For example, repeated sequences of starting and chaining might suggest undirected viewing (moving back and forth visiting links on a starting page); while sequences of differentiating and extracting might suggest informal search (going to a bookmarked site and doing a local search). Each viewing/searching mode also implies different information needs and information-use goals.

Two other observations can be made. The first concerns "Monitoring," which is keeping up in an area by regularly following particular core or important sources. Two forms of monitoring are possible on the Web: "pull" monitoring is when a user selects a bookmark or enters a URL to revisit a site; "push" monitoring is when a user automatically receives alerts that a monitored site has been updated. Common methods of push monitoring on the Web include subscribing to email newsletters or alerts from the monitored site; setting up a personalized profile or channel; and subscribing to services that track content changes on selected sites. Although most participants in this study would be considered as being Web-savvy, very few of the participants made use of push monitoring techniques: one did use an email alert service; three others tried out a push service, but only for a limited time.

The second observation concerns "Extracting." Extracting on the Web is systematically searching through one or more sites in order to locate information of interest at those sites. In this study, most episodes of extracting employed basic searching strategies. For the most part, search formulations were relatively simple, with advanced features such as Boolean operators, and word truncation or proximity operators rarely utilized. This was the case even when participants appeared to be working in the formal search mode. There were no instances of participants accessing search-engine help instruction pages to improve their searches.

6.6 Effect of Web Training on Organizational Web Use

Granting physical access to the Internet is only one step organizations can take to help users find the information they need to do their work. As a means of facilitating better utilization of the Web as an information seeking tool, some organizations are providing their employees with Web browser training. Recently there has been some discussion in the academic literature on the benefits of providing Web browser training. For example, one study by Bruce (1998) identified no relationship between formal Web training and the satisfaction of users in utilizing the Web for information seeking purposes.

To understand better the effect of Web browser training on organizational Web use, a follow-up study was carried out by the authors on a subset of 17 participants from one organization called TRAINCo (a pseudonym). Unlike the other companies in the larger study, TRAINCo underwent two separate Web tracking monitoring periods and interviews both prior and after an advanced training course on the use of Netscape Navigator. The course was designed and conducted by the company's internal library/information center. The purpose of this follow-up study was to explore and compare patterns in World Wide Web use for participants both prior and after taking the training and to rate the general effectiveness of the training course.

The subset of 17 participants represented a more diverse sample population than the other 35 participants who took part in the larger study. Of the 17 participants at TRAINCo, nine were manager/supervisors, two were consultants, five held information technologist/analyst job titles, and one was an administrative assistant. Overall, the participants in the TRAINCo sample were less technically-oriented and less skilled in using the World Wide Web in daily work practice. For example, though both population groups reported that Web usage accounted for 18% of their daily work activity on average, TRAINCo participants collectively reported themselves at the "intermediate" level in terms of their *computer background* (mean=3.18, sd=0.95) and *Web expertise* (mean=2.65, sd=1.0) as compared to the other companies' rating at the "intermediate/expert" level for their *computer background* (mean=3.86, sd=0.97) and *Web expertise* (mean=3.80, sd=0.96). A two-sample T-test revealed the *computer background* difference to be significant at the 5% significance level and the *Web expertise* difference to be statistically significant at the 0.1% significance level.

The results of the TRAINCo's questionnaire were compared with the results of the 35 other participants. In comparison, TRAINCo's participants utilized all information sources to a greater extent except for the World Wide Web. Specifically, other companies ranked the World Wide Web as their second-most frequently used source (mean=5.43, sd=0.65) while TRAINCo ranked it third-most frequent (mean=5.0, sd=0.87). A two sample T-test identified this difference not to be statistically significant.

TRAINCo also had slightly lower quality ratings for the more highly-ranked information sources and slightly higher quality ratings for the lesser ranked information sources. Of interest is that TRAINCo participants rated the World Wide Web slightly lower in relevance and reliability (mean=8.0, sd=1.22). However, a two sample T-test revealed this difference in perceived source quality not to be statistically significant.

In comparison to other companies, notable differences are evident in the TRAINCo's participants' perception of accessibility for the World Wide Web. TRAINCo ranked the World Wide Web eighth-most highly rated (mean=7.0, sd=2.0) as compared to the other companies' ranking of third-most highly rated (mean=7.69, sd=2.03). However, a two sample T-test indicated that this difference was not statistically significant.

Thus, compared to the results of the 35 participants from other companies, TRAINCo participants experienced lower frequency of use, lower perceived source quality, and lower perceived source accessibility for the World Wide Web. The results also indicated a greater reliance on non-Web information sources and a greater perception of both quality and accessibility of non-Web sources. One explanation for these findings may be the broader spectrum of non-technical participants in TRAINCo's sample population as compared to that of the participants from other companies. This was likely an influencing factor in the ratings of the twelve information sources in the questionnaire.

Table 6.11 below summarizes the results of the participants' Web usage activity from the WebTracker logs collected over the pre- and post-training periods. Of the 17 participants, one declined to participate in the tracking portion of the study. Of these 16, all surfed the Web regularly during the pre-training period, while only seven searched the Web on a regular basis during the post-training period in August. This lower usage made it more difficult to make comparisons in Web usage before and after the training course. Overall, there were three reasons for the decreased usage in the post-tracking period: 1) August was the prime month for people to take vacations; 2) the fiscal year end for the company was September, translating into more work and less time for Web scanning activity by the managers and supervisors participating in the study; and 3) technical difficulties with the company's firewall in August inhibited use of the Web by some participants. As a result of these constraints, the pre-training period was more successful in terms of the amount of data collected.

Table 6.11 displays the overall averages for frequency and duration of Web use in both the pre- and post-tracking periods per participant. Though the post-tracking period was longer in duration, the average number of days WebTracker monitored participants in each period was roughly the same (pre-training = 7.4 days; post-training = 7.7 days). Overall, the results indicate sizeable increases in the number of Uniform Resource Locators (URLs) or Web page visited in the post-training period. Interestingly, more varied searching and browsing activity occurred in the post phase of the study as reflected by the over 70% rise in the number unique URLs and doubling of unique URL hosting domains visited after the training course. Further, the number of sessions (i.e. periods of Web use without gaps in time over 30 minutes) increased as well in the post-training period indicating that participants searched longer and more intensively in the second round of tracking.

	# of Days Web Used	# of URLs Visited	# of URLs Visited per Day	# of Unique URLs Visited	# of Unique Domains Visited	# of Sessions	# of Sessions per Day
Pre-Training Average (N=16)	7.4	314.3	42.6	153.4	36.9	14.0	1.9
Post-Training Average (N=7)	7.7	491.0	63.7	263.0	72.0	21.0	2.7
Post-Training % Increase	4.5%	56.2%	49.5%	71.4%	94.9%	50.0%	43.6%

Table 6.11 TRAINCo Pre & Post Web Usage Activity

In terms of the content visited on the Web, analysis of the tracking logs showed more substantial and efficient information seeking episodes in the period after the training course. A notable example of post-training Web activity was increased usage of the internal library's web site off the company's intranet. In these instances, participants utilized the links off the intranet page to access external articles concerning the organization. Another typical instance in the post-training period was the utilization of many of the tips & techniques taught during the course. For example, the logs showed substantial usage by most participants of meta search engines which helped participants find information on the Web more quickly; in most cases, the pre-training logs showed no previous use of these sites.

Despite the general increase in Web use by participants after the training course, two of the seven participants in the post-training period experienced a decrease in usage. The reason some participants did not show an increase may be due to the short data collection time during both the pre- and post-training periods. A more longitudinal study would be required to yield more substantial evidence. However, analysis of the interview data suggests that participants who used the Web to a lesser extent searched the Web more effectively after the training course, while other participants increased their usage because they became more comfortable with using the Web itself.

Overall, the course had a positive influence on participant Web behaviour. Generally it was found that participants applied their new learnings from the course which in turn led to more effective information searches, increased user confidence, and a more realistic understanding of the Web itself. For example, several participants stated that they used the tips and techniques learned from the training course when on the Internet, namely the ability to open two Netscape windows simultaneously, check for valid URLs in their bookmark files, use meta search engines, and focus their information searches with boolean terms. Interestingly, many remarked on the use of the company's list of hot sites and NEWSEDGE—two services they did not know existed prior to taking the training. These new learnings led to improved Web habits. For example, one participant commented that he now used the bookmark functionality offered in Netscape Navigator since the course taught him that bookmarks could save him from performing unnecessary searches in the future.

Many participants reported their ability to conduct more effective information searches. One participant reported that people who took the training searched the Internet in better ways—they now used the Web more logically in terms of their search approach which led to improved searches, the use of better search engines, and the utilization of the internal library's list of hot Web sites on the company's intranet. Another participant described her increased ability to plan a search strategy by being able to think ahead of the appropriate search parameters and search engines to use. Overall, most participants commented on their ability to find information "quicker" as a result of taking the course.

Another benefit of the course was increased participant confidence. Two participants stated the course made them feel so at ease with Web technology they decided to get Internet access at home. Several participants reported the course reconfirmed their understanding of what they knew about the Internet, thus easing anxieties about using the Web to find information. Many participants reported they were more comfortable with using Internet technology: one participant stated she viewed the Web as less threatening; another stated the course had enlightened him about the various functionalities of the Web. Overall, most participants reported the course helped them achieve a more realistic understanding of the Web itself in terms of its limitations as an information source.

6.7 Conclusion

The World Wide Web represents a new kind of information resource space that is more open, accessible, and versatile than its online predecessors. The reach and richness of the Web poses management challenges. The Web is not only a place where one can look up answers to questions, but also a vast information commons where one can browse, make chance discoveries, and learn more about issues. The risk is that unbridled information on the Web can just as easily confound, mislead, and overwhelm the undiscriminating user. A new technology elicits new patterns of behaviors from its users. The corollary is that managing the Web as a new technology will be most effective when it is based on a clear understanding of how people are in fact adapting Web use into their work practice.

This chapter presented the findings and methodology of a study of how knowledge workers in business organizations use the Web as part of their day-to-day work activities. The study was of interest because it focused on participants' actual experiences of using the Web in their natural work settings over extended periods of time. The study provided a nuanced view of how people actually use the Web: it found that people who use the Web as part of their work engage in four complementary modes of information seeking, ranging from undirected viewing, conditioned viewing, to informal searching, and formal searching. In each of these modes people perceive information needs, adopt information seeking strategies, and use the information found in distinctive ways. Moreover, the study was able to characterize each information seeking mode in terms of specific sequences of browser-based actions and events made by users. These findings together have significant implications for the *design* and *evaluation* of the Intranet or other Web-based infrastructure for supporting knowledge work.

In *designing* a Web-based information infrastructure, the study suggests that the design needs to facilitate not only the finding or searching for information (perhaps the more common goal of website implementation), but also the browsing or viewing of information. Browsing—as in undirected and conditioned viewing—is the principal way by which organizational participants develop, elaborate, and prioritize their emergent information needs. Browsing is also an important way for users to make serendipitous connections and acquire peripheral vision. As organizations thrive in complex environments where actors and agencies step out of their traditional domains, cross industry boundaries, and create non-traditional linkages, the information skill to watch and assess emergent trends and phenomena, through scanning and the broadening of peripheral vision, will become increasingly salient.

For *evaluating* a Web-based information infrastructure, the study suggests that an analysis of browser-based actions and events initiated by users as they look for information may be a viable method for evaluating the usability and usefulness of the infrastructure. By elucidating typical patterns of browser actions or moves — cycles of stepping backward and forward between Web pages, or climbing upward or downward between levels of a Web site hierarchy; following new links; bookmarking; printing; and so on — we are able to observe the preferences of users, their information seeking styles, their strategies for finding information, as well as the occasions when they fail to locate useable information. This consitutes fine-grained feedback based on actual use that can be analyzed to enhance the design, structure, and functionality of the Web site or Intranet.

The Web is an "informating" system (Zuboff 1988) in the sense that it generates data about its use even as it is being used. For this reason, most organizational web sites have adopted tools and methodologies to examine Web site traffic and user interactions on a site (sometimes in real-time) in order to constantly evaluate and enhance the content and functionality of their sites. (The study presented here used a specialized software [WebTracker]. Other methods are available, including: modifying the browser application; re-directing Web traffic through a proxy server and analyzing the proxy log file; using a cookie or a text file; examining the history file; rewriting URLs; embedding invisible HTML fields to maintain basic state information. A growing number of software companies are offering specialized tools to analyze site traffic and usage.)

The project presented in this chapter also points to a methodological approach for studying Web information seeking and use. In line with our perspective that information is a subjectively constructed relationship between the person and the information artifact he or she is encountering, the data collection in the project is *multimodal*, embracing both *interpretive* data solicited from the person, and *interaction* data generated by software. Thus, users' personal stories of their episodes of finding and making use of significant information furnish the narrative frameworks in which the detailed data on browser actions and site visits are interpreted. These users' stories sometimes elaborate the thinking processes, emotional states, and situational constraints that contextualize the episodes of encountering information. Our experience in this study indicates that a research methodology that integrates qualitative and quantitative data can offer the depth and detail needed to make sense of Web-based information seeking and use.

The Web use study as well as our discussions throughout the book suggests some principles for increasing effective Web use at the organizational level:

1. The Web should be a vital component of an organization's enabling IT infrastructure (Weill and Broadbent 1998). An enabling infrastructure provides functionality beyond current operational needs to capabilities that support adaptive learning, informed decision making, and the achievement of longer-term goals. Weill and Broadbent observe that an enabling infrastructure is characterized by: "over-investment" in the IT infrastructure beyond current needs; a main focus on flexibility; reaching across business units and to customers; and providng extensive range of services.

2. The Web is not just an information network, but a shared work space where information is accessed, communicated, and acted upon. Management needs to adopt a broader view of Web use by employees. A more liberal policy and fewer controls about access to internal and external Web sites can promote self-directed learning and problem solving. It can encourage employees to plough the Web freely, see the initially unseen, and connect the initially unconnected.

3. For organizations that have established intranets, this infrastructure may be leveraged to promote information and knowledge sharing. In particular, organizations may support self-organizing communities of practice (Wenger 1998) by providing dedicated Web areas where these communities can share the information they find on the Web, exchange stories and discoveries, and in general extend their conversations online.

4. Although much has been written about the ease-of-use of the Web, perhaps just as much can be said about users who are grappling with questions such as: How can I manage information overload? How do I evaluate the quality of online information? How can I retrieve more relevant information? As users ply the Web more intensively, these issues will loom larger. Users increasingly need training and assistance to become more efficient and effective Web mavens. Thus, they need to learn how to diagnose search results and fine-tune their search strategies; assess the quality of information on Web pages; and understand when and how to complement Web use with information sources and services that are *not* available online.

5. The current study found that the way people use the Web tends to be conditioned by the functions that are built into their browser clients. System designers may consider enhancing and extending Web information seeking by developing customized functionality that is tailored to the requirements of Web work in their organizations.

6. For example, subject taxonomies ("knowledge maps") could be designed to categorize Web-based information and facilitate the browsing and sharing of Web pages and bookmarks. Workflow applications could embed Web use within task stages and activities. Group memory spaces could be created for users to contribute and compare information. Searching, alerting and recommending functions could exploit the chaining/linking between Web pages frequented by project group members and other communities. (Chaining and citation analysis techniques are being used by two search engine projects at Stanford University and IBM Almaden Research Center to locate authoritative Web sources: Stanford's Google engine uses forward chaining to move from link to link; IBM's Clever Project uses both forward and backward chaining, including looking back from an authoritative page to see who points to that page.)

At an operational level, we may postulate ways of supporting and enhancing the information seeking of Web users as they engage in the four modes of information seeking portrayed in this study. Example suggestions are shown in the table below.

Web Use Mode	Enhancing Web Use
Undirected viewing: starting and chaining	• Introduce systems that can search or recommend new jumpsites or "similar-to" sites • Encourage people in a group to share bookmarks, Web pages, URLs • Design corporate portals to support undirected, serendipitous viewing
Conditioned viewing: browsing, differentiating, monitoring	• Train users to evaluate and escalate priority or importance of information • Make it easy for users to share Web-based information via email or in online forums • Introduce users to services that allow them to subscribe to and be notified about new content on Web pages
Informal search: differentiating, monitoring, extracting	• Pre-select high quality sources and search engines for quick, informal searches • Prepackage good search strategies developed by subject matter experts; allow users to view these strategies and learn from them • Educate users on how to evaluate information provenance and quality
Formal search: extracting	• Educate users about full range of information sources that should be considered for comprehensive search: print, online, human sources • Educate users about when to use: commercial online database services; the library or information resource center; information brokers/professionals • Train users on advanced search techniques: narrowing or broadening a search; balancing precision and recall; backward and forward chaining.

Table 6.12 Enhancing Web Use

(This research is supported by a grant from the Social Sciences and Humanities Research Council of Canada. The WebTracker application was developed by Ross Barclay, then a master's student at the Faculty of Information Studies, University of Toronto.)

Coda

Knowledge work consists of transforming data into information, information into knowledge, and then using this knowledge to take action and obtain results:

Data -> Information -> Knowledge -> Action -> Results

Near the beginning of the book we saw how the conversion of data into knowledge involved increasing the order and structure of information through increasing levels of human enactment, interpretation, and reflection. Information seeking lies at the very core of this process, and we sketched a multi-layered view of information seeking as including the experiencing of information needs, the gathering of information, and the utilization of information.

The mobilization of knowledge into action and results requires the "integration" of complementary categories of knowledge resources (the tacit, explicit, and cultural) through connected knowledge processes (knowledge creation, diffusion, and utilization). Two models of "integration" were examined: in one, organizations generate new capabilities by combining existing knowledge and integrating the knowledge of their members; in the other, organizational knowing is the emergent outcome of a network of information processes that links knowledge creation to sensemaking and decision making.

Information technology can facilitate and accelerate the information-to-action transformation process in a number of ways. It can provide fast, direct access to a vast array of electronic information resources. It can allow users not only to consult many more sources, but to filter information selectively; monitor trends and developments; discover hidden patterns in large sets of data; and share, discuss, and interpret new information. Technology can also support action-taking by managing information and making the appropriate information available for an individual or a group during task performance or project collaboration.

A major theme of the book is the vital role of information technology in building an enabling infrastructure for supporting knowledge work. We suggested that the effective design of an knowledge-enabling infrastructure would be based on a firm understanding of the information ecology of the organization as well as the information behaviors and work practices of the organization's members. Thus, a knowledge infrastructure, be it an intranet, a groupware system, or some other platform, would be designed to complement the strengths of an organization's information ecology (its information culture, politics, and information management framework), and to compensate for its weaknesses. Similarly, by focusing on user behaviors, practices and perceptions, the infrastructure would be designed to promote the use of technology rather than to promote the technology itself.

The World Wide Web has transfigured the online information environment into a hypertextual information commons that knows no boundaries, and recognizes little control or authority. As a new kind of information medium, the Web is constantly eliciting new behaviors from its users. Users in turn shape the evolution of the Web, so that the way they respond to innovations on the Web will determine which trajectories the Web will follow. For the new digerati, being able to navigate the Web, find and evaluate information, track and follow issues, manage personal information, have all become essential competencies. Interestingly, the Web itself is addressing some of these needs: visited sites can be remembered; related sites can be recommended; relevant information can be retrieved automatically; and so on.

The final two chapters of the book present a glimpse of the research on how people actually use the Web. Our message is that we need more of such research urgently to inform our attempts to design knowledge work platforms on the Web. Our belief is that such research could usefully combine qualitative and quantitative methods which leverage our knowledge about human information behavior, and take advantage of the Web's tools and architecture to collect fine-grained data.

Making the Web work requires not only working the information web, but also working the human and social webs that endow information with meaning and purpose.

References

Abraham, Jorij. 1998. *The Business Value of Intranets: An Exploratory Research Study into the Value of Intranets in Organisations*. Ph.D. dissertation, Department of Information Management, University of Amsterdam, Amsterdam.

Adler, Paul S. and Robert E. Cole. 1993. Designed for Learning: A Tale of Two Auto Plants. *Sloan Management Review* 34, no. 3: 85-94.

Aguilar, Francis J. 1967. *Scanning the Business Environment*. New York, NY: Macmillan.

Aguilar, Francis J. 1988. *General Managers in Action*. New York, NY: Oxford University Press.

Allen, Bryce L. 1996. *Information Tasks: Toward a User-Centered Approach to Information Systems*. Edited by H. Borko. San Diego, CA: Academic Press.

Allen, Thomas J. 1977. Managing the Flow of Technology: Technology Transfer and the Dissemination of Technological Information within the R & D Organization. Cambridge, MA: MIT Press.

Almind, Tomas C. and Peter Ingwersen. 1997. Informetric Analysis on the World Wide Web: Methodological Approaches to "Webometrics". *Journal of Documentation* 53, no. 4: 404-426.

Alvesson, Mats. 1993. Organizations as Rhetoric: Knowledge-Intensive Firms and the Struggle with Ambiguity. *Journal of Management Studies* 30, no. 6: 997-1015.

Argyris, Chris. 1994. Good Communication That Blocks Learning. *Harvard Business Review* 71, no. 4: 77-90.

Audi, Robert. 1998. Epistemology: A Contemporary Introduction to the Theory of Knowledge. New York: Routledge.

Auster, Ethel and Chun Wei Choo. 1993. Environmental Scanning by CEOs in Two Canadian Industries. *Journal of the American Society for Information Science* 44, no. 4: 194-203.

Badaracco, Joseph L. 1991. *The Knowledge Link: How Firms Compete Through Strategic Alliances*. Boston, MA: Harvard Business School Press.

Baecker, Ronald M., ed. 1993. *Groupware and Computer Supported Collaborative Work*. New York: Morgan Kaufmann Publishers.

Baecker, Ronald M., Jonathan Grudin, William A.S. Buxton, and Saul Greenburg, eds. 1995. *Readings in Human Computer Interaction: Toward the Year 2000.* 2nd ed. San Fransico, CA: Morgan Kaufmann.

Bandura, A. 1977. Self Efficacy: Towards A Unifying Theory of Behavioural Change. *Psychological Review* 84: 191-215.

Bannon, Liam J., and Kjeld Schmidt. 1991. CSCW: Four characters in search of a context. In *Studies in computer supported cooperative work: Theory, practice, and design*. Proceedings of the First European Conference on Computer Supported Cooperative Work, 1989, edited by J. M. Bowers and S. D. Benford. North-Holland: Elsevier Science.

Bartlett, Frederic C. 1932. *Remembering: A Study in Experimental and Social Psychology.* Cambridge, UK: Cambridge University Press.

Bayne, Rowan. 1995. The Myers-Briggs Type Indicator: A Critical and Practical Guide. London, UK: Chapman and Hall.

Belkin, N. J., R. N. Oddy, and H. M. Brooks. 1982a. Ask for Information Retrieval: Part I. Background and Theory. *Journal of Documentation* 38, no. 20: 61-71.

Belkin, N. J., R. N. Oddy, and H. M. Brooks. 1982b. Ask for Information Retrieval: Part II. Results of a Design Study. *Journal of Documentation* 38. no. 3: 145-164.

Bentley, R., W. Appelt, U. Busbach, E. Hinrichs, D. Kerr, K. Sikkel, J. Trevor, and G. Woetzel. 1997a. Basic Support for Cooperative Work on the World Wide Web. *International Journal of Human-Computer Studies* 46: 827-846.

Bentley, Richard, Thilo Horstmann, and Jonathon Trevor. 1997b. The World Wide Web as Enabling Technology for CSCW: The Case of BSCW. *Computer Supported Cooperative work: The Journal of Collaborative Computing* 6, no. 2-3): 111-134.

Berners-Lee, Tim, Robert Cailliau, Ari Luotonen, Henrik Frystyk Nielsen, and Arthur Secret. 1994. The World Wide Web. *Communications of the ACM* 37, no. 8: 76-82.

Boisot, Max H. 1995. Information Space: A Framework for Learning in Organizations, Institutions and Culture. London, UK: Routledge.

Boisot, Max. 1998. Knowledge Assets: Securing Competitive Advantage in the Information Economy. New York: Oxford University Press.

Bourdieu, Pierre. 1988. *The Logic of Practice.* Stanford: Stanford University Press.

Bowers, John. 1994. The Work to Make a Network Work: Studying CSCW in Action. In *Proceedings of CSCW '94*, edited by R. Furuta and C. Neuwirth. Chapel Hill, NC: ACM Press.

Bradford, S.C. 1934. Sources of Information on Specific Subjects. *Engineering* 137: 85-86.

Broadbent, Marianne, and Peter Weill. 1997. Management by Maxim: How Business and IT Managers Can Create IT Infrastructures. *Sloan Management Review* Spring: 77-92.

Brookes, B. C. 1973. Numerical Methods of Bibliographic Analysis. *Library Trends*: 18-43.

Brown, John Seely. 1991. Research That Reinvents the Corporation. *Harvard Business Review* 69, no. 1: 102-111.

Brown, John Seely. 1993. Session II - Papers Submitted by, Presentation by, Main Themes Generated by John Seely Brown. *In Proceedings of Learning in Organizations Workshop* held in London, Ontario, edited by Mary M. Crossan, Henry W. Lane, James C. Rush, and Roderick E. White, Vol. 81-115. University of Western Ontario.

Brown, John Seely and Paul Duguid. 1991. Organizational Learning and Communities-of-Practice: Toward a Unified View of Working, Learning, and Innovation. *Organization Science* 2, no. 1: 40-57.

Bruce, Harry. 1998. User Satisfaction with Information Seeking on the Internet. *Journal of the American Society for Information Science* 49, no. 6: 541-556.

Catledge, L. D., & Pitkow, J. E. 1995. Characterizing Browsing Strategies in the World-Wide Web. *Computer Networks and ISDN Systems* 27: 1065-1073.

Chang, Shan-Ju and Ronald E. Rice. 1993. Browsing: A Multidimensional Framework. In *Annual Review of Information Science and Technology*, ed. Martha E. Williams. Medford, NJ: Learned Information.

Choo, Chun Wei, Brian Detlor, and Don Turnbull. 2000. Working the Web: An Empirical Model of Web Use. In Proceedings of the 33rd Hawaii International Conference on System Science (HICSS) held in Maui, Hawai, Jan 4-7.

Choo, Chun Wei, Brian Detlor, and Don Turnbull. 1998. A Behavioral Model of Information Seeking on the Web: Preliminary Results of a Study of How Managers and IT Specialists Use the Web. In *Proceedings of the 61st Annual Meeting of the American Society for Information Science,* ed. C. M. Preston, 35: 290-302. Medford, NJ: Information Today.

Choo, Chun Wei and Ethel Auster. 1993. Scanning the Business Environment: Acquisition and Use of Information by Managers. In *Annual Review of Information Science and Technology* , ed. Martha E. Williams. Medford, NJ: Learned Information, Inc. for the American Society for Information Science.

Choo, Chun Wei. 1993. Environmental Scanning: Acquisition and Use of Information by Chief Executive Officers in the Canadian Telecommunications Industry. Ph.D. dissertation, University of Toronto.

Choo, Chun Wei. 1998. Information Management for the Intelligent Organization: The Art of Scanning the Environment. Second ed. Medford, NJ: Information Today, Inc.

Choo, Chun Wei. 1998. The Knowing Organization: How Organizations Use Information to Construct Meaning, Create Knowledge, and Make Decisions. New York: Oxford University Press.

Ciborra, Claudio. 1998. Towards a Contigency View of Infrastructure and Knowledge: An Exploratory Study. In *Proceeding of the 19th Annual International Conference on Information Systems*, "Crossing boundaries: Managing Virtual Enterprises", Helsinki, Finland, December 13th-16th.

CIO Communications. 1998a. It Takes a Village. *CIO WebBusiness Magazine*, February 1st. Available at http://www.cio.com/archive/webbusiness/020198_village_content.html (last accessed Jan 21st, 2000).

CIO Communications. 1998b. The List of Winners: 1998 CIO WebBusiness 50/50 Award Winners - Intranet Winners. CIO *WebBusiness Magazine* July. Available at http://www.cio.com/archive/webbusiness/070198_intranet_winners.html (last accessed Jan 21st, 2000).

Clement, Andrew, and Ina Wagner. 1995. Fragmented Exchange: Disarticulation and the Need for Regionalized Communication Spaces. In *Fourth European Conference on Computer Supported Cooperative Work,* Stockholm, Sweden, September 10-14, edited by H. Marmolin, Y. Sundblad and K. Schmidt. Dordrecht, The Netherlands: Kluwer Academic Publishers.

CMP Media. 1998. Best Intranet: Coopers & Lybrand. *InternetWeek*, March 9th. Available at http://www.internetwk.com/trends/boti5.htm (last accessed Jan 21st, 2000).

Collins, Harry. 1998. Cultural Competence and Scientific Knowledge. In *Exploring Expertise: Issues and Perspectives* , ed. Robin Williams, Wendy Faulkner, and James Fleck, 121-142. London, UK: Macmillan Press.

Conklin, Jeffrery E. 1992. Capturing Organizational Memory. In *Proceedings of Groupware '92,* edited by D. Colemman. CA: Morgan Kaufmann.

Cook, Scott D. N., and Dvora Yanow. 1996. Culture and Organizational Learning. In *Organizational Learning*, edited by M. D. Cohen and L. S. Sproull. Thousands Oaks, CA: Sage.

Cortese, Amy. 1996. Here Comes the Intranet. *Business Week* Feb 26, Cover story: Special Report. Available at http://www.businessweek.com/1996/09/b34641.htm (last accessed Jan 21st, 2000).

Cronin, B., and C. Hert. 1995. Scholarly foraging and network discovery tools. *Journal of Documentation* 51 (4):388-403.

Crovella, Mark, and Azer Bestavros. 1996. *Self-Similarity in World Wide Web Traffic: Evidence and Possible Causes.* Paper read at SIGMETRICS '96: The International Conference on Measurement and Modeling of Computer Systems, Philadelphia.

Cuhna, C.R., A. Bestavros, and M.E. Crovella. 1995. *Characteristics of WWW Client-Based Traces.* Available at http://www.cs.bu.edu/techreports/abstracts/95-010 (last accessed Jan 21st, 2000).

Culnan, Mary J. 1983. Environmental Scanning: The Effects of Task Complexity and Source Accessibility on Information Gathering Behavior. *Decision Sciences*, 14: 194-206.

Culnan, Mary J. 1985. The Dimensions of Perceived Accessibility to Information: Implications for the Delivery of Information Systems and Services. *Journal of the American Society for Information Science* 36, no. 5: 302-308.

Cyberspace. 59th ASIS Annual Meeting, Baltimore, Maryland.

Cyert, Richard and James G. March. 1963/1992. *A Behavioral Theory of the Firm*. 2nd ed. Oxford, UK: Blackwell.

Daft, R. L., J. Sormunen and D. Parks. 1988. Chief Executive Scanning, Environmental Characteristics, and Company Performance: An Empirical Study. *Strategic Management Journal* 9: 123-139.

Daft, Richard. L. & Weick, Karl. E. 1984. Toward a Model of Organizations as Interpretation Systems. *Academy of Management Review* 9, no. 2: 284-295.

Davenport, Thomas H. 1994. Saving IT's Soul: Human-Centered Information Management. *Harvard Business Review* (March-April):119-131.

Davenport, Thomas H. 1997. Information Ecology: Mastering the Information and Knowledge Environment. New York: Oxford University Press.

Davenport, Thomas H., and Laurence Prusak. 1998. *Working Knowledge: How Organizations Manage What They Know*. Boston, Massachusetts: Harvard Business School Press.

Davenport, Thomas H., Robert G. Eccles, and Laurence Prusak. 1992. Information Politics. *Sloan Management Review* 34, no. 1: 53-63.

Davenport, Thomas H., Sirkka L. Jarvenpaa, and Michael C. Beers. 1996. Improving Knowledge Work Processes. *Sloan Management Review* (Summer):53-65.

Dervin, Brenda, and Michael Nilan. 1986. Information Needs and Uses. In *Annual Review of Information Science and Technology (ARIST)*, edited by M. E. Williams. White Plains, New York: Knowledge Industry Publications.

Dervin, Brenda. 1977. Useful Theory for Librarianship: Communication, Not Information. *Drexel Library Quarterly* 13, no. 3:16-32.

Dervin, Brenda. 1983a. An Overview of Sense-Making: Concepts, Methods, and Results to Date. In *Proceedings of International Communication Association Annual Meeting*, May 1983 held in Dallas, Texas, USA. Available at: http://communication.sbs.ohio-state.edu/sense-making/art/artdervin83.html (last accessed Jan 21st, 2000).

Dervin, Brenda. 1983b. Information As A User Construct: The Relevance of Perceived Information Needs to Synthesis and Interpretation. In *Knowledge Structure and Use: Implications for Synthesis and Interpretation*, ed. Spencer A. Ward and Linda J. Reed, 153-184. Philadelphia, PA: Temple University Press.

Dervin, Brenda. 1992. From the Mind's Eye of the 'User': The Sense-Making Qualitative-Quantitative Methodology. In *Qualitative Research in Information Management*, ed. Jack D. Glazier and Ronald R. Powell. Englewood, CO: Libraries Unlimited.

Detlor, Brian. 2000. The Corporate Portal as Information Infrastructure: Towards a Framework for Portal Design. *International Journal of Information Management*, April.

Detlor, Brian. 1998a. Basing Intranet Design on the Organizational Information Environment and User Information Behaviour. In the *Proceedings of the 26th Annual Conference of the Canadian Association for Information Science (CAIS)* "Information Science at the Dawn of the Millennium", June 3rd-5th, at Université d'Ottawa, Ottawa, Ontario, 93-106.

Detlor, Brian. 1998b. Facilitating Organizational Information Access in Global Network Environments: Towards a New Framework for Intranet Design. In the *Proceedings of the American Society for Information Science (ASIS) Annual Conference*, "Information Access in the Global Economy", Oct 25th-Oct 29th, at Pittsburgh, PA.

Diodato, V. 1994. *Dictionary of Bibliometrics*. New York: The Haworth Press.

Dix, Alan. 1997. Challenges for Cooperative Work on the Web: An Analytical Approach. *Computer Supported Cooperative Work: The Journal of Collaborative Computing* 6, no. 2-3:135-156.

Douglas, Mary. 1975. *Implicit Meanings: Essays in Anthropology*. London: Routledge.

Downie, J. Stephen. 1996. Informetrics and the World Wide Web: A Case Study and Discussion. In *Proceedings of Canadian Association for Information Science* held at the University of Toronto, Ontario, edited by Charles Meadow et. al., 130-141.

Doz, Yves and Gary Hamel. 1997. The Use of Alliances in Implementing Technology Strategies. In *Managing Strategic Innovation and Change*, ed. Michael Tushman and Philip Anderson, 556-589. New York: Oxford University Press.

Dretske, Fred I. 1981. *Knowledge and The Flow of Information*. Cambridge, MA: MIT Press.

Drott, M. C. 1981. Bradford's Law: Theory, Empiricism and the Gaps Between. *Library Trends* 30, no. 1: 41-52.

Duncan, Robert B. 1972. Characteristics of Organizational Environments and Perceived Environmental Uncertainty. *Administrative Science Quarterly* 17, no. 3: 313-327.

Eckerson, W.W. 1999. Plumtree Blossoms. New Version Fulfills Enterprise Portal Requirments. Product Profile. Patricia Seybold Group.

Eich, B., et. al. (1998). *Mozilla.org*. Available at http://www.mozilla.org/ (last accessed Jan 21st, 2000).

Eisenberg, Michael and Linda Schamber. 1988. Relevance: The Search for a Definition. In *Proceedings of Proceedings of the 51st ASIS Annual Meeting* held in Medford, NJ, edited by Christine L. Borgman and Edward Y.H. Pai, 164-168. Learned Information.

Ellis, C.A., S.J. Gibbs, and G.L. Rein. 1991. Groupware: Some Issues and Experiences. *Communications of the ACM* 34, no. 1:39-58.

Ellis, David and Merete Haugan. 1997. Modelling the Information Seeking Patterns of Engineers and Research Scientists in an Industrial Environment. *Journal of Documentation* 53, no. 4: 384-403.

Ellis, David, D. Cox, and K. Hall. 1993. A Comparison of the Information Seeking Patterns of Researchers in the Physical and Social Sciences. *Journal of Documentation* 49, no. 4: 356-369.

Ellis, David. 1989. A Behavioural Model for Information Retrieval System Design. *Journal of Information Science* 15, no. 4/5: 237-247.

Etzioni, Amitai. 1967. Mixed-Scanning: A "Third" Approach to Decision-Making. *Public Administration Review* 27, no. 5:385-392.

Finholt, Tom, and Lee S. Sproull. 1990. Electronic Groups at Work. *Organization Science* 1, no. 1.

Fielding, R., U.C. Irvine, J. Gettys, J. Mogul, H. Frystyk, and T. Berners-Lee. 1997. Hypertext Transfer Protocol - HTTP/1.1. *Network Working Group*. Requests for Comments: 2068. Category: Standards Track. (January). Available at http://ds.internic.net/rfc/rfc1945.txt (last accessed Jan 21st, 2000).

Flanagan, John C. 1954. The Critical Incident Technique. *Psychological Bulletin* 51, no. 4: 327-358.

Fleck, James. 1998. Expertise: Knowledge, Power and Tradeability. In *Exploring Expertise: Issues and Perspectives* , ed. Robin Williams, Wendy Faulkner, and James Fleck, 143-172. London, UK: Macmillan Press.

Fletcher, Patricia Tobaka. 1991. *An Examination of Situational Dimensions in the Information Behaviors of General Managers*. Ph.D. dissertation, School of Information Studies, Syracuse University, Syracuse, New York.

Foucault, Michel. 1980. *Power/Knowledge: Selected Interviews and Other Writings 1972-1977*. New York: Pantheon Books.

Francik, Ellen, Susan Ehrlich Rudman, Donna Cooper, and Stephen Levine. 1995. Putting Innovation to Work: Adoption Strategies for Multimedia Communications Systems. In *Readings in Human Computer Interaction: Toward the Year 2000*, edited by R. M. Baecker, J. Grudin, W. A. S. Buxton and S. Greenburg. San Fransico, CA: Morgan Kaufmann.

Gardner, Howard. 1985. The Mind's New Science: A History of the Cognitive Revolution. New York: Basic Books.

Garud, Raghu and Michael A. Rappa. 1994. A Socio-Cognitive Model of Technology Evolution: The Case of Cochlear Implants. *Organization Science* 5, no. 3: 344-362.

Gerson, Elihu, and Susan Leigh Star. 1986. Analyzing Due Process in the Workplace. *ACM Transactions on Office Information Systems* 4, no. 3:257-270.

Gerstberger, Peter G. and Thomas J. Allen. 1968. Criteria used by Research and Development Engineers in the Selection of an Information Source. *Journal of Applied Psychology* 52, no. 4: 272 -279.

Ghoshal, Sumantra. 1988. Environmental Scanning in Korean Firms: Organizational Isomorphism in Practice. *Journal of International Business Studies* 19, no. 1: 69-86.

Giddens, Anthony. 1984. *The Constitution of Society*. Berkeley, CA: University of California Press.

Ginsburg, Mark, and Katherine Duliba. 1997. Enterprise-Level Groupware Choices: Evaluating Lotus Notes and Intranet-Based Solutions. *Computer Supported Cooperative Work: The Journal of Collaborative Computing* 6:201-225.

Goldman, Alvin I. 1986. *Epistemology and Cognition*. Cambridge, MA: Harvard University Press.

Gonzalez, Jennifer Stone. 1997. *The 21st-Century Intranet*. Upper Saddle River, NJ: Prentice Hall.

Grant, Robert M. 1996a. Toward a Knowledge-based Theory of the Firm. *Strategic Management Journal* 17, Special Issue: 109-122.

Grant, Robert M. 1996b. Prospering in Dynamically-Competitive Environments: Organizational Capability as Knowledge Integration. *Organization Science* 7: 375-387.

Grasso, Antonietta, Jean-Luc Meunier, Daniele Pagani, and Remo Pareschi. 1997. Distributed Coordination and Workflow on the World Wide Web. *Computer Supported Cooperative Work: The Journal of Collaborative Computing* 6, no. 2/3: 175-200.

Greenberg, Saul. 1993. *The Computer User as Toolsmith: The Use, Reuse, and Organization of Computer-based Tools*. Cambridge, UK: Cambridge University Press.

Grudin, Jonathan. 1990. Groupware and Cooperative Work: Problems and Prospects. In *The Art of Human Computer Interface Design*, edited by B. Laurel: Addison-Wesley.

Grudin, Jonathan. 1994. Groupware and Social Dynamics: Eight Challenges for Developers. *Communications of the ACM* 37, no.1:92-105.

Guengerich, Steve, Douglas Graham, Mitra Miller, and Skipper McDonald. 1997. *Building the Corporate Intranet*. New York: John Wiley & Sons.

Halbwachs, M. 1980. *The Collective Memory*. Translated by 1950. Edited by F. J. Ditter and V. Y. Ditter. New York: Harper Colophon.

Halpern, David and Michael S. Nilan. 1988. A Step Toward Shifting the Research Emphasis in Information Science from the System to the User: An Empirical Investigation of Source-Evaluation Behavior, Information Seeking and Use. In *Proceedings of the American Society for Information Science* held in Medford, NJ, edited by Christine L. Borgman and Edward Y.H. Pai, Vol. 169-175. Learned Information.

Harper, R. 1992. Looking at Ourselves: An Examination of the Social Organization of Two Research Laboratories. In *Proceedings of CSCW '92,* edited by J. Turner and R. Kraut. New York: ACM Press.

Harter, Stephen P. 1986. Online Information Retrieval: Concepts, Principles, and Techniques. Toronto: Academic Press.

Harter, Stephen P. 1992. Psychological Relevance and Information Science. *Journal of the American Society for Information Science* 43, no. 9: 602-615.

Haynal, Russ. 1996. Understanding the Intranet: Enterprise Reengineering.

Hewins, Elizabeth T. 1990. Information Need and Use Studies. In *Annual Review of Information Science and Technology (ARIST)*, edited by M. E. Williams. Amsterdam, The Netherlands: Elsevier.

Hildebrand, Carol. 1997. Designing an Intranet is Different From Designing an External Web Site. But Its No Less Important. *WebMaster Magazine* (February). Available at http://www.cio.com/archive/webbusiness/020197_facts_content.html (last accessed Jan 21st, 2000).

Hinrich, Randy J. 1997. Intranet 101. *The Intranet Journal.* Available at http://www.intranetjournal.com/newbie.html (last accessed Jan 21st, 2000).

Horton, Forrest Woody Jr. 1979. *Information Resources Management: Concept and Cases*. Cleveland, OH: Association for Systems Management.

Huber, G.P. 1990. A Theory of the Effects of Advanced Information Technologies on Organizational Design, Intelligence, and Decision Making. *Academy of Management Review* 15, no. 1:47-71.

Huber, George P. 1996. Organizational Learning: The Contributing Processes and the Literatures. In *Organizational Learning*, edited by M. D. Cohen and L. S. Sproull. Thousand Oaks, CA: Sage.

Huber, George P., and Richard L. Daft. 1987. The Information Environments of Organizations. In *Handbook of Organizational Communications*, edited by F. Jablin and L. L. Putnam. Newbury Park, CA: Sage Publications.

Huberman, Bernardo A., Peter L. Pirolli, James E. Pitkow, and Rajan M. Lukose. 1998. Strong Regularities in World-Wide Web Surfing. *Science* 280, no. 5360: 94-97.

Hummingbird. 1996. The Intranet: Implementation of Internet and Web Technologies in Organizational Information Systems.

INET. 1996. *Intranets: Internet Technologies Deployed Behind The Firewall For Corporate Productivity*. Framingham, MA: Process Software Corporation. Available at http://www.process.com/intranets/wp2.htp (last accessed Jan 21st, 2000).

Ingwersen, P. 1998. The Calculation of Web Impact Factors. *Journal of Documentation* 54, no. 2: 236-243.

James, Geoffrey. 1996. Intranets Rescue Reengineering. *Datamation* (December).

Janis, Irving. 1982. *Groupthink: Psychological Studies of Policy Decision*. Boston, MA: Houghton Mifflin.

Johnson-Laird, P. N. 1983. Mental Models: Towards A Cognitive Science of Language, Inference, and Consciousness. Cambridge, MA: Harvard University Press.

Johnson-Lenz, Peter, and Trudy Johnson-Lenz. 1982. Groupware: The Process and Impact of Design Choices. In *Computer-Mediated Communication Systems: Status and Evaluation*, edited by E. Kerr and S. Hiltz: Academic Press.

Katz, Ralph and Thomas J. Allen. 1982. Investigating The Not Invented Here (NIH) Syndrome: A Look At The Performance, Tenure, And Communication Patterns Of 50 R & D Project Groups. *R&D Management* 12, no. 1: 7-19.

Katzer, Jeffrey, and Patricia T. Fletcher. 1992. The Information Environment Of Managers. In *Annual Review of Information Science and Technology (ARIST)*, edited by M. E. Williams. Medford, New Jersey: Learned Information, Inc.

Keegan, W. J. 1974. Multinational Scanning: A Study Of The Information Sources Utilized By Headquarters Executives In Multinational Companies. *Administrative Science Quarterly* 19: 411-421.

Kehoe, C., J. Pitkow, and J. Rogers. 1998. *GVU's Ninth WWW User Survey Report*. Available at http://www.gvu.gatech.edu/user_surveys/survey-1998-04 (last accessed Jan 21st, 2000).

Kelly, G. A. 1963. *A Theory of Personality: The Psychology of Personal Constructs*. New York: W. W. Norton & Co.

Kessler, M.M. 1963. *Comparison of the Results of Bibliographic Coupling and Analytic Subject Indexing*. Report. Massachusetts Institute of Technology (January 28th).

Kiesler, C. A. 1971. *The Psychology of Commitment*. New York: Academic Press.

Kirkpatrick, D. 1994. Why Microsoft Can't Stop Lotus Notes. *Fortune* 12, (December):141-157.

Kirton, M. J., ed. 1989. *Adaptors and Innovators*. London: Routledge.

Kling, Rob. 1996a. Learning About the Possible Futures of Computerization from the Present and the Past. In *Computerization and Controversy: Value Conflicts and Social Choices,* 2nd edition, edited by R. Kling, pp. 26-31. San Diego, CA: Academic Press.

Kling, Rob. 1996b. Computerization at Work. In *Computerization and Controversy: Value Conflicts and Social Choices,* 2nd edition, edited by R. Kling, pp. 278-308. San Diego, CA: Academic Press.

Kogut, Bruce and Udo Zander. 1992. Knowledge of the Firm, Combinative Capabilities, and the Replication of Technology. *Organization Science* 3, no. 3: 383-397.

Kornblith, Hilary, ed. 1994. *Naturalizing Epistemology*. Cambridge, MA: MIT Press.

Kraut, Robert E., Robert S. Fish, Robert W. Root, and Barbara L. Chalfonte. 1990. Informal Communications In Organizations: Form, Function, And Technology. In *People's Reactions To Technology In Factories, Offices, And Areospace*, edited by S. Oskamp and S. Spacapan. The Claremont Symposium on Applied Social Psychology: Sage Publications.

Krohne, H. W. 1986. Coping With Stress: Dispositions, Strategies, and the Problem of Measurement. In *Dynamics of Stress*, ed. C. D. Spielberger and I. G. Sarason. New York: Plenum.

Krohne, H. W. 1989. The Concept of Coping Modes: Relating Cognitive Person Variables to Actual Coping Behavior. *Advances in Behavioural Research and Theory* 11: 235-249.

Kuhlthau, Carol C. 1991. Inside The Search Process: Information Seeking From The User's Perspective. *Journal of the American Society for Information Science* 42, no. 5:361-371.

Kuhlthau, Carol Collier. 1993. *Seeking Meaning: A Process Approach to Library and Information Services*. Norwood, NJ: Ablex Publishing.

Kuhn, Thomas S. 1970. *The Structure of Scientific Revolutions*. Chicago, IL: University of Chicago Press.

Kuutti, Kari. 1996. Debates In IS And CSCW Research: Anticipating System Design For Post-Fordist Work. In Information Technology And Changes In Organizational Work. *In the Proceedings Of The IFIP WG8.2 Working Conference On Information Technology And Changes In Organizational Work*, December 1995, edited by W. J. Orlikowski, G. Walsham, M. R. Jones and J. I. DeGross. London: Chapman & Hall.

Larson, Ray R. 1996. Bibliometrics of the World Wide Web: An Exploratory Analysis of the Intellectual Structure of Cyberspace. In the *Proceedings of 59th ASIS Annual Meeting* held in Baltimore, Maryland, edited by Steve Hardin, 33: 71-78.

Lave, Jean and Etienne Wenger. 1991. *Situated Learning: Legitimate Peripheral Participation.*. Cambridge, UK: Cambridge University Press.

Lave, Jean, and Etienne Wenger. 1995. Situated Learning: Legitimate Peripheral Participation. Edited by R. Pea and J. Seely Brown. Vol. first published in 1991, *Learning In Doing: Social, Cognitive, And Computational Perspectives*. New York: Cambridge University Press.

Leonard, Dorothy; Sensiper, Sylvia. 1998. The Role Of Tacit Knowledge In Group Innovation. *California Management Review* 40, no. 3: 112-132.

Leonard-Barton, Dorothy. 1995. *Wellsprings of Knowledge: Building and Sustaining the Sources of Innovation*. Boston, MA: Harvard Business School Press.

Lester, Ray and Judith Waters. 1989. *Environmental Scanning and Business Strategy*. London, UK: British Library, Research and Development Department.

Liu, Cricket, Jerry Peek, Russ Jones, Bryan Buss, and Adrian Nye. 1994. *Managing Internet Information Services*. Sebastopol, CA: O'Reilly & Associates.

Lotka, A.J. 1926. The Frequency Distribution of Scientific Productivity. *Journal of the Washington Academy of Sciences* 16: 317-323.

Mace, Scott, Udo Flohr, Rick Dobson, and Tony Graham. 1998. Weaving A Better Web: The Features That Made HTML So Popular Are Causing The Web To Fall Apart. What's Next? *Byte Magazine* (March).

MacMullin, Susan E. and Robert S. Taylor. 1984. Problem Dimensions and Information Traits. *Information Society* 3, no. 1: 91-111.

Malone, Thomas W., Kenneth R. Grant, Kum-Yew Lai, Ramana Rao, and David A. Rosenblitt. 1989. The Information Lens: An Intelligent System For Information Sharing And Coordination. In *Technological Support For Work Group Collaboration*, edited by M. Olson: Lawrence Erlbaum Associates.

March, James G. 1994. *A Primer on Decision Making: How Decisions Happen*. New York, NY: Free Press.

March, James G. and Herbert A. Simon. 1993. *Organizations*. 2nd ed. Oxford, UK: Blackwell.

Marchionini, Gary. 1995. *Information Seeking In Electronic Environments*. Edited by J. Long, Cambridge Series on Human-Computer Interaction. Cambridge, UK: Cambridge University Press.

Marshakova, I. V. 1973. A System Of Document Connection Based On References. *Scientific and Technical Information Serial of VINITI* 6, no. 2: 3-8.

Martin, Joanne. 1992. *Cultures in Organizations: Three Perspectives*. New York: Oxford University Press.

Miller, S. M. and C. E. Mangan. 1983. Interesting Effects of Information and Coping Style in Adapting to Gynecological Stress: Should a Doctor Tell All? *Journal of Personality and Social Psychology* 45: 223-236.

Moser, Paul K., Dwayne H. Mulder, and J. D. Trout. 1998. *The Theory of Knowledge*. New York: Oxford University Press.

Mouzelis, Nicos P. 1995. Sociological Theory: What Went Wrong? Diagnosis and Remedies. London: Routledge.

Mullich, Joe. 1997. Turning The Focus Outward: C&L Leverages Intranet For Access To External Info Services. *PCWeek Online* (August 28). Available at http://www.zdnet.com/pcweek/builder/0825/25cl.html (last accessed Jan 21st, 2000).

Nelson, Richard and Sidney Winter. 1982. *An Evolutionary Theory of Economic Change*. Cambridge, MA: Belknap Press.

Netscape. 1996a. Intranets Redefine Corporate Information Systems: Netscape Solutions Enterprise.

Netscape. 1996b. *U S West Communications Uses Netscape Software For Corporate Intranet*. Available at http://www.netscape.com/newsref/pr/newsrelease265.html (last accessed Jan 21st, 2000).

Netscape. 1998. Building Technology Competence Across The Organization.

Nilan, Michael S., Robin P. Peek, and Herbert W. Snyder. 1988. A Methodology for Tapping User Evaluation Behaviors: An Exploration of Users' Strategy, Source and Information Evaluating. In *Proceedings of Proceedings of the American Society for Information Science (ASIS) 51st Annual Meeting* held in Medford, NJ, edited by Christine L. Borgman and Edward Y. H. Pai, 152-159. Learned Information.

Nonaka, Ikujiro and Hirotaka Takeuchi. 1995. The Knowledge-Creating Company: How

Japanese Companies Create the Dynamics of Innovation. New York, NY: Oxford University Press.

Nonaka, Ikujiro, and Noboru Konno. 1998. The Concept Of "Ba": Building A Foundation For Knowledge Creation. *California Management Review* 40, no. 3: 40-54.

Olsen, Michael D., Bvsan Murthy, and Richard Teare. 1994. CEO Perspectives on Scanning the Global Hotel Business Environment. *International Journal of Contemporary Hospitality Management* 6, no. 4: 3-9.

O'Reilly, Charles A. III. 1982. Variation In Decision Makers' Use Of Information Sources: The Impact Of Quality And Accessibility Of Information. *Academy of Management Journal* 25, no. 4: 756-771.

O'Reilly, Charles A. III and Michael L. Tushman. 1997. Using Culture for Strategic Advantage: Promoting Innovation Through Social Control. In *Managing Strategic Innovation and Change*, eds. Michael Tushman and Philip Anderson, 200-216. New York: Oxford University Press.

Orlikowski, Wanda J. 1992. Learning From Notes: Organizational Issues In Groupware Implementation. In the *Proceedings of CSCW '92*, Toronto, Ontario, Canada, October 31-November 4, edited by J. Turner and R. Kraut. New York: ACM Press.

Orlikowski, Wanda J. 1995. *Evolving With Notes: Organizational Change Around Groupware Technology*. Cambridge, MA: Massachusetts Institute of Technology.

Ottenlips, Sam, Thomas A. Browdy, and David Carrithers. 1997. *Let's Talk!: An Intranet For Gathering Intelligence And Facilitating Corporate Communications*. Society For Information Management (SIM) International Paper Awards Competition.

Paisley, William. 1968. Information Needs and Uses. In *Annual Review of Information Science and Technology*, ed. Carlos A. Cuadra, 1-30. Chicago, IL: Encyclopaedia Britannica, Inc.

Pejtersen, Annelise Mark, and J. Rasmussen. 1997. Effectiveness Testing Of Complex Systems. In the *Handbook of Human Factors and Ergonomics*, edited by G. Salvendy. London: John Wiley.

Pejtersen, Annelise Mark. 1996. Empirical Workplace Evaluation Of Complex Systems. In the *Proceedings of the Second MIRA Workshop*, University of Glasgow Computing Science Research Report TR-1997-2, edited by M. D. Dunlop. Monselice, Italy.

Perrin, Constance. 1991. Electronic Social Fields In Bureaucracies. *Communications of the ACM* 34, no. 12: 75-82.

Perrow, Charles. 1967. A Framework for the Comparative Analysis of Organizations.

American Sociological Review 32, no. 2: 194-208.

Pirolli, Peter and Stuart Card. 1995. Information Foraging in Information Access Environments. In the *Proceedings of Conference on Human Factors in Computer Systems CHI-95* held in Denver, Colorado, USA, 51-58. ACM Press.

Pirolli, Peter, James Pitkow, and Ramana Rao. 1996. Silk from a Sow's Ear: Extracting Usable Structures from the Web. In the *Proceedings of Conference on Human Factors in Computer Systems CHI-96* held in Vancouver, BC, Canada. ACM Press.

Pitkow, Jim. 1997. In Search of Reliable Usage Data on the WWW. In the *Proceedings of the Sixth International World Wide Web Conference*, Santa Clara, CA.

Pitkow, Jim and M. Recker. 1994. Results From The First World-Wide Web Survey. *Journal of Computer Networks and ISDN Systems* 27, no. 2.

Plumtree. 1999. Corporate Portals: A Simple View of a Complex World. (White Paper).

Polanyi, Michael. 1962. *Personal Knowledge Towards a Post-Critical Philosophy.* Chicago: University of Chicago Press.

Polanyi, Michael. 1966. *The Tacit Dimension*. London, UK: Routledge & Kegan Paul.

Preble, J. F., A. Pradeep, and A.Reichel. 1988. The Environmental Scanning Practices of US Multinationals in the Late 1980s. *Management International Review* 28: 4-14.

Price, D. 1976. A General Theory of Bibliometric and Other Cumulative Advantage Processes. *Journal of American Society of Information Science* 27, (Sept-Oct): 292-306.

Price, N. and Schiminovich, S. 1968. A Clustering Experiment: First Step Towards a Computer-Generated Classification Scheme. *Information Storage Retrieval* 4:271-280.

PricewaterhouseCoopers. 1998. Coopers & Lybrand Expanded Intranet Site Now Drawing More That 10 Million Hits A Month. (March 9th).

Quine, W. V. 1969. *Ontological Relativity and Other Essays*. New York: Columbia University Press.

Rasmussen, J., A.M. Pejtersen, and L.P. Goodstein. 1994. *Cognitive Systems Engineering*. London: John Wiley.

Rice, Valeri. 1996. Building The Case For Your Intranet. *PC Week* (April 29th). Available at http://www.zdnet.com/pcweek/archive/960429/pcwk0052.htm (last accessed Jan 21st, 2000).

Roberts-Witt, S.L. 1999. Making Sense of Portal Pandemonium. *Knowledge Management*. July. Available at http://www.kmmag.com/kmmagn2/km199907/featurea1.htm (last accessed Jan 21st, 2000).

Robinson, M. 1991a. Computer Supported Co-Operative Work: Cases And Concepts. In *Groupware 1991: The Potential Of Team And Organisational Computing*, edited by P. Hendriks. P.O. Box 424, 3500 AK Utrecht, The Netherlands: Software Engineering Research Centre (SERC).

Robinson, Mike. 1991b. Double Level Languages And Co-Operative Working. *AI & Society* 5: 34-60.

Rogers, Everett M. 1983. *Diffusion of Innovations*. 3rd ed. New York, NY: The Free Press.

Rogers, Everett M. 1995. *Diffusion of Innovations*. 4th ed. New York, NY: The Free Press.

Rogers, Yvonne. 1994. Exploring Obstacles: Integrating CSCW in Evolving Organizations. In the *Proceedings of CSCW '94*, Chapel Hill, NC, October 22-26, edited by R. Furuta and C. Neuwirth. New York: ACM Press.

Rosenbaum, Howard. 1993. Information Use Environments And Structuration: Towards An Integration Of Taylor And Giddens. In the *Proceedings of the 56th ASIS Annual Meeting*, Columbus, Ohio, October 24-October 28, edited by S. Bonzi. Medford, NJ: Learned Information.

Rosenbaum, Howard. 1996. Managers And Information In Organizations: Towards A Structurational Concept Of The Information Use Environment Of Managers. Ph.D. dissertation, School of Information Studies, Syracuse University, Syracuse, New York.

Rosenberg, V. 1967. Factors Affecting The Preferences Of Industrial Personnel For Information Gathering Methods. *Information Storage and Retrieval*, 3: 119-127.

Russell, Bertrand. 1912. *The Problems of Philosophy*. New York: Henry Holt.

Ryan Garcia, Mary. 1997. Knowledge Central: Services Vendors In Intranets To Speed Data Sharing. *InformationWeek Online* (September 22nd). Available at http://www.informationweek.com/649/profes.htm (last accessed Jan 21st, 2000).

Sackmann, Sonja A. 1991. *Cultural Knowledge in Organizations*. Newbury Park, CA: Sage.

Sackmann, Sonja A. 1992. Culture and Subcultures: An Analysis of Organizational Knowledge. *Administrative Science Quarterly* 37, no. 1: 140-161.

Salancik, G.R. 1977. Commitment and the Control of Organizational Behavior and Belief. In *New Directions in Organizational Behavior*, ed. B.M. Staw and G.R. Salancik, 1-54. Chicago: St. Clair.

Sanchez, Ron. 1997. Managing Articulated Knowledge in Competence-based Competition. In *Strategic Learning and Knowledge Management*, ed. Ron Sanchez and Aime Heene, 163-188. New York: John Wiley.

Sandstrom, Pamela Effrein. 1994. An Optimal Foraging Approach to Information Seeking and Use. *Library Quarterly* 64, no. 4: 414-449.

Saracevic, Tefko. 1970. The Notion of 'Relevance' in Information Science. In *Introduction to Information Science*, ed. Tefko Saracevic, 111-151. New York, NY: R.R. Bowker Co.

Saracevic, Tefko. 1975. Relevance: A Review of and a Framework for the Thinking on the Notion in Information Science. *Journal of the American Society for Information Science* 26, no. 6: 321-343.

Schamber, Linda. 1994. Relevance and Information Behavior. In *Annual Review of Information Science and Technology*, ed. Martha E. Williams. Medford, NJ: Learned Information, Inc.

Schamber, Linda, Michael B. Eisenberg, and Michael S. Nilan. 1990. A Re-examination of Relevance: Toward a Dynamic, Situational Definition. *Information Processing & Management* 26, no. 6: 755-776.

Schatz, Bruce R. 1991-1992. Building an Electronic Community System. *Journal of Management Information Systems* 8, no. 3: 87-107.

Schein, Edgar H. 1997. *Organizational Culture and Leadership*. 2nd ed. San Francisco, CA: Jossey-Bass.

Schein, Edgar H. 1991. What Is Culture. In *Reframing Organizational Culture* , ed. Peter J. Frost, Larry F. Moore, Meryl Reis Louis, Craig C. Lundberg, and Joanne Martin, 243-253. Newbury Park, CA: Sage Publications.

Schiminovich, S. 1971. Automatic Classification and Retrieval of Documents by Means of a Bibliographic Pattern Discovery Algorithm. *Information Storage and Retrieval* 6: 417-435.

Schön, Donald A. 1983. The Reflective Practitioner: How Professionals Think in Action. New York: Basic Books, Inc.

Schuler, Douglas, and Aki Namioka, eds. 1993. *Participatory Design: Principles and*

Practices. Hillsdale, New Jersey: Lawrence Erlbaum Associates.

Schumpeter, Joseph A. 1934. *The Theory of Economic Development.* Cambridge, MA: Harvard University Press.

Senker, Jacqueline. 1998. The Contribution of Tacit Knowledge to Innovation. In *Exploring Expertise: Issues and Perspectives* , ed. Robin Williams, Wendy Faulkner, and James Fleck, 223-244. London, UK: Macmillan Press.

Simon, Herbert A. 1997. *Administrative Behavior: A Study of Decision-Making Processes in Administrative Organization*. 4th ed. New York, NY: The Free Press.

Simon, Herbert A. 1979. Information Processing Models of Cognition. *Annual Review of Psychology* 30: 363-96.

Small, H. 1973. Co-Citation in the Scientific Literature: A New Measurement of the Relationship Between Two Documents. *Journal of the American Society of Information Science* 24, no. 4: 265-269.

Smith, Douglas K. and Robert C. Alexander. 1988. *Fumbling The Future: How Xerox Invented, Then Ignored, The First Personal Computer*. New York, NY: William Morrow.

Spender, J.-C. 1996. Competitive Advantage from Tacit Knowledge? Unpacking the Concept and Its Strategic Implications. In *Organizational Learning and Competitive Advantage,* ed. Bertrand Monigeon and Amy Edmondson. Thousand Oaks, CA: Sage Publishers.

Spender, J.-C. 1998. The Dynamics of Individual and Organizational Knowledge. In *Managerial and Organizational Cognition: Theory, Methods and Research*, ed. Colin Eden and J.-C. Spender. Thousand Oaks, CA: Sage.

Spertus, E. (1997, April 7-11). ParaSite: Mining Structural Information on the Web. In the *Proceedings of the Sixth International World Wide Web Conference*, Santa Clara, CA.

Sproull, Lee, and Sara Kiesler. 1991a. Computers, Networks and Work. *Scientific American* 265, no. 3 (September 1991): 116-123.

Sproull, Lee, and Sara Kiesler. 1991b. Increasing Personal Connections. In *Connections: New Ways Of Working In The Networked Organization*, edited by L. Sproull and S. Kiesler: MIT Press.

Sprout, Alison, and Ruth Coxeter. 1995. The Internet Inside Your Company. *Fortune* (Nov 27th).

Stata, R. 1989. Organizational Learning: The Key to Management Innovation. *Sloan*

Management Review (Spring): 63-74.

Staw, Barry M. and Jerry Ross. 1987. Knowing When to Pull the Plug. *Harvard Business Review* 65, no. 2: 68-74.

Stein, E. W., & Zwass, V. (1995). Actualizing organizational memory with information systems. *Information Systems Research, 6*(2), 85-117.

Stephens, D. W., & Krebs, J. R. 1986. *Foraging Theory*. Princeton, N.J.: Princeton University Press.

Strom, David. 1995. *Creating Private Intranets: Challenges And Prospects For IS.* Available at http://www.strom.com/pubwork/intranetp.html (last accessed Jan 21st, 2000).

Sullivan, Patrick H., ed. 1998. *Profiting From Intellectual Capital*. New York: John Wiley.

Sutton, Stuart A. 1994. The Role of Attorney Mental Models of Law in Case Relevance Determinations: An Exploratory Analysis. *Journal of the American Society for Information Science* 45, no. 3: 186-200.

Tauscher, Linda and Saul Greenberg. 1997. How People Revisit Web Pages: Empirical Findings and Implications for the Design of History Systems. *International Journal of Human-Computer Studies* 47: 97-137.

Tauscher, Linda and Saul Greenberg. 1997. Revisitation Patterns in World Wide Web Navigation. In the *Proceedings of CHI 97 Human Factors in Computing Systems* held in Atlanta, Georgia, USA, edited by Steven Pemberton, Vol. 399-406. CHI 97.

Taylor, Robert S. 1968. Question-Negotiation and Information Seeking in Libraries. *College & Research Libraries* 29, no. 3: 178-194.

Taylor, Robert S. 1986. *Value-added Processes in Information Systems*. Norwood, NJ: Ablex Publishing Corp.

Taylor, Robert S. 1991. Information Use Environments. In *Progress in Communication Science*, ed. Brenda Dervin and Melvin J. Voigt, 217-254. Norwood, NJ: Ablex Publishing Corporation.

Telleen, Steven L. 1996a. *The Intranet Architecture: Managing Information In The New Paradigm*. Sunnyvale, CA: Amdahl Corporation. Available at http://www.amdahl.com/doc/products/bsg/intra/infra.html (last accessed Jan 21st, 2000).

Telleen, Steven L. 1996b. *Intranet Organization: Strategies for Managing Change.* (online book). Available at http://www.iorg.com/intranetorg/ (last accessed Jan

21st, 2000).

Telleen, Steven L. 1996c. *Intranets and Adaptive Innovation.* Sunnyvale, CA: Amdahl Corporation. Available at http://www.amdahl.com/doc/products/bsg/intra/adapt.html (last accessed Jan 21st, 2000).

Thyfault, Mary E. 1996. The Intranet Rolls In. *InformationWeek.*

Tsoukas, H. 1996. The Firm as a Distributed Knowledge System: A Constructionist Approach. *Strategic Management Journal* 17, (Special Issue): 11-26.

Tversky, Amos and David Kahneman. 1974. Judgment Under Uncertainty: Heuristics and Biases. *Science* 185: 1124-1131.

Verity. 1999. The Verity Corporate Portal: Organize Your Intranet The Way You Organize Your Business. (White Paper).

von Krogh, Georg. 1998. Care In Knowledge Creation. *California Management Review* 40, no. 3: 133-153.

Voos, H. 1974. Lotka and Information Science. *Journal of the American Society of Information Science* 25: 270-273.

Walsh, James P., and Gerardo R. Ungson. 1991. Organizational Memory. *Academy of Management Review* 16, no. 1: 57-91.

Weick, Karl E. 1995. *Sensemaking In Organizations.* Thousand Oaks, CA: Sage Publications.

Weick, Karl E. and Richard L. Daft. 1983. The Effectiveness of Interpretation Systems. In *Organizational Effectiveness: A Comparison of Multiple Models*, ed. Kim S. Cameron and David A. Whetten, 71-93. New York, NY: Academic Press.

Weill, Peter and Marianne Broadbent. 1998. *Leveraging the New Infrastructure: How Market Leaders Capitalize on IT.* Cambridge, MA: Harvard Business School Press.

Wenger, Etienne. 1998. *Communities of Practice: Learning, Meaning and Identity.* Cambridge, UK: Cambridge University Press.

Wilson, Patrick. 1977. Public Knowledge, Private Ignorance: Toward a Library and Information Policy. Westport, CT: Greenwood Publishing Group.

Wilson, Tom D. 1981. On User Studies and Information Needs. *Journal of Documentation* 37, no. 1: 3-15.

Wilson, Tom D. 1994. Information Needs and Uses: Fifty Years of Progress? In *Fifty*

Years of Information Progress: A Journal of Documentation Review, ed. Brian C. Vickery, 15-51. London, UK: Association for Information Management.

Wilson, Tom D. 1997. Information Behaviour: An Interdisciplinary Perspective. *Information Processing & Management* 33, no. 4: 551-572.

Winterhalder, B. 1981. Foraging Strategies in the Boreal Forest: An Analysis of Cree Hunting and Gathering. In *Hunter-Gather Foraging Strategies*, eds. B. Winterhalder and E. Smith, 66-98. Chicago: University of Chicago Press.

Witkin, H. A. and D. R. Goodenough. 1981. Cognitive Styles: Essence and Origins, Field Dependence and Field Independence. *Psychological Issues* 14, no. 51: whole issue.

Witkin, H. A., C. A. Moore, D. R. Goodenough, and P. W. Cox. 1977. Field-Dependent and Field-Independent Cognitive Styles and Their Educational Implications. *Review of Educational Research* 1977: 1-64.

Wolesky, Patricia. 1996. An Info*Engine White Paper: Business-Driven Intranets.

Woodruff, Allison, Paul M Aoki, Eric Brewer, Paul Gauthier, and Lawrence A. Rowe. 1996. An Investigation of Documents from the World Wide Web. Paper read at *5th International WWW Conference* (WWW5), at Paris.

Wulfekuhler, M. R. and. P., William F. 1997. Finding Salient Features for Personal Web Page Categories. In the *Proceedings of the Sixth International World Wide Web Conference*, Santa Clara, CA.

Zipf, George Kingsley. 1949. Human Behavior and the Principle of Least Effort: An Introduction to Human Ecology. Cambridge, MA: Addison-Wesley.

Zmud, Robert W. 1978. An Empirical Investigation of the Dimensionality of the Concept of Information. *Decision Sciences* 9, no. 2: 187-195.

Zuboff, S. 1988. *In The Age Of The Smart Machine*. New York: Basic Books.

Index

The letters *f* and *t* following page numbers denote figure and table respectively.

Abraham, J., 71–72, 101–2
Abstraction. *See* Knowledge diffusion
Action-oriented behaviors, 111
ActiveX, 78
Adaption-Innovation Theory, 17
Adler, P. and Cole, R., 47
Affective factors, 4f, 8f, 15f
Aguilar, F., 151–52, 160, 177
Allen, B., 5, 8, 128
Allen, T., 12, 87, 149, 166
Almaden Research Center (IBM), 187
Almind, T. and Ingwersen, P., 144–46. *See also* Bibliometrics, Webometrics
AltaVista, 146, 176, 178
Alto, 45
Alvesson, M., 45
America Online (AOL), 157
Anarchy. *See* information politics
API (Application Programming Interface), 76, 78
Argyris, C., 18, 25
Audi, R., 31
Auster, E. and Choo, C., 160, 162–63, 166

Ba, 91–92
Badaracco, J., 46–48
Bandura, A., 12
Bannon, L. and Schmidt, K., 81, 90, 95
Barclay, R., 187
Bartlett, F., 30
Bayne, R., 16
Behavioral Model of Information Seeking, 177–81
  episodes of activity from case study, 177f
Behavioral Model of Web Information Seeking, 152–54, 153f
Behavioral-Ecological Framework, 117–23, 118f
  empirical testing of, 123–28
Belief-forming processes, 32
Belkin, N., Oddy, N. and Brooks, H., 103
Bentley, R., Appelt, W., Busbach, U., Hinrichs, E., Kerr, D., Sikkel, K., Trevor, J. and Woetzel, G., 80
Bentley, R., Horstmann, T. and Trevor, J., 74, 80
Berners-Lee, T., Cailliau, R., Luotonen, A., Nielsen, H. and Secret, A., 73
Bibliometrics, 137–47
  and Web documents, 142–44
  bibliometric coupling, 138
  bibliometric laws, 139–42
  bibliometrics of use, 137–38
  co-citation analysis, 138–39
  measures of group web use, 146–47
  Webometrics, 144–46
Boeing, 129. *See also* Intranet case studies.
Boisot, M., 33, 43, 49, 52–54, 56, 66
Boolean, 146, 180, 183
Bourdieu, P., 62
Bowers, J., 92–93
Bradford, S., 141, 174
Bradford's Law of Scattering, 139, 141–42. *See also* Bibliometrics, bibliometric laws
Bravo, 45
British Petroleum (BP), 54
  exploration arm (BPX), 54–56
Broadbent, M. and Weill, P., 82–83
Broker pages. *See* Intranets, broker pages
Brookes, B., 141–42
Brown, J., 34, 49
Brown, J. and Duguid, P, 49
Bruce, H., 181

C (computer language), 76
C++, 76
Canada Newswire Site, 178
CANOE, 178
Carnegie Mellon University, 95
Catledge, L. and Pitkow, J., 155–56, 167, 172
CGI (Common Gateway Interface), 76, 78
Chang, S. and Rice, R., 149
Choo, C., 7, 13, 33, 63–64, 67, 149
Choo, C. and Auster, E., 7
Choo, C., Detlor, B. and Turnbull, D., 159
Ciborra, C., 84
CIO Communications, 96, 99
Clement, A. and Wagner, I., 81
Clever Project (IBM), 187
Client/server model, 73, 74f, 75–78
CMP Media, 97
Co-citation analysis. *See* Bibliometrics, co-citation analysis
Codification. *See* Knowledge diffusion
Cognitive factors, 4f, 8f, 15f
Cognitive gaps, 4
Cognitive style, 16, 24–26
Collins, H., 43
Communities of practice, 56–60, 58f, 186. *See also* Knowledge utilization; Wenger, E.

Conditioned viewing. *See* Scanning Model
Conklin, J., 92–93
Content pages. *See* Intranets, content pages
Cook, S. and Yanow, D., 89
Coopers & Lybrand, 96–7, 100–1. *See also* Intranet case studies, Coopers & Lybrand
Corporate intranets. *See* Portals
Cortese, A., 72, 102
Critical Incident Technique (Flanagan), 175
Cronin, B. and Hert, C., 136
Crovella, M. and Bestavros, A., 156–57
CSCW (Computer Supported Cooperative Work), 71, 90, 95–96
  lessons learned from, 92–96
Cuhna, C., Bestavros, A. and Crovella, M., 167
Culnan, M., 12–13, 160
Cultural knowledge, 34t, 43–48. *See also* Organizational knowledge
CyberLYB. *See* KnowledgeCurve
Cyert, R. and March, J., 19–20, 25, 39–40, 65

Daft, R., Sormunen, J. and Parks, D., 160
Daft, R. and Weick, K., 151
Data, Information and Knowledge, 30f
Data mining, 144
Davenport, T., 88, 112–17, 123, 128
Davenport, T., Eccles, R. and Prusak, L., 21, 25, 119
Davenport, T., Jarvenpaa, S. and Beers, M., 79
Davenport, T. and Prusak, L., 79
DejaNews, 178
Delphi Group, 72
Denmark, 129, 145
Dervin, B., 4–5, 16, 22, 103, 120, 123
Dervin, B. and Nilan, M., 110
Detlor, B., 71, 117
Diffusion. *See* Knowledge Diffusion
Diodato, V., 141
Dix, A., 80
Douglas, M., 45–46
Dow Jones Interactive, 97
Downie, J., 146–47
Doz, Y. and Hamel, G., 47
Dretske, F., 31
Drott, M., 141
Duncan, R., 7

Eckerson, W., 72
Eich, B. et al., 167
Eisenberg, M. and Schamber, L., 9
Electronic Browsing Model (Marchionini), 147–48
Electronic Commerce Framework, 178
Ellis, C., Gibbs, S. and Rein, G., 81, 95
Ellis, D., 148–50, 152, 177–78, 180
Ellis, D. and Haugan, M., 148
Ellis, D., Cox, D. and Hall, K., 148, 150
Environment Protection Agency, 178
Etzioni, A., 152
Explicit knowledge, 34t, 39–43. *See also* Organizational knowledge
Extensible Markup Language. *See* XML

Federalism. *See* Information politics.
Feudalism. *See* Information politics.
Field dependence / independence, 16–17, 25
Fielding, R., Irvine, U., Gettys, J., Mogul, J., Frystyk, H. and Berners-Lee, T., 74
Finholt, T. and Sproull, L., 80, 91
FIS. *See* University of Toronto
Flanagan, J., 175
Fleck, J., 43
Fletcher, P., 107
Foraging Theory (Stephens and Krebs), 133. *See also* Information foraging.
Formal search. *See* Scanning Model
Forrester Research, 178
Fortune 500, 72
Foucault, M., 43
Francik, E., Rudman, S., Cooper, D. and Levine, S., 95

GAOO. *See* Matsushita case, GAOO.
Gartner Group, 72
Garud, R. and Rappa, M., 44
General Motors, 46–47
Georgia Tech., 155
Gerson, E. and Star, S., 90
Gerstberger, P. and Allen, T., 12, 166
Ghoshal, S., 7
Giddens, A., 110–11. *See also* Theory of Structuration
Ginsburg, M. and Duliba, K., 79–80, 95
Global Village. *See* Intranet case studies, USWest
Goldman, A., 32
Gonzalez, J., 80, 99
Google engine (Stanford University), 187
Grant, R., 39, 49, 61, 67
Grasso, A., Meunier, J., Pagani, D. and Pareschi, R., 80
Greenberg, S., 156
Greif, I. and Cashman, P., 90
Groupthink, 20–21
Groupware, 80–81, 90, 92–96
  barriers to adoption and use of, 92–94
Grudin, J., 92–93, 95, 103
Guengerich, S., Graham, D., Miller, M. and McDonald, S., 76

Halbwachs, M., 89

Halpern, D. and Nilan, M., 10
Harper, R., 92–93
Harter, S., 9–10
Haynal, R., 72
Heuristics, three sets of, 17
Hewins, E., 110
Hildebrand, C., 102
Hinrich, R., 71
Horton, F., 112
HTML (Hypertext Markup Language), 73–78
HTTP (Hypertext Transfer Protocol), 73–77
Huber, G., 84, 87–90
Huber, G. and Daft, R., 90
Huberman, B., Pirolli, P., Pitkow, J. and Lukose, R., 140, 157
Human Behavior & the Principle of Least Effort (George K. Zipf), 139
Human Electronics. *See* Matsushita case, Human Electronics

IBM (International Business Machines), 176, 187
Informal search. *See* Scanning Model
Information,
  as food, 137. *See also* Information foraging
  dimensions of, 9
Information behaviors, 109–13, 116t, 120–22, 123t. *See also* Information traits
Information culture, 113, 117–18
  empirical findings, 125, 126t
Information ecology, 117–19, 121,
  and creation of value-added processes, 126t
  empirical findings, 123–25, 123t, 127
Information Ecology Model (Davenport), 112–15, 117
Information environment, 112–17. *See also* Organizational information environment
  common elements of four models, 115–17
  major tenets of four models, 116t
Information Environment of Managers (Katzer & Fletcher), 109–10
Information foraging, 133–37
Information needs, 3–7, 4f, 22–23
  affective dimensions, 5–6
  cognitive dimensions, 4–5
  levels of, 5–6
  situational dimensions, 6–7
Information needs and uses, 117, 119–120
Information needs and uses studies, 4
Information politics, 21, 25–26, 113
Information processes, 114
Information relevance, 9
Information search process (Kuhlthau), 10–11
  six sets of implications, 11
  six stages, 10–11
Information seeking, 5, 8–14, 8f, 21–27
  affective dimensions, 10–12
  cognitive dimensions, 9–10
  integrated model, 21–27, 22f
  perceived source accessibility and quality, 14f
  situational dimensions, 12–14
Information Seeking Model (Ellis), 148–51
  six categories, 148–50
Information Source Usage, frequency of, 163f
Information Sources Used, 161t
Information Space (I-Space) Model (Boisot), 52–56, 55f
Information staff, 114, 119
Information traits, 9, 108, 115–16, 116t, , 120–21, 123–24, 123t, 127 *See also* Information behaviors
  and creation of value-added processes, 127t
Information use, 5, 14–21, 15t, 24–26
  affective dimensions, 17–19
  cognitive dimensions, 16–17
  eight categories, 15–16
  situational dimensions, 19–21
Information Use Environment (IUE) (Taylor), 107–12, 115–6
Information users, 119–20
Informavores, 136. *See also* Information foraging
Ingwersen, P., 145–46
Inktomi search engine, 142
Internet protocol (IP). *See* TCP/IP
Interpretive perspective. *See* Organizational learning
Intranet case studies, 96–100, 129
  Coopers & Lybrand, 96–98, 101
  Maritz, 98–99
  US West, 99–100
Intranet design approaches,
  CSCW, 103–4
  PD 103–4
  traditional, 102–3
Intranets, 71–130
  as collaboration space, 87f, 90–91
  as communication space, 87f, 88–90
  as content space, 87f, 87–88
  as IT infrastructure, 82–86
  as shared information workspace, 86–92, 87f
  as socio-technical systems, 103
  benefits and challenges, 79–82
  broker pages, 72
  content pages, 72
  design principles, 123t
  obtaining database information, 77f
  stages of design and implementation, 101–3
  underlying technology, 71–79
  value-added processes, 120–22

James, G., 73

Janis, I., 20–21
Java applets, 78
JavaScript, 76
Johnson-Laird, P., 30
Johnson-Lenz, P. and Johnson-Lenz, T., 81
Jung, C., 16

Katz, R. and Allen, T., 19
Katzer, J. and Fletcher, P., 109–110, 115
Keegan, W. , 160
Kehoe, C., Pitkow, J. and Rogers, J., 159
Kelly, G., 11
Kessler, M., 138
Kiesler, C., 19
Kirton, M., 17
Kling, R., 103–4
Knowledge, *See also* Organizational knowledge
  creating, diffusing and using, 48f
  data to information, 29–30
  individual-automatic, 38
  information to knowledge, 31–33
  propositional / non-propositional, 31, 33
  signals to data, 29
  social-collective, 39
Knowledge creation, 49–52
  four modes, 49–51
  knowledge conversion cycle, 52f
  social constructionist approach, 89
Knowledge diffusion, 52–56, 55f
Knowledge discovery, 144
Knowledge gaps, 5
Knowledge utilization, 56–60. *See also* Communities of Practice; Wenger, E.
KnowledgeCurve, 96–97
Knowledge-in-use, 58f
Kogut, B. and Zander, V., 39, 49, 60–61, 67
Kornblith, H., 31
Kraut, R., Fish, R., Root, R. and Chalfonte, B., 90
Krohne, H., 6
Kuhlthau, C., 5, 10–11, 22, 24, 103
Kuhn, T., 44
Kuutti, K., 90

Larson, R., 144
Lave, J. and Wenger, E., 57, 89
Leonard, D. and Sensiper, S., 36
Leonard-Barton, D., 34, 45
Lester, R. and Waters, J., 7
Let's Talk! *See* Intranet case studies, Maritz
Life Situations database. *See* Intranet case studies, US West
Likert scale, 161–62
Link Density, 145. *See also* Bibliometrics
Liu, C. Peek, J., Jones, R., Buss, B. and Nye, A., 75
Logs. *See* Web use studies, logs
Lotka, A., 140
Lotka's Law, 139–41, 145. *See also* Bibliometrics, bibliometric laws
Lotus Notes, 79–80, 94–95
Lycos 250, 144

MacMullin, S. and Taylor, R., 23, 107–8, 115, 120, 123
Malone, T., Grant, K., Lai, K., Rao, R. and Rosenblitt, D., 91
Management by deals, 83
Management by maxim, 83
March, J., 65
March, J. and Simon, H., 65
Marchionini, G., 103, 147–48, 150
Maritz, 98–99. *See also* Intranet case studies, Maritz
Markup languages, 75–76
Marshakova, I., 138
Martin, J., 20, 25
Matsushita case, 34, 49–51
  GAOO, 51
  Human Electronics, 51
Merrill Lynch, 72
META tags, 144
Microsoft, 76, 78, 167, 174, 174t, 176, 178–79
Microsoft Internet Explorer, 72
Miller, S. and Mangan, M., 6.
MIT (Massachussets Institute of Technology), 138
Monarchy. *See* Information politics
Moser, P., Mulder, D. and Trout, J., 31
Mouzelis, N., 62
Mozilla project, 167
Mullich, J., 97
Myers-Briggs Type Indicator (MBTI), 25

Nelson, R. and Winter, S., 36, 40
Netscape, 168t, 174, 174t, 183
Netscape Navigator, 72, 181, 184
NewsEdge, 177, 184
NIH (Not-Invented Here) syndrome, 19, 25
Nilan, M., Peek, R. and Snyder, H., 10
Nonaka, I. and Konno, N., 91–92
Nonaka, I. and Takeuchi, H., 39, 49, 51–52, 61, 66, 85–86, 88
Non-propositional knowledge. *See* Knowledge, propositional / non-propositional
Notes. *See* Lotus Notes
Novell, 178
NSCA Mosaic, 156
NUMMI (New United Motor Manufacturing, Inc.), 46–48. *See also* General Motors

Olsen, M., Murthy, B. and Teare, R., 7

O'Reilly, C., 9, 87
O'Reilly, C. and Tushman, M., 47
Organizational culture, 20–21, 25, 27, 39, 44, 47–48, 93
Organizational information environment, 107–17, 123. *See also* Information environment
Organizational intelligence, 83
Organizational knowledge, 29–67
and sense making, decision making, 63–66
categories, 34t
cultural, 43–48
explicit, 39–43
integration, 60–62
structure of, 33–48
tacit, 35–39
Organizational learning, 47, 84–85, 88–90
interpretive perspective, 89
Organizational memory, 85, 88, 93, 98
Organizational Web use, empirical study, 159–187
Correlation between frequency of source use and perceived source accessibility, 166t
Correlation between frequency of source use and perceived source quality, 165t
Orlikowski, W., 92–94
Ottenlips, S., Browdy, T. and Carrithers, D., 98
Osaka International Hotel, 50

Paisley, W., 12
Participatory Design (PD). *See* Intranet design approaches
Pejtersen, A., 129
Pejtersen, A. and Rasmussen, J., 129
Perceived environmental uncertainty. *See* Situational complexity
Perceived source accessibility, 162, 165f, 165–66, 182
Perceived source quality, 161, 164f, 182
PERL, 76
Perrin, C., 92–93
Perrow, C., 13
Pirolli, P. and Card, S., 134–36
Pirolli, P., Pitkow, J. and Rao, R., 135–36
Pitkow, J., 157, 167
Plumtree, 72
Polanyi, M., 35, 38
Portals, 71–73
Preble, J., Pradeep, A. and Reichel, A., 160
Price, D., 138, 143
Price Waterhouse, 96
PricewaterhouseCoopers, 98
Problem dimensions, 7t, 107–8, 121, 127
and creation of value-added processes, 126t
Problem situations, 120, 122
Propositional knowledge. *See* Knowledge, propositional / non-propositional

Quine, W., 31

Rasmussen, J., Pejtersen, A. and Goodstein, L., 129
RDF (Resource Description Framework), 76
Rice, V., 102
Risø Labs (Denmark), 129
Roberts-Witt, S., 72
Robinson, M., 90
Rogers, E., 42, 92–93, 96
Rosenbaum, H., 110–12, 115
Rosenberg, V., 166
Rumor Mill. *See* Intranet case studies, USWest
Russell, B., 31
Ryan Garcia, M., 97

Sackmann, S., 44
Salancik, G., 19
Sanchez, R., 41–42
Sandstrom, P., 133–34, 136
Saracevic, T., 9–10
Satisficing (Simon), 136
Scanning Model (Aguilar), 151–52
conditioned viewing, 151, 153, 177f, 179–80, 184–85, 187t
formal search, 152, 153f, 154, 177f, 178–80, 184, 187t
informal search, 152, 153f, 154, 177f, 178–80, 184, 187t
undirected viewing, 151, 177f, 179–180, 184–5, 187t
Scatter/Gather interface, 136
Schamber, L., 10
Schatz, B., 81
Schein, E., 20, 25, 44
Schiminovich, S., 138
Schön, D., 35, 37
Schuler, D. and Namioka, A., 103
Schumpeter, J., 60
Science Citation Index, 137
Scripting languages, 76
Senker, J., 37–38
Sensemaking gaps, 4–5, 5t
Sensemaking, knowledge creating and decision making, 64f
SGML (Standard Generalized Markup Language), 75
Signals, 29
Simon, H., 65, 136
Situational factors, 4f, 8f, 15f
Situational complexity, 7
Small, H., 138
Smith, D. and Alexander, R., 45
Social learning theory, 12
Social Science Citation Index, 137

Spender, J., 33, 38
Spertus, E., 144
Sproull, L. and Kiesler, S., 95
Sprout, A. and Coxeter, R., 73
SQL (Structured Query Language), 78
Stanford University, 187
Stata, R., 89
Staw, B. and Ross, J., 18
Stein, E. W. and Zwass, V. 88
Stephens, D. and Krebs, J., 133
Strom, D., 73
Structurationally Informed Value-Added Model (Rosenbaum), 110–12
Sullivan, P., 40–41
Sun Microsystems, 178
Sutton, S., 150

Tacit knowledge, 34t, 35–39. *See also* Organizational knowledge
Tanaka, Ikuko, 50
Tauscher, L. and Greenberg, S., 155–6
Taylor, R., 5, 10, 15–16, 23–24, 104–8, 110–12, 115–17, 119–20, 124, 128, 149
TCP/IP (transmission control protocol/internet protocol), 74
Technological utopianism. *See* Information politics
Telleen, S., 72–73, 78–79, 81–82, 101
Theory of Structuration (Giddens), 110–11
Thyfault, M., 81, 102
Toyota, 46–47
TQM (Total Quality Management) techniques, 18
Training. *See* Web training
Tsoukas, H., 61–62
Tversky, A. and Kahneman, D., 17, 25

Uddevalla. *See* Volvo
UDP (User Data Protocol), 75
Undirected viewing. *See* Scanning Model
University of Toronto, Faculty of Information Studies, 167, 187
University of Washington, Graduate School of Library and Information Science, 129
User browsing, 147–54
User-centered approach, 128. *See also* Intranet design approaches
USWest, 99–100. *See also* Intranet case studies, USWest

Value-added approach to information systems, 105f,
Value-Added Model (Taylor), 104–6, 110, 112, 117
Value-added processes, 104, 117, 123–24, 127–28
VBScript (Microsoft), 76
Verity, 72
Volvo, 47
von Krogh, G., 32
Voos, H., 141

W3C (World Wide Web Consortium), 75
Wall Street Journal, 176
Walsh, J. and Ungson, G., 88
Web client/server model, 74f
Web-IF (Web Impact Factors), 145. *See also* Bibliometrics
Web training, 181–84
  Web Usage Activity, 183t
Web use,
  how to enhance, 187t
Web use studies, 154–58
  history mechanisms (Tauscher and Greenberg), 155–56
  logs (Pitkow), 157
  network traffic (Crovella and Bestavros), 156–57
  session boundaries (Catledge and Pitkow), 155
  surfing patterns (Huberman et al.) 157–58
WebTracker, 167–75, 177–79, 185, 187
  Button Browser Actions, 168t
  Expanded Window, 171f
  Key Browser Actions, 169t
  Log File Format, 168f
  Log View, 172t
  Main Window, 170f
  Menu Browser Actions, 169t
  Participant Examples of Web Use, 173t
  Search Engine Use Distribution, 175f
  Search Engine Visits, 174t
  Setup Window, 170f
  Total Time of Web Use, 173t
Weick, K., 63
Weick, K. and Daft, R., 151
Weill, P. and Broadbent, M., 186
Wenger, E., 49, 57–61, 66, 186
Wilson, T., 3, 6, 12, 23–24
Winterhalder, B., 134
Witkin, H. and Goodenough, D., 17
Wolesky, P., 72
Woodruff, A., Aoki, P., Brewer, E., Gauthier, P. and Rowe, L., 142–43
Wulfekuhler, M. and William, F., 143

Xerox, 34, 102, 157
  Xerox PARC, 45
XML (Extensible Markup Language), 75
XMosaic, 155, 167

Yahoo, 72, 138, 176, 178

ZDnet, 178
Zipf, G., 13, 139
Zipf's Law or Principle of Least Effort, 13, 139–40. *See also* Bibliometrics, bibliometric laws
Zmud, R., 9
Zuboff, S., 35–36, 92–93, 185